Learning and Teaching British Values

Sadia Habib

Learning and Teaching British Values

Policies and Perspectives on British Identities

Sadia Habib
Manchester, UK

ISBN 978-3-319-60380-3   ISBN 978-3-319-60381-0   (eBook)
DOI 10.1007/978-3-319-60381-0

Library of Congress Control Number: 2017949200

Cover illustration: © Harvey Loake

Printed on acid-free paper

This Palgrave Macmillan imprint is published by Springer Nature
The registered company is Springer International Publishing AG
The registered company address is: Gewerbestrasse 11, 6330 Cham, Switzerland

To my nieces—Hannah and Inayat—and my husband's
nieces—Madihah, Samihah and Adilah—for taking great interest in my
research, asking pertinent critical questions and sharing their stories.
To the trainee teachers, Art students and teachers who granted me the
privilege of listening to and learning from their narratives.
To the young people and teachers of multicultural Britain, keep on
critically reflecting and seeking social justice.

Foreword

It was a pleasure to be invited to write the foreword for this book. I had the great privilege of reading and examining Sadia's doctoral thesis analysing young people's constructions of British identity. The visual depictions were beautiful, compelling and extremely interesting. The analysis of the artwork and the narratives of Sadia's young student participants and that of their teachers exquisitely illuminated the life and identity construction of young Londoners. This book, and the thesis it is based upon, make for compelling reading. This book is very timely and makes an original contribution to the field of social justice and equality in particular to the ongoing debate of how Britishness is perceived by teachers and young people. There is no doubt that more work, like this, is required to extend our knowledge of how young people perceive their identities; particularly so after the imposition of the duty to teach "Fundamental British Values" (FBV) in schools by teachers who are themselves unsure about the concept of Britishness but very aware of the dangers of racism and xenophobia that may be instigated through the study of Britishness. I applaud Sadia for making such a contribution to the field and for privileging the narratives of young people and *their* interpretations of Britishness.

This book is based on two very interesting empirical studies. The recent one is related to student teachers at a university in London and their reflections on the requirement to teach FBV. The earlier study, which generated data from artwork on the theme of Britishness followed by interviews with young people and their Art teachers, was conducted in a South-East London secondary school before the mandate to teach

British values. The young people's narratives on their sense of belonging and Britishness make fascinating reading. Sadia has effectively integrated the academic literature related to race, class, identity and nation as well as critical pedagogy, to foreground how this teaching approach can be utilised to draw out how pre-service and in-service teachers and the young people they have the privilege to teach construct Britishness. The art-based ethnographic study explored the complexities of teaching and learning Britishness, and how identity and belonging are articulated by young people reflecting their racialised, classed and localised constructions of identity. In her analysis of the empirical data, Sadia utilises the theoretical construct of critical pedagogy and race to create a picture of how the teachers and their students were "liberated" through the use of critical pedagogy and how the young students were given space to exercise their agency to express their identity as young Britons through art.

The young pupils' notions of Britishness are multi-layered, fluid and still under development as they negotiate family and cultural heritage, which they position alongside their belonging as Londoners. The analysis and interpretation of the data are compared to existing theories to demonstrate the lived experience of being young and British in twenty-first-century London. The young people's depictions of Britishness in their artwork are presented by the author in a careful, sensitive and ethical manner. Her empathy with her participants and her openness to share her own feelings about her British identity enabled the students to validate their own sense of Britishness. The later chapters identify the key factors that have shaped the young participants' perceptions of their British identity, which contrasts with the confusion and scepticism of the pre-service teachers towards the teaching of FBV in the earlier chapter.

This book adeptly examines the theoretical notions of Britishness and contrasts it to the bygone debates associated with assimilation, multiculturalism and integration. The author eloquently argues, with the support of an extensive and robust theoretical framework that (i) the imposition of the duty on teachers to "not undermine fundamental British values" within the Teachers' Standards Department for Education (2011) in England; (ii) the subsequent adaptation of the Ofsted Framework for inspection, which specifies that if a school does not teach FBV, it can be placed in special measures; (iii) placed alongside the mandate to teach FBV within the curriculum particularly in relation to Spiritual, Social Moral and Cultural Education, leave teachers no options, thereby limiting their ability to exercise their professionalism. The Government's counter-terrorism strategy Prevent (HM Government 2011) defines an extremist as someone who voices opposition to or acts to oppose "FBV". So the phrase has migrated from counter-terrorism legislation to the Teachers' Standards and is now governing their personal and professional conducts in relation to the curriculum, and thereby classrooms.

This is why critical pedagogies offer a means to teachers and their students to engage with a contentious topic through the medium of art. In the earlier chapter, Sadia's reflective student teachers critique the notion of FBV highlighting the contradictions inherent between the rhetoric of values such as liberty and tolerance and how they play out in reality. As one young teacher in training notes it is "tolerance in theory but not in practice". The "insidious imposition of a political securitization agenda, onto an unsuspecting profession and pupil population" (Lander 2016: 274) through policy is palpable in the discomfort expressed by student teachers as they try to reconcile notions of contemporary multicultural Britain with those of colonialism and imperialism associated with Britain's past and the common tropes used to depict Britishness such as the Tower of London, Beefeaters and the monarchy. The student teachers, Sadia shows, considered the notion of Britishness as divisive, exclusionary and wholly inappropriate for preparation to live in a diverse multicultural country. Sadia notes that these teachers were from a range of ethnic and cultural backgrounds and they were learning to teach in multicultural London schools. She is mindful that not all pre-service or in-service teachers would critique the teaching of Britishness in the same vein, consciously or dysconsciously (King 2004) opting to assert the assimilationist thrust underpinning the teaching of Britishness.

Within Sadia's book, the artwork undertaken by the young school students was considered "meaningful, healing, therapeutic" and cathartic, but also affirming. The Art teachers, whose classes formed the research site for the second empirical study, reflected on their own identities to in turn support their young students' explorations of identity. It was interesting to read how some young people from the White majority group articulated how they owned Britishness thus rooting it in a White identity. One young man, Joe, was a fervent adherent to White Britishness and its attendant privileges. While one young White woman depicted her identity through fashion labels, dress and the association of these signifiers with the derogatory label of "chav", a term of derision used for White working-class people. In her artwork and her narrative, Ellie expresses her resentment against such a label positioning her in class terms as the abject "Other". This exclusionary discourse affects her sense of self and ascribes her sense of belonging to her locality and class.

In this way, Sadia's work shows how the notion of Britishness while associated with being White is not only a raced, but also a "class situated" notion. Joe and his articulation of Britishness continue to worry me long after reading the thesis and the manuscript of this book. Some of his utterances are worrying and racist, for example, he says, "I consider White people as like the first race...". The expression of his identity underscores the power of whiteness and in parts; his expressions of identity are based on White supremacy. For example, Joe felt it is only the Black and minority ethnic students who have to work to develop their Britishness when he does not really consider them to be truly British indicates there is, in his mind, and perhaps others, a hierarchy of Britishness where those who are White occupy the highest position in this hierarchy or supremacist framework. The book highlights that the study of identity might furnish students like Joe with a stage for his racist whiteness, particularly if it took place in school, and if teachers and student teachers are not properly trained to deal with racism and xenophobia.

The Black minority ethnic young people in the study expressed their identity and feelings of belonging in terms of their cultural heritage as well as a local sense of belonging. Their articulations of being British alluded to hyphenated identities and they saw little conflict between the two or more ethnic and cultural aspects of their hybrid British identity. They expressed pride in each facet of their British identity refusing to be subjugated by the hegemonic notion of a White British identity. One young woman, Kadisha, and her strident challenge to Joe have left an inedible impression. Her challenge of Joe's White supremacist views is an example, as Sadia points out of "talking-back", in the example provided Kadisha metaphorically "puts Joe in his place" by telling him that we all originated from Africa and didn't he know that? Thus, pointing out the baselessness of his supremacist views.

Kadisha's courage to do this is indeed an example of her multicultural Britishness borne, no doubt, from the struggles to mediate her sense of belonging to the nation and to her ethnic, cultural and religious identities, which she manages to negotiate everyday even when she is positioned as an outsider by her classmate. Her identity, and that of others, stems from who they say they are and also in terms of what they do in their everyday lives. The chapters examining young people's narratives of their identity in relation to Britishness are simultaneously fascinating and yet worrying given the current geopolitical climate following the rise of racism as a result of the EU Referendum, the election of Trump as President of the USA and the subsequent emboldening of the political Right and Far Right.

There are clear implications of this study for teachers, teacher training and schools with respect to the important task of preparing young citizens to live in and belong to multicultural Britain. It is imperative as Sadia argues so well to educate teachers not only to understand "race", class and identity formation but also to educate their students to engage critically with these concepts to develop a secure sense of self, a sense of belonging to Britain and to have pride in asserting their Britishness as equal citizens of Britain regardless of their skin colour, class or religion. Sadia urges teachers to resist reproducing notions of Britishness based on White identities, which would merely serve to re-inscribe the "notion of insider-outsider citizen" (Lander 2016: 275), or might inadvertently endorse "a stratification of citizenship into those who really belong, namely the indigenous majority; those who can belong namely those of minority ethnic heritage who have assimilated or integrated and those who really don't quite belong, or those we tolerate up to a point, namely the Muslim 'Other'" (Lander 2016: 275).

This important, timely and significant book should be compulsory reading on all teacher education programme reading lists. All teachers who are struggling to "teach" British values in their classroom need to engage with this book, to embrace the messages the young people are communicating and then to have the professional courage to engage with the philosophy and methodologies of critical pedagogy to ensure young people who will be citizens of the future develop a secure sense of belonging to, and pride in, an inclusive multicultural Britain.

Vini Lander
Professor in Education
Edge Hill University
Ormskirk, Lancashire, UK

REFERENCES

HM GOVERNMENT. 2011. Prevent Strategy.

King, J.E. 1991. Dysconscious Racism: Ideology, Identity, and the Miseducation of Teachers. *Journal of Negro Education* 60: 133–146.

Lander, V. 2016. Introduction to Fundamental British Values. *Journal of Education for Teaching* 42: 274–279.

ACKNOWLEDGEMENTS

This book came to be because of the unwavering support of my parents, Abdul and Zubaida Bari, my sister and brother, Asifa and Tayyub and my husband Ghulam, as well as my faith in God Almighty.

I am indebted to my doctoral supervisors Vicky Macleroy and Anna Carlile. They are amazing critical pedagogues. I must also thank colleagues at Goldsmiths, including Charmian Kenner and Chris Kearney (my supervisors initially before they retired) as well as Carrie Paechter, Rosalyn George, Clare Kelly, Paul Dash, Julia Hope, Sheryl Clark and Amanda Kipling. And of course my examiners—Vini Lander and Les Back—who offered constructive advice and supported and challenged me to be bolder.

My academic identity has been enriched by advice from friends or colleagues: Garth Stahl, Shazad Amin, Heather Mendick, Gwen Redmond, Gemma Casserly, Jessica Elizabeth Peters, Tait Coles, Ian Roberts, Zalan Alam, Shamim Miah, Aqsa Dar, Bill Bolloten, Debbie Epstein, Michaela Benson and Mark Carrigan; and by technological help from Naadir (my brother in law), Mark Leigh Edmondson and Shaf Choudry.

Contents

CHAPTER 1

Introduction

Abstract This chapter introduces background information about schools, teachers and students increasingly being required to develop knowledge and understanding of Britishness and Fundamental British Values (FBV). Since 2007, politicians have offered hegemonic ideas about the meanings of Britishness and called upon the teaching and learning of Britishness as necessary for social cohesion. This endorsement of national identity has in recent years evolved into the Fundamental British Values (FBV) duty where schools have now been placed in a position where they must actively promote FBV. This chapter also examines how identity, national identity and nation are defined in the literature, as well as the intersections of multicultural and White Britishness.

Keywords Britishness · Fundamental British values · Multiculturalism Identity · Nation

This chapter introduces background information about schools, teachers and students increasingly being required to develop knowledge and understanding of Britishness and Fundamental British Values (FBV). Since 2007 politicians have offered hegemonic ideas about the meanings of Britishness and called upon the teaching and learning of Britishness as necessary for social cohesion. This endorsement of national identity has in recent years evolved into the FBV duty where schools have now been placed in a position where they must actively promote FBV.

© The Author(s) 2018
S. Habib, *Learning and Teaching British Values*,
DOI 10.1007/978-3-319-60381-0_1

1

The chapter also examines how identity, national identity and nation are defined in the literature, as well as the intersections of multicultural and White Britishness.

TEACHING BRITISHNESS AND FUNDAMENTAL BRITISH VALUES

In the past, perhaps governments may have discouraged citizenship education, preferring docile subjects to radical citizens who challenge the status quo (Heater 2001; Andrews and Mycock 2008), but today critically examining and embracing new conceptions of belongings and identities is becoming more and more necessary. Educationalists witness Britishness and British values debated in popular, academic and political spheres (House of Lords 2008; Brunel University 2016) "at unprecedented levels" (Ward 2009: 3). This is a contrast to decades before when there was "relatively little public debate about the meaning of Britishness" (Carrington and Short 1995: 221) when political rhetoric seemed to doggedly cling onto defence of an exclusive White Britishness (Ward 2004). Yet paradoxically, the government reacted angrily when The Parekh Report suggested that symbols of Englishness or Britishness represented Whiteness (Gilroy 2004), denying the intersections of Britishness, Whiteness and racism.

Emphasising the reasons it is important to listen to stories about Britishness, in this book, I report on the outcomes of employing a critical pedagogy framework when exploring identities, as well as on the expectations and experiences of trainee teachers, and young people and their Art teachers when it comes to learning and teaching about Britishness. With its non-hierarchical and non-elitist approach, critical pedagogy empowers teachers and students to collaborate; they can work together to create a schooling space that emboldens students' voices, stimulates dialogue and recommends reflection and action to attain goals of social justice. Education should strive to seek "the opening up of possibilities through the exploration of alternative understandings, the critical application of evidence and argument and the development of the skills and dispositions necessary to act on the possibilities" (Sears and Hughes 2006: 4). This book will therefore describe how education can promote the pedagogy of possibility through advocating the alternative and championing the critical.

In this chapter, I introduce the backdrop against which schools, teachers and students are required to develop knowledge and understanding of FBV. By writing this book, I aim to "make hegemonic forms of subjectivity and identity strange" by "problematizing and relativizing" (Weedon 2004: 4) concepts of Britishness and FBV, while remaining mindful of race, nation and ethnicity as "constructed (not inherited) categories, shaped by political interests exploiting social antagonisms" (Cohen 1995: 2). "Melancholic nostalgia" seeps into contemporary discourses of Britishness harking back "for a monochrome Britishness that probably never existed" (Gidley 2014: n.p.). To counter this monochrome and melancholic depiction of a mythical Britishness of the past that has seeped into our national imaginary, this book moves forwards by including the voices of ethnic minority and White working-class communities as they seek to rethink and redefine contemporary (national) belongings and identities. Rather than teaching students about politicised and hegemonic versions of Britishness, I draw upon the ways teachers can choose to galvanise young people to speak boldly about what it means to be British. This book addresses the ways (trainee) teachers are working out how they might best incorporate exploration of identities in their lessons. Teachers and students working together can counteract "the power of the rhetoric of 'Britishness'" (Andrews and Mycock 2008: 143) for, as this book substantiates, there is no singular way to experience Britishness.

Chapter 2 outlines features of educational, urban and critical ethnography, arts-based educational research (ABER), as well as critical race methodology (CRM) and critical pedagogy which I believe are necessary in enabling participant voice and empowerment, thereby advancing social justice and social change. Chapter 3 explains the potential of critical pedagogies for teachers and students wanting to explore identities, social experiences and belongings. Drawing upon empirical research conducted with trainee teachers, and school students and their teachers, Chaps. 4–7 detail how Britishness and FBV teaching are perceived by trainee teachers and experienced by young people and their Art teachers. I aim to present rarely heard voices (Gregory 2005; Smyth and McInerney 2013) on Britishness and FBV. While we are frequently reminded of government policy and perspectives on FBV, we urgently need empirical evidence about the experiences and views of those most immersed in schooling at the classroom level in their everyday lives: teachers, trainee teachers and students.

Chapter 4 describes trainee teachers' experiences of FBV, who rejecting reification and homogeneity, view FBV as undefined and perplexing. Evident in the trainee teacher responses to teaching FBV are complex notions about identities. Wary of the problematic "ideological aura attached to nationhood" (Billig 1995: 4), they think of identity as never stagnant or stationary but in a state of rapid flux (Hall 1992; May 1999). Worryingly, dialogue and debate about FBV are not encouraged among teachers, nor is there sufficient training on how to tackle the jingoistic or indoctrinating nature of FBV policies and practices (Elton-Chalcraft et al. 2017). A big challenge for schools and teacher education institutions is how to respond to trainee teachers and existing classroom teachers consistently reporting that they are inadequately guided or trained to teach young people about multiculturalism and social inequalities.

Chapters 5, 6 and 7 reveal the benefits of seeking reflections about identities that are meaningful, open and patient, and conducted through structured classroom activities. I proposed a project on Britishness to the Head of the Art department at a South East London school, and we decided there would be educational, moral, cultural and social value in exploring Britishness through GCSE[1] coursework. The artwork produced by students would contribute to their final GCSE grade, giving the project gravity and significance.[2] Chapter 7 lays bare some of the young Londoner's conceptions of Britishness as they deliberate over what it means to be British; I particularly draw upon paired interviews conducted with students Chris, Ellie, Kadisha and Joe.[3] The concluding chapter argues for the importance of further research on everyday lived experiences of Britishness, as well as on learning about teaching about localised and globalised British identities.

Teaching Britishness: Policy, Process and Practice

Teaching Britishness 2007–2010

The research detailed in Chaps. 5–7 was conducted during a time when the Labour government was buoyant about the possibilities of Britishness teaching in schools, especially as a solution to social problems (Garner 2007; BBC News 2007; Ajegbo et al. 2007). Complexities and uncertainties surrounding notions of immigration, identity, multiculturalism and the Union's future were seen as resolvable by promoting Britishness in civic, social and educational spaces (Andrews and Mycock 2008). The terror attacks in the USA on 11 September 2001, and in

London in July 2005 amplified debates about Britishness (Kiwan 2012). The British people would witness senior politicians "stress the importance of education in uniting the nation" (Osler 2008: 11). Gordon Brown, even before he was Prime Minister, appealed to Britons to be patriotic (Golmohamad 2009), as he sought to position Britishness "at the top of the public agenda" (Parekh 2008: 69), defining Britishness as an issue needing addressing in policy. His conception of British values, though, was "tolerance, fairness and enterprise, none of which is unique to the country" (Parekh 2008: 69).

An underlying uneasiness about hegemonic attempts to impose an unwelcome patriotic—or even racist—agenda on schools troubled me. I was becoming aware of the political discourses of Britishness as "officially constructed patriotism" by the powerful elite (Colley 1992: 145), at a time when the President of the National Union of Teachers critiqued politicians for reinforcing racist rhetoric by ordering schools to teach Britishness (Eason 2007). During that time the Ajegbo Report (2007) came about because government combined a "need to counter terrorist activity and the strengthening of national identity and British values through the curriculum" (Osler 2015: 7). By 2009, though, the "wave of patriotic rhetoric" from politicians calling for Britishness to be promoted in schools and society had "begun to break on the shores of public indifference" (Hand and Pearce 2009: 464). Britishness sometimes becomes fashionable, while other times it is presented by politicians as mandatory—thus, rising, falling and rising again in public rhetoric and political ideologies. The zeal for national identity might fade into the background until the next politician arrives to propose new policies, as happened when the new government came into power in 2010.

Fundamental British Values 2011–2015

After the Coalition government of 2010 came into power,[4] debates about immigration, place and national identities continued to amplify. Communities Secretary, Eric Pickles, demanded the end of "state-sponsored multiculturalism", crusading to popularise "British Values" by bolstering up a vision of Christianity and the English language as core to British identity (Walford 2012; Communities and Local Government 2012; Grayson 2012). In changes to teacher education, the "Teachers' Standards" enjoined teachers not to *undermine fundamental British values* (Department for Education 2011), while Ofsted has gone further by encouraging school management to "actively" promote Fundamental British Values (FBV), not just to undermine FBV (Elton-Chalcraft et al. 2017). Such directives raise obvious questions about how teachers and school managers might respond to policies that ratify neoliberal regulation of teachers both as professionals and as citizens.

In 2014, the Coalition government announced schools in England were expected—in line with Spiritual, Moral, Social and Cultural (SMSC) education—to actively promote FBV (Easton 2014), defined as "democracy, the rule of law, individual liberty and mutual respect and tolerance of those with different faiths and beliefs" (Department for Education 2014). It is important to critically assess political motivations concerning educational policies, for example when it comes to FBV, Osler (2008: 12) argues that "in commissioning the Ajegbo report, the government made a direct link between the need to counter terrorist activity and to strengthen national identity and British values through the curriculum". The FBV guidance (HM Government 2015) originates from unexpected and controversial beginnings. It does not root from education policy, but from Home Office documents on "extremism" (Richardson 2015), where extremism is defined by the government as "vocal or active opposition to fundamental British values..." (HM Government 2015: 2). Britishness discourses might initially have emerged from the political elite's anxieties about Scotland and Wales seeking independence, but by 2011 "unintegrated" ethnic minorities—particularly Muslims—became the target of FBV policies (Maylor 2016).

The ways teachers are appraised on this professional duty not to *undermine FBV* is undoubtedly complicated by the relationship between FBV and Counter Terrorism and Security (Revell and Bryan 2016). Teacher educators are concerned about the profession becoming increasingly politicised, with teachers coerced into monitoring students (Elton-Chalcraft et al. 2017). Teachers' Standards therefore come to be perceived as political tools serving to promote government approved ideologies of Britishness (Maylor 2016), and administering government's hard-line approach: "We are saying it isn't enough simply to respect these values in schools – we're saying that teachers should actively promote them. They're not optional; they're the core of what it is to live in Britain" (Cameron 2014). Schools are warned they might "face action if they fail to promote 'British Values'", and that they are "expected to confront pupils, parents or school staff that express intolerant or extremist views" (The Yorkshire Post 2014). Questions continue to arise—and will keep on emerging—about who defines "British Values", and whether religiously, ethnically and culturally diverse Britons are permitted and welcome to contribute to the conversation on British belongings and identities (Bragg 2006; Berkeley 2011; Miah 2015; Hoque 2015).

Multicultural British Identities

Identity and Belonging

Identity, a relatively new concept, concerning who we are and what defines or distinguishes us as individuals (Parekh 2000a), has become a key conceptual lens employed by academics (Solomos 2001; Sarup 2005). Perceived as important for being human and for our sense of agency (Cokley 2002), identity is a broad concept with distinctive connotations (Brubaker and Cooper 2000; Deaux 2001). The basic tenets consist of belonging, commonalities and differences (Solomos 2001), and identity is often "defined in a relation of difference to what it is not"(Weedon 2004: 19). *Belonging* refers to acceptance and recognition within a group or society. Its multiple layers are illustrated by "the interplay of the subjective self, collective agency and structural positioning", while its multiple facets mean we can "belong to a community, a locality or a nation", but also experience "a transnational sense of belonging" (Vasta 2013: 198). *Community* concerns the right to feel you belong within the boundaries of the community, that you matter and make a difference in that space, and your needs are fulfilled while you share emotional experiences with other community members (McMillan and Chavis 1986).

Within debates about (national) identities, referring to multiple identities is now the norm (Hussain and Bagguley 2005), where "complex affiliations, meaningful attachments and multiple allegiances to issues, people, places and traditions that lie beyond the boundaries of their resident nation-state" are recognised and valued (Vertovec and Cohen 2002: 2). Within communities and nations, identity "is always being reconstituted in a process of becoming and by virtue of location in social, material, temporal and spatial contexts" (Edensor 2002: 29). Jacobson (1997) and Vadher and Barrett (2009) present fluid, context-dependent multiple positionings as the norm for young Britons. Following Baumann (1996), Vadher and Barrett (2009: 443) describe national identification as a "dynamic process through which the values, beliefs, traditions and indeed the boundaries of the national group are being renegotiated and redefined" in different times and places. The conviction that a "proud, much proclaimed identity" can "give way to another" over time (Modood 2005: 464), is particularly pertinent when considering young people's relationship with Britishness. Some scholars, therefore, prefer to describe *identifications* of social agents, thereby, emphasising fluidity, process and change, rather than *identity* which seems too firm, fixed and final (Hall 1996c). Even if identities are evolving, it is vital to remember that they are not "free-floating", but "limited by borders and boundaries" (Sarup 2005: 95). Identities and identifications are sometimes limiting and limited, and other times expansive, as we might actively choose to co-opt and resist fluctuating features of identities.

National Identity and Nation

National identity has become a popular notion since the 1950s (Parekh 2000a); importantly, this was a time when people from the Commonwealth were arriving to make Britain their home. It has come to replace eighteenth- and nineteenth-century terms such as *national character* and *national consciousness* (Smith 2010: 18), not merely as a theoretical concept, but also invoking "notions and categories of practice" (Smith 2010: 19). National identity is "historically specific" and "plural, fractured and refigured by gender, ethnic and class relations" (Weedon 2004: 20). In the past, promoting national identities was seen as controversial (Day and Thompson 2004), perhaps this explains why we seem to know more about nations and nationalism than about national identity (Bechhofer and McCrone 2010). Members of a nation tend to witness their politicians skilfully manipulating national identity to reflect politically elitist attitudes, values and goals (Cameron 1999). Of great consequence for teaching Britishness, and what this book highly recommends, is for teachers and students to explore how national identity—contrary to political rhetoric that attempts to fix, essentialise and reify it—is frequently contested, complex and difficult to define (Jacobson 1997; Scourfield et al. 2006; Maylor 2010; Anderson 2012; Burkett 2013).

Exploration of national identity should not be mistaken for nationalism, nor is professing a national identity equal to a strong attachment to the nation, for being a member of a nation can be a general taken-for-granted status, or might even reveal young people's apathy (Fenton 2007). Nation, nationality and nationalism are terms not only hard to define, but also difficult to analyse (Anderson 2006). Throughout this book, I document how students, teachers and trainee teachers conceive Britishness as nuanced, multifaceted and incomplete. National identities are thus "too complex and elusive to be reduced to a set of easily identifiable features or summed up in a few neat propositions"(Parekh 2000a: 6). If national identity is ambivalent and ambiguous, to progress as individuals, as communities and as a society, we can seek to understand redefinitions of Britishness contextually. Rethinking Britishness will "require a deep historical knowledge of the country and a feel for its past, as well as a rigorous and realistic assessment of its present circumstances and future aspirations" (Parekh 2000a: 6).

Nation, like national identity, is a contested and problematic concept (Cameron 1999). Prevailing narratives insist the West "has always had 'nations' and 'histories', while the Rest had 'tribes', 'ethnic groups' and 'traditions'" (Žarkov 2015: 5). Others argue it is a relatively new concept unknown in ancient times: "Classical antiquity had republics, municipal kingdoms, confederations of local republics and empires, yet it can hardly be said to have had nations in our understanding of the term" (Renan 1990: 9). Some scholars define the nation in relation to linguistic identity (Oakes 2001; Rydgren 2004; Kamusella 2008; Gellner and Breuilly 2008). Others recount resplendent nation-building, for example establishing systems of education, health and welfare for citizens (Carnegie 2002). Although some political theorists attempt to define a nation as dynastic, it is not a dynasty, nor can nation be defined by exclusivity of race or of language, as some have misguidedly asserted, for there is no linguistic or racial purity (Renan 1990). Brubaker (2004: 11) recommends race, nation and ethnicity to be defined "not as substances or things or entities or organisms or collective individuals... but rather in relational, processual, dynamic, eventful, and disaggregated terms".

Then, there is the "ambivalence" of the narration of nation: "the language of those who write of it and the lives of those who live it" (Bhabha 1990: 1) might radically differ. For Renan and French Enlightenment thinkers, belonging to a nation was voluntary, while German Romanticism presented nation as "predetermined community bound by blood and heredity" (Malik 1996: 131). For Gellner, nations were far from natural, thus, the "horror of nationalist excesses" entered

Gellner's narrations (Day and Thompson 2004: 42). Media discourses often neglect to present the nation's borders as "arbitrary dividing lines that are simultaneously social, cultural and psychic", instead nations and their borders are depicted as "territories to be patrolled against those who whom they construct as outsiders, aliens, the Others" (Brah 1996: 198).

Political discourses also frequently present a narration of nation closely tied to Othering. Parekh incisively deconstructs Margaret Thatcher's "uncritical" version of British identity, where "her words imply that continental Europeans are gravely deficient in such virtues as individuality, initiative, fairness and equity" (Parekh 2008: 64). Thatcherism[5] unashamedly "powerfully organized itself around particular forms of patriarchy and cultural or national identity" (Hall 1996a: 235). Politicians might claim national ties are powerful bonds, almost familial, or like religious connections with God (Kedourie 1993); however, nations are not eternal, for they begin and end, thus humanity becomes the highest ideal in the eyes of some philosophers and historians (Renan 1990).

The nation then is "a powerful historical idea" which emerged from "impossibly romantic and excessively metaphorical" political and literary thought (Bhabha 1990: 1). The most popular definition for nation seems to be an "imagined political community", where "even the smallest nation will never know most of their fellow-members, meet them, or even hear of them, yet in the minds of each lives the image of their communion" (Anderson 2006: 6). This imagined community consists of "economic, political, linguistic, cultural, religious, geographical, historical" relationships (Hroch 2012: 79). Nations "have always been culturally and ethnically diverse, problematic, protean and artificial constructs that take shape very quickly and can come apart just as fast" (Colley 1992: 5), perhaps then the nation is "important only in the moment where its cultural imperatives are being carnivalized, subverted and challenged" (Back 1996: 250).

Discursive ideas on Britishness are popular among academics (Andrews and Mycock 2008), yet Britishness remains contested (Saeed et al. 1999; Croft 2012; Thurston and Alderman 2014; Mason 2016). National identity and nation are not just difficult concepts for minority ethnic communities to define, but also for indigenous Britons (Vadher and Barrett 2009). Nevertheless, Britain is "constantly engaged in debates about race, racism and national identity" (Malik 2002: 1). If teachers are wary of presenting "unthinking patriotism, discredited imperialism or an exclusive nationalism" (Osler and Starkey 2005: 12), urgent questions emerge about how schools might respond to policy calls to teach Britishness and FBV. This book investigates the reflections of trainee teachers, Art teachers and students regarding the pedagogical processes involved in the exploration of Britishness in the classroom. At a time when FBV is a requirement placed upon educational institutions, thinking over how British identities might be explored with ethnically, religiously and culturally diverse students becomes increasingly important for trainee and in-service teachers, as well as teacher educators.

White Britishness

When Commonwealth citizens from India, Pakistan and the Caribbean came to establish homes in post-war Britain it became exceedingly difficult to "uphold the idea that a British identity was exclusively a white identity" (Cohen 1994: 18). Yet—open a tabloid newspaper—and somehow the supposed "common sense" view still prevails today that Britishness is "a finite collective identity" unable to "accommodate all of these immigrants" (Ward 2004: 125). Britishness discourses can normalise and privilege Whiteness, pitting White Britons against those who are Othered (Wemyss 2009). Often the voices of ethnic minority communities are invisible and marginalised in political and policy conversations on Britishness. Simultaneously there is "over-racialisation of visible minorities at the expense of a de-racialization of ethnic majorities" resulting in White identity crises (Nayak 2003: 139). The processes causing ethnic minorities to be both invisible and visible when it comes to belonging in Britain result in conflicted and contradictory policies often enforcing assimilation.

Successive second, third, fourth and even fifth generations settled in Britain are still asked about "back home": What is life like back home? How often do you go back home? Where is back home? I, therefore, attempt to write with awareness of hundreds of years of colonial rule and postcolonial posturing fashioning modern Britishness. Politicians appoint themselves as vanguards of "shaping, defining and guarding 'Britishness'" (Grube 2011: 628): "Patriotism and ideas of national identity have long been the playthings of politicians" (Ward 2004: 93). Yet colonial rule in distant lands, and here in Britain, complicates 'Britishness', defying the simplicity attributed to national identities by politicians. Seamus Heaney, for example, took offence and vehemently rejected the label "British" poet (Cullen 2000; Thurston and Alderman 2014):

"be advised/My passport's green./No glass of ours was ever raised/To toast *The Queen*" (Heaney 1983).

During World War Two, embracing and maintaining Britishness was embedded in "the national war effort" (Burletson 1993: 120); since then Britishness has been frequently reinvented by media, political and popular discourses, often imagined in opposition to and as needing preservation from the Other (Croft 2012). Politicians are responsible for creating "rhetorical frames through which to define how the public sees policy issues, how they decide on who is a friend and who is an enemy, and how they assess who are outsiders and who are insiders" (Grube 2011: 628). Citizenship education and social cohesion have been high on Britain's agenda (Sears and Hughes 2006), and intense debates on the impact of migration and multiculturalism on national cohesion are still rampant (Murji and Solomos 2015). The right-wing blame multicultural policies for social exclusion and urban riots, yet these allegations lack empirical evidence (Finney and Simpson 2009; Wright and Bloemraad 2012; Watson and Saha 2012; Heath and Demireva 2014).

Some politicians ignore the relationship between Britishness, Whiteness and racism (Back et al. 2002), refuting that British cultural nationalism was historically "a language of race" (Gilroy 1992: 56). Such denials about the historical and contemporary links between Britishness, Whiteness and racism are often conscious political acts that seriously hinder racial equality and contribute to alienation and oppression of British ethnic minorities. Even if "Whiteness nowhere features as an explicit condition" of Britishness, we know Englishness and Britishness are "racially coded": "Race is deeply entwined with political culture and with the idea of nation, and underpinned by a distinctive kind of British reticence—to take race or racism seriously, or even to talk about them at all, is bad form..." (Parekh 2000b: 38).

Following critical race methodology principles, we must take race and racism seriously, and we must have spaces where we can talk about historical and contemporary racisms and how these tie in with notions of nation and belonging. In the spirit of critical methodology, I explore ambiguous British identities by arguing we must question "the relevance, substance and validity of what is commonly termed national identity today" (Ware 2009: 8). Ideas about teaching Britishness arose from social concerns like young people's political disenfranchisement, fragmented multicultural society (Golmohamad 2009), "radicalisation" of young Muslim males and the educational failure of White working-class males (Jerome and Clemitshaw 2012). I write knowing (racist) tropes about troubled, failing and lost generations of youth is nothing new: "there is a long history of social anxiety that finds its crystallising focus in a preoccupation with the rising youth generation, and the crime and violence for which it is responsible" (Pearson 2012).

POLITICISED BRITISHNESS

Britishness is undeniably presented, produced and contested through political influences and policy decisions. Distinct minority groups, despite claims of equality, have historically been placed somewhere in a "hierarchy of Britishness" by political elites, which impacted upon how they "experienced" Britishness (Paul 1997: xii): "...white UK residents were directed to the Commonwealth in order to maintain Britishness abroad... migrating citizens of color were rejected as members of British society because they had never been and could never become 'really' British" (Paul 1997: xv). Where a Briton fits into this hierarchy of Britishness will impact upon how she perceives experiences and even contests Britishness as it intersects with her ethnicity, religion, gender and class.

Margaret Thatcher, British Prime Minister from 1979 to 1990, "prided herself on her patriotism" (Ward 2004: 38) yearning to put the "Great" back into "Great Britain" (Croft 2012: 161). She declared schools should teach Empire "without apology, as a story of the nation's 'civilizing' mission in the world at large" (Morley and Robins 2001: 6). Parekh (2008: 64) critically analysed Thatcher for using "the language of national identity... to foreclose a wide variety of views" arguing, she "breathes the spirit of intolerance": "Thatcher places post-Elizabethan colonial expansion at the centre of British history, sees it as a wholly beneficial influence, and equates the English with British history". Another Conservative politician, Norman Tebbit, unhelpfully suggested the 'cricket test' could determine loyalty levels of British ethnic minorities according to the support of international cricket teams, yet what of the Scots: Would they pass the 'cricket test'? (Croft 2012).

Some politicians have attempted to counter quaint imagery of pastoral Britishness. William Hague, ex-leader of the Conservatives, celebrated urban multi-ethnic Britain (The Guardian 1999). New Labour of the 1990s was created with emphasis on Britishness as an underlying and important value (Croft 2012), resulting in "entangled" Britpop and

Blairism, and clumsy attempts to thrust upon the nation a new, inclusive and multicultural Britishness, alongside reclaiming of the Union Jack flag from the far right (Huq 2010). Kunzru (2006: 14) refers to New Labour as "enforcing nationalism with the carrot of 'belonging' and the stick of exclusion". This symbolic alliance of Britpop and Blairism was "almost exclusively white" (Morley and Robins 2001: 9), and male-dominated (Whiteley 2010). Where did ethnic minority men and women, with Bhangra, Bollywood, reggae and rap repertoires, situate themselves in Blair's *Britpop Cool Britannia* vision? *Britpop* not only excluded ethnic minority communities and women; most of the music bands promoted were English, and mainly London-based (Scott 2010; Percival 2010).

In 1999, Labour Prime Minister, Tony Blair also declared "I am a patriot. I love my country" (Croft 2012: 160). Parekh (2008: 68) explains though Blair's vision was "free from the Thatcherite gloating over how it had 'civilized' the inferior races of Asia and Africa and 'saved' the rest of Europe from its internal Barbarians", nonetheless, like Thatcher, Blair viewed British colonialism as "on the whole a good thing, and that the country should continue to give 'leadership' to the rest of Europe and the world". Within New Labour discourses there were "competing narratives" of Britishness (Karvounis et al. 2003: 313): (i) Imperial or transcontinental nationalism locating British identity "in the wider, geopolitical context of traditional allies of Britain… Here, Britain's political and spiritual home is within the British Commonwealth and/or the Anglo-American alliance" and (ii) Euro-nationalism placing British identity "solidly within the European Union, where Britain is prepared to 'pool' sovereignty, but only as a means to maintain national identity". And now Brexit[6] has revealed deep divisions in the nation between those who are pro-Europe and those asserting their Britishness as separate from Europe.

The Swann Report (1985: 7), over thirty years ago, highlighted Britishness as "dynamic and ever changing, adapting and absorbing new ideas and influences". The Cantle Report (2001) and The Runnymede Report (2015) both explain "there is no inherent and/or homogenous ethnic construction of Britishness", thereby recommending "civic values, based on Human Rights conventions, as the basis for a cohesive national collectivity" (Yuval-Davis et al. 2005: 525). The Cantle Report (2001) and the White Paper (2002) could only provide universal liberal values when attempting to define core values of Britain and British citizenship (Joppke 2004), yet over fifty years ago, Kedourie viewed nationalism as "always inherently illiberal and in constant tension with universalism" (Anthias and Yuval-Davis 1992: 39).

British values though are not uniquely "British" (Rosen 2014; Iordanou 2014), but "a grab-bag of universal values that can no longer effectively bind the nation together" (Grube 2011: 632). Addressing the then Education Secretary Michael Gove, Rosen (2014) writes: "Your checklist of British values... I can't attach the adjective 'British' to these. In fact, I find it parochial, patronising and arrogant that you think it's appropriate or right to do so". The President of the National Union of Teachers had similarly once questioned Education Secretary Alan Johnson: "In what way are values of free speech, tolerance and respect for the rule of law not also the values of other countries?" (Eason 2007). Britishness is frequently articulated in a new context where "western culture comes to be recognised as but one particular form of modernity, rather than as some universal template for humankind", in an age where Britain is no longer as influential, and increasingly ethnically diverse (Morley and Robins 2001: 3):

...this lack of unified concept has been explained in terms of the collapse of the British empire and the United Kingdom's declining economic role on the world stage, globalization, increased devolution and increased pluralism (Runnymede Trust 2000). (Kiwan 2012: 52)

Politicians who, in grand speeches, equate Britishness with worthy principles like equality, tolerance, justice and human rights are critiqued for foreign policy decisions that result in Britons feeling "betrayal and disillusionment that the principles they associated with British society were being neglected by its institutions" and politicians (Yousuf 2007: 371). Resisting politicians' attacks on the very British identity that government claims it is protecting becomes a valid societal concern.[7]

"Black in the Union Jack": Where Are We Now?

The London 2012 Olympics illustrated everyday British multiculturalism (Modood 2014), with athletes like Mo Farah, wrapped in the Union Jack flag, cheered on by the nation (Werbner 2013). The Union Jack flag is perceived by some ethnic minorities as representing racist ideologies of far right groups like the BNP. Bradford's ethnic minority youth, for example, preferred to fly the St George's flag during the 2002 World Cup football tournament (Hussain and Bagguley 2005). Yet Mo Farah made an intentional performative gesture of embracing his Britishness through donning the Union Jack. His multiple attachments were not seen as the norm. Farah's pride in his Muslim African heritage resulted in his belonging and loyalty questioned. He was asked by journalists if he would have preferred to represent Somalia (Wagg 2015). Though seemingly loved by Britons, Farah's Somalian Muslim Otherness was emphasised by a British media that frequently denigrates Somalia "with the negative signifiers of civil war, poverty, piracy and unwelcome (often 'asylum seeking') immigration" (Wagg 2015: 155). More recently, *The Great British Bake Off* (Love Productions 2015) winner, Nadiya Hussain, received racist and Islamophobic threats on social media. Though she "stole the nation's heart", it "didn't stop cruel Twitter trolls targeting her because of her faith" (Gordon 2016).

Diversity—"a fundamental characteristic of the universe"(Kedourie 1993: 49)—inevitably arises in analyses of nation and identity. Yet diversity no longer commands respect in a post-9/11 and 7/7 world where it "has become conditional on a new duty to integrate at the level of shared values"(McGhee 2008: 3). Inconclusive messages about belonging harbour tensions and ambiguities regarding multicultural Britain; politicians applaud diversity and integration, while simultaneously their policies perpetuate assimilationist rhetoric (Back et al. 2002). Superpatriotism (Zinn 2013) is evident in FBV policy that aims to "deradicalise" Muslim students judged as unwilling to assimilate, as indisposed to the very British values that have been pronounced by policymakers and politicians as irrevocable and obligatory. For a long time, British Muslims have increasingly been seen in terms of "negativity, deprivation, disadvantage and alienation" (Alexander 2000: 6).

Hall (1996b: 449) referring to Gilroy's *There Ain't No Black in the Union Jack* writes: "Fifteen years ago we didn't care, or at least I didn't care, whether there was any black in the Union Jack. Now not only do we care, we *must*". Yet there exists "a crisis of belonging", where "more and more people feel as though they do not belong. More and more people are seeking to belong, and more and more people are not counted as belonging" (Miller 2008: 1). Political perceptions of belonging and Britishness translate into policies, which impact upon the lives of young Britons. Therefore, this book values young people's identities and belongings, problematising notions of shared values, belonging and Britishness. Can we probe the meanings of everyday Britishness through creative encounters in the classroom?

A Note on Problematising Identity Categories and Labels

Race, understood to be difference "associated with migration, origin and colour" (Finney and Simpson 2009: 5), is a highly problematic and contested concept (Gunew 2004; James 2006; Fredman 2011): "An individual's race is determined socially and psychologically, not biologically" (James 2006: 44). The concept of race entered the European vocabulary in the eighteenth century, before then it was not used in Africa; though Africa was ethnically and linguistically diverse, there existed "cultural unity that allowed for an African worldview that did not facilitate a spirit of conquest, exploitation, and enslavement of people based on such an arbitrary physical marker as skin color" (Cokley 2002: 30). *Ethnicity*—the historical, political and cultural construction of identities (Hall 1996b)—consists of "the rituals of daily life, including language and religion" (Gunew 2004: 21). Even with shared ethnic identities, individual experiences differ (Maylor et al. 2007), since ethnic groups themselves are not monolithic (Bhavnani et al. 2005; Fredman 2011).

Black and White cultures and identities are not homogenous, thus essentialising cultures and identities is problematic (Cokley 2002; Yancy 2005). Regarding the complex language of race, it seems "conventions governing the capitalization of racial identifiers are currently in flux" (Watson 2013: ix). Some scholars intentionally avoid capitalising racial categories. Lewis (2004) refers to "white", "whiteness", "black" and "blackness" , while Allen (2009), maybe because of marginalised Appalachian White roots, capitalises Whiteness. White students benefit from racial ideologies (Lewis 2004), but White working-class students frequently do not experience the power and privilege associated with elite hegemonic Whiteness. Therefore, capitalising Whiteness in presenting this research was a conscious decision. As my White British research participant, Ellie, highlights, she is Othered as the White working-class *chav* by humiliating wider social discourses. The young people I interviewed are aware White working-class students are sometimes perceived as "backward" in contrast with White middle-class "respectable" students (Preston 2003: 7). Young people's discourses of belonging might reveal paradoxical ways of negotiating notions of respectability, authenticity and value as they resist and embrace conflicted conceptions of class and locale (Stahl and Habib 2017).

Writing about Blackness, scholars might make a political statement with a capital B. We can similarly empower White working-class students. I want to draw attention to Whiteness as a social construct by capitalising the W (Ignatiev and Garvey 1996; Shore 2001; Foster 2003; Lee 2004; Kuehnel 2009; Lund and Carr 2010). Writers sometimes refer to "race" using quotation marks to problematise the unnatural notion (Rowe 2012). Some advocates of critical race theory, like Delgado or Ladson-Billings, do not employ quotation marks when referring to race (Bhopal and Preston 2012). To avoid clumsy and cumbersome stylistics of placing quotation marks around all social categories, following Jiwani (2006) and DaCosta (2007), I highlight from the beginning my commitment to deconstruct the flawed construct of race without continually employing quotation marks or italicising. The derogatory label of chav is also a problematic social construction reflecting class prejudices and discrimination, but again, I will not be italicising it throughout the book.

NOTES

1. The General Certificate in Secondary Education typically taken at age sixteen.
2. Culturally relevant pedagogy (Ladson-Billings 1995)—which I discuss in later chapters—recognises that academic competence and success are necessary for students, alongside raising self-confidence about identity.
3. For more on these students and other South East London students' ideas of belonging, see Stahl and Habib (2017).
4. In 2010, the General Election in the UK resulted in a hung parliament. A coalition government was formed between the Conservatives and Liberal Democrats.
5. Thatcherism refers to the policies of Prime Minister Margaret Thatcher's government from 1979 to 1990.
6. Brexit refers to Britain exiting the European Union.
7. When Gordon Brown requested the British Library to create an exhibition to celebrate Britishness, the British Library responded with a "clever snub" in the form of an exhibition entitled "Taking Liberties"; government policies on ID cards and detention of suspects were explored in the exhibition (Hastings et al. 2008).

REFERENCES

Ajegbo, K., D. Kiwan, and S. Sharma. 2007. *Diversity and Citizenship: Curriculum Review*. London: Department for Education and Skills.

Alexander, C.E. 2000. *The Asian Gang: Ethnicity, Identity, Masculinity*. Oxford and New York: Berg.

Alexander, C., D. Bernard-Weekes, and J. Arday. 2015. The Runnymede School Report: Race, Education and Inequality in Contemporary Britain. The Runnymede Trust.

Allen, R.L. 2009. What About Poor White People? In *Handbook of Social Justice in Education*, ed. W. Ayers, T.M. Quinn, and D. Stovall. New York: Routledge.

Anderson, B. 2006. *Imagined Communities: Reflections on the Origin and Spread of Nationalism*. London: Verso.

Anderson, B. 2012. Introduction. In *Mapping the Nationm*, ed. G. Balakrishnan. London: Verso Books.

Andrews, R., and A. Mycock. 2008. Dilemmas of Devolution: The 'Politics of Britishness' and Citizenship Education. *British Politics* 3: 139–155.

Anthias, F., and N. Yuval-Davis. 1992. *Racialized Boundaries: Race, Nation, Gender, Colour and Class and the Anti-Racist Struggle*. London and New York: Routledge.

Back, L. 1996. *New Ethnicities and Urban Culture: Racisms and Multiculture in Young Lives*. London: Routledge.

Back, L., M. Keith, A. Khan, K. Shukra, and J. Solomos. 2002. New Labour's White Heart: Politics, Multiculturalism and the Return of Assimilation. *The Political Quarterly* 73: 445–454.

Baumann, G. 1996. *Contesting Culture: Discourses of Identity in Multi-ethnic London*. Cambridge: Cambridge University Press.

BBC News. 2007. *Schools 'Must Teach Britishness'* [Online]. Available: http://news.bbc.co.uk/1/hi/education/6294643.stm.

Bechhofer, F., and D. Mccrone. 2010. Choosing National Identity. *Sociological Research Online* [Online], 15. Available: http://www.socresonline.org.uk/15/3/3.html.

Berkeley, R. 2011. True Multiculturalism Acts as a Bulwark Against Further Extremism [Online]. *Left Foot Forward*. Available: http://leftfootforward.org/2011/02/david-cameron-wrong-on-multiculturalism/. Accessed 24 Feb 2016.

Bhabha, H.K. (ed.). 1990. *Nation and Narration*. Abingdon: Routledge.

Bhavnani, R., H.S. Mirza, V. Meetoo, and J.R. Foundation. 2005. *Tackling the Roots of Racism: Lessons for Success*. Bristol: The Policy Press.

Bhopal, K., and J. Preston. 2012. *Intersectionality and "Race" in Education*. New York and London: Routledge.

Billig, M. 1995. *Banal Nationalism*. London: Sage.

Bragg, B. 2006. *The Progressive Patriot*. London: Transworld.

Brah, A. 1996. *Cartographies of Diaspora: Contesting Identities*. London: Routledge.

Brubaker, R. 2004. *Ethnicity Without Groups*. Cambridge and London: Harvard University Press.

Brubaker, R., and F. Cooper. 2000. Beyond "Identity". *Theory and Society* 29: 1–47.

Brunel University. 2016. *Debate Questions British Values—But Evidence of EU Impact Should Decide Our Fate* [Online]. Available: http://www.brunel.ac.uk/news-and-events/news/news-items/ne_468559. Accessed 21 Mar 2016.

Burkett, J. 2013. *Constructing Post-imperial Britain: Britishness, 'Race' and the Radical Left in the 1960s*. Basingstoke: Palgrave Macmillan.

Burletson, L. 1993. The State, Internment and Public Criticism in the Second World War. In *The Internment of Aliens in Twentieth Century Britain*, ed. D. Cesarani and T. Kushner. London and New York: Routledge.

Cameron, D. 2014. British Values Aren't Optional, They're Vital. That's Why I Will Promote Them in EVERY School: As Row Rages Over 'Trojan Horse' Takeover of Our Classrooms, the Prime Minister Delivers This Uncompromising Pledge... [Online]. *The Mail on Sunday*. Available: http://www.dailymail.co.uk/debate/article-2658171/DAVID-CAMERON-British-values-arent-optional-theyre-vital-Thats-I-promote-EVERY-school-As-row-rages-Trojan-Horse-takeover-classrooms-Prime-Minister-delivers-uncompromising-pledge.html. Accessed 26 June 2014.

Cameron, K. (ed.). 1999. *National Identity*. Exeter: Intellect.

Carnegie, C.V. 2002. *Postnationalism Prefigured: Caribbean Borderlands*. New Brunswick: Rutgers University Press.

Carrington, B., and G. Short. 1995. What Makes a Person British? Children's Conceptions of Their National Culture and Identity. *Educational Studies* 21: 217–238.

Cohen, R. 1994. *Frontiers of Identity: The British and the Others*. London and New York: Longman.

Cohen, R. 1995. Fuzzy Frontiers of Identity: The British Case. *Social Identities* 1: 35–62.

Cokley, K. 2002. To Be or Not to Be Black: Problematics of Racial Identity. In *The Quest for Community and Identity: Critical Essays in Africana Social Philosophy*, ed. R.E. Birt. Lanham: Rowman & Littlefield.

Colley, L. 1992. *Britons: Forging the Nation, 1707–1837*. New Haven: Yale University Press.

Communities and Local Government. 2012. *Creating the Conditions for Integration*. Department for Communities and Local Government.

Croft, S. 2012. *Securitizing Islam: Identity and the Search for Security*. Cambridge: Cambridge University Press.

Cullen, F. (ed.). 2000. *Sources in Irish Art: A Reader*. Cork: Cork University Press.

DaCosta, K. 2007. *Making Multiracials: State, Family, and Market in the Redrawing of the Color Line*. Stanford: Stanford University Press.

Day, G., and A. Thompson. 2004. *Theorizing Nationalism*. Houndmills: Palgrave Macmillan.

Deaux, K. 2001. *Social Identity. Encyclopedia of Women and Gender*. San Diego: Academic Press.

Department for Education. 2011. Teachers' Standards: Guidance for School Leaders, School Staff and Governing Bodies.

Department for Education. 2014. *Promoting Fundamental British Values as Part of SMSC in Schools*, ed. D.F. Education. DFE-00679-2014 ed

Eason, G. 2007. Britishness Lessons 'Fuel Racism' [Online]. *BBC News*. Available: http://news.bbc.co.uk/1/hi/education/6535089.stm. Accessed 7 July 2014.

Easton, M. 2014. Should Teachers 'Promote' British Values? [Online]. *BBC News*. Available: http://www.bbc.co.uk/news/uk-27784747. Accessed 20 June 2014.

Edensor, T. 2002. *National Identity, Popular Culture and Everyday Life*. Oxford: Berg.

Elton-Chalcraft, S., V. Lander, L. Revell, D. Warner, and L. Whitworth. 2017. To Promote, or Not to Promote Fundamental British Values?—Teachers' Standards, Diversity and Teacher Education. *British Educational Research Journal* 43: 29–48.

Fenton, S. 2007. Indifference Towards National Identity: What Young Adults Think About Being English and British*. *Nations and Nationalism* 13: 321–339.

Finney, N., and L. Simpson. 2009. *'Sleepwalking to Segregation'? Challenging Myths About Race and Migration*. Bristol: Policy Press.

Foster, L. 2003. The Capitalization of Black and White. *Share: Canada's Largest Ethnic Newspaper* [Online], 26. Available: http://www.yorku.ca/lfoster/documents/Foster%20Scanned%20Articles/The%20Capitalization%20of%20Black%20And%20White_Foster_Share_21.08.03.pdf.

Fredman, S. 2011. *Discrimination Law*. Oxford: Oxford University Press.

Garner, R. 2007. Schools must Teach British Values to Beat 'Big Brother'-Style Bigotry, Says Minister [Online]. *The Independent*. http://www.independent.co.uk/news/education/education-news/schools-must-teach-british-values-to-beat-big-brother-style-bigotry-says-minister-6229006.html. Accessed 7 July 2014.

Gellner, E. and J. Breuilly. 2008. *Nations and Nationalism*. Ithaca: Cornell University Press.

Gidley, B. 2014. Integration. In *Migration: The COMPAS Anthology*, ed. B. Anderson and M. Keith. Oxford: COMPAS.

Gilroy, P. 1992. The End of Antiracism. In *Race, Culture and Difference*, ed. J. Donald and A. Rattansi. London: Sage.

Gilroy, P. 2004. *After Empire: Multiculture or Postcolonial Melancholia*. London and New York: Routledge.

Golmohamad, M. 2009. Education for World Citizenship: Beyond National Allegiance. *Educational Philosophy and Theory* 41: 466–486.

Gordon, A. 2016. Great British Bake-Off Winner Nadiya Hussain Reveals Police Had to Check Her Home Because She was Targeted by Anti-Islamic Hate Mob After She Won the Show [Online]. *Mail Online*. Available: http://www.dailymail.co.uk/news/article-3388379/Great-British-bake-winner-Nadiya-Hussain-reveals-police-guarded-home-targeted-anti-Islamic-hate-mob.html. Accessed 27 Mar 2016.

Grayson, J. 2012. The Strange Xenophobic World of Coalition Integration Policy [Online]. *Institute of Race Relations*. Available: http://www.irr.org.uk/news/the-strange-xenophobic-world-of-coalition-integration-policy/. Accessed 06 July 2014.

Gregory, E. 2005. Introduction: Tracing the Steps. In *On Writing Educational Ethnographies: The Art of Collusion*, ed. J. Conteh, E. Gregory, C. Kearney, and A. Mor-Sommerfeld. Stoke on Trent: Trentham Books.

Grube, D. 2011. How Can 'Britishness' Be Re-made? *The Political Quarterly* 82: 628–635.

Gunew, S. 2004. *Haunted Nations: The Colonial Dimensions of Multiculturalisms*. Abingdon: Routledge.

Hall, S. 1992. The Question of Cultural Identity. In *Modernity and Its Futures*, ed. S. Hall, D. Held, and T. McGrew. Cambridge: Polity Press.

Hall, S. 1996a. The Meaning of New Times. In *Stuart Hall: Critical Dialogues in Cultural Studies*, ed. K.-H. Chen and D. Morley. London: Routledge.

Hall, S. 1996b. New Ethnicities. In *Stuart Hall: Critical Dialogues in Cultural Studies*, ed. K.-H. Chen and D. Morley. London: Routledge.

Hall, S. 1996c. Who Needs 'Identity'? In *Questions of Cultural Identity*, ed. S. Hall and P. Du Gay. London: Sage.

Hand, M., and J. Pearce. 2009. Patriotism in British Schools: Principles, Practices and Press Hysteria. *Educational Philosophy and Theory* 41: 453–465.

Hastings, C., B. Jones, and S. Plentl. 2008. Gordon Brown 'Snubbed' Over His Britishness Exhibition at the British Library [Online]. *The Telegraph*. Available: http://www.telegraph.co.uk/news/2569642/Gordon-Brown-snubbed-over-his-Britishness-exhibition-at-the-British-Library.html. Accessed 20 June 2014.

Heaney, S. 1983. *An Open Letter*. Derry: Field Day Theatre Company.

Heater, D. 2001. The History of Citizenship Education in England. *The Curriculum Journal* 12: 103–123.

Heath, A., and N. Demireva. 2014. Has Multiculturalism Failed in Britain? *Ethnic and Racial Studies* 37: 161–180.

HM Government. 2015. Revised Prevent Duty Guidance: For England and Wales.

Home Office. 2001. *Community Cohesion: A Report of the Independent Review Team*, Chaired by Ted Cantle. London: HMSO.

Hoque, A. 2015. *British-Islamic Identity: Third Generation Bangladeshis from East London*. London: IOE Press.

House of Lords. 2008. Debate: "To Call Attention to the Concept of Britishness in the Context of the Cultural, Historical, Constitutional and Ethical Tradition of the Peoples of These Islands".

Hroch, M. 2012. From National Movement to the Fully-Formed Nation: The Nation-building Process in Europe. In *Mapping the Nation*, ed. G. Balakrishnan. London: Verso Books.

Huq, R. 2010. Labouring the Point? The Politics of Britpop in 'New Britain'. In *Britpop and the English Music Tradition*, ed. A. Bennett and J. Stratton. Farnham: Ashgate.

Hussain, Y., and P. Bagguley. 2005. Citizenship, Ethnicity and Identity: British Pakistanis after the 2001 'Riots'. *Sociology* 39: 407–425.

Ignatiev, N., and J. Garvey (eds.). 1996. *Race Traitor*. New York and London: Routledge.

Iordanou, G. 2014. Not Very British #BritishValues: How David Cameron is Silencing Minorities [Online]. *Huff Post Politics*. Available: http://www.huffingtonpost.co.uk/george-iordanou/not-very-british-britishv_b_5499524.html. Accessed 3 July 2015.

Jacobson, J. 1997. Perceptions of Britishness. *Nations and Nationalism* 3: 181–199.

James, C.E. 2006. Race, Ethnicity, and Cultural Identity. In *Identity and Belonging: Rethinking Race and Ethnicity in Canadian Society*, ed. B.S. Bolaria and S.P. Hier. Toronto: Canadian Scholars' Press.

Jerome, L., and G. Clemitshaw. 2012. Teaching (About) Britishness? An Investigation into Trainee Teachers' Understanding of Britishness in Relation to Citizenship and the Discourse of Civic Nationalism. *Curriculum Journal* 23: 19–41.

Jiwani, Y. 2006. *Discourses of Denial: Mediations of Race, Gender, and Violence.* Vancouver: UBC Press.

Joppke, C. 2004. The Retreat of Multiculturalism in the Liberal State: Theory and Policy. *The British Journal of Sociology* 55: 237–257.

Kamusella, T. 2008. *The Politics of Language and Nationalism in Modern Central Europe*. Basingstoke: Palgrave Macmillan.

Karvounis, A., K. Manzo, and T. Gray. 2003. Playing Mother: Narratives of Britishness in New Labour Attitudes Toward Europe. *Journal of Political Ideologies* 8: 311–325.

Kedourie, E. 1993. *Nationalism*. Oxford: Blackwell.

Kiwan, D. 2012. Multicultural Citizenship and Social Cohesion: Reflecting on the Case Study of England. In *Rethinking Education for Social Cohesion: International Case Studies*, ed. M. Shuayb. Basingstoke: Palgrave Macmillan.

Kuehnel, S.S. 2009. Abstinence-Only Education Fails African American Youth. *Washington University Law Review* 86: 1241–1271.

Kunzru, H. 2006. *The Values on the Ground: Multiculturalism and the War on Terror*, 2. Mute: Culture and Politics After the Net.

Ladson-Billings, G. 1995. But That's Just Good Teaching! The Case for Culturally Relevant Pedagogy. *Theory into Practice* 34: 159–165.

Lee, B.T. 2004. The Network Economic Effects of Whiteness. *American University Law Review* 53: 1259–1304.

Lewis, A.E. 2004. What Group? Studying Whites and Whiteness in the Era of "Color-Blindness". *Sociological Theory* 22: 623–646.

Lund, D.E., and P.R. Carr. 2010. Exposing Privilege and Racism in The Great White North: Tackling Whiteness and Identity Issues in Canadian Education. *Multicultural Perspectives* 12: 229–234.

Malik, K. 1996. *The Meaning of Race: Race, History and Culture in Western Society*. New York: NYU Press.

Malik, S. 2002. *Representing Black Britain: Black and Asian Images on Television*. London: Sage.

Mason, R. (ed.). 2016. *Muslim Minority-State Relations: Violence, Integration, and Policy*. Basingstoke: Palgrave Macmillan.

May, S. (ed.). 1999. *Critical Multiculturalism: Rethinking Multicultural and Antiracist Education*. London: Falmer Press.

Maylor, U. 2010. Notions of Diversity, British Identities and Citizenship Belonging. *Race Ethnicity and Education* 13: 233–252.

Maylor, U. 2016. 'I'd Worry About How to Teach It': British Values in English Classrooms. *Journal of Education for Teaching* 42: 314–328.

Maylor, U., B. Read, H. Mendick, A. Ross, and N. Rollock. 2007. Diversity and Citizenship in the Curriculum: Research Review. Research Report 819. London: The Institute for Policy Studies in Education, London Metropolitan University.

McGhee, D. 2008. *End of Multiculturalism: Terrorism, Integration and Human Rights*. Maidenhead: Open University Press.

McMillan, D.W., and D.M. Chavis. 1986. Sense of Community: A Definition and Theory. *Journal of Community Psychology* 14: 6–23.

Miah, S. 2015. *Muslims, Schooling and the Question of Self-Segregation*. Basingstoke: Palgrave Macmillan.

Miller, T. 2008. *Cultural Citizenship: Cosmopolitanism, Consumerism, and Television in a Neoliberal Age*. Philadelphia: Temple University Press.

Modood, T. 2005. Ethnicity and Political Mobilization in Britain. In *Ethnicity, Social Mobility, and Public Policy: Comparing the USA and UK*, ed. G.C. Loury, T. Modood, and S.M. Teles. Cambridge: Cambridge University Press.

Modood, T. 2014. Multiculturalism and Britishness: Provocations, Hostililities and Advances. In *The Politics of Ethnic Diversity in the British Isles*, ed. R. Garbaye and P. Schnapper. Basingstoke: Palgrave Macmillan.

Morley, D. and K. Robins. 2001. Introduction: The National Culture in its New Global Context. In *British Cultural Studies: Geography, Nationality and Identity*, ed. D. Morley and K. Robins. Oxford: Oxford University Press.

Murji, K., and J. Solomos (eds.). 2015. *Theories of Race and Ethnicity*. Cambridge: Cambridge University Press.

Nayak, A. 2003. *Race, Place and Globalization: Youth Cultures in a Changing World*. Oxford: Berg.

Oakes, L. 2001. *Language and National Identity: Comparing France and Sweden*. Amsterdam: J. Benjamins Publishing Company.

Osler, A. 2008. Citizenship Education and the Ajegbo Report: Re-imagining a Cosmopolitan Nation. *London Review of Education* 6: 11–25.

Osler, A. 2015. The Stories We Tell: Exploring Narrative in Education for Justice and Equality in Multicultural Contexts. *Multicultural Education Review* 7: 12–25.

Osler, A., and H. Starkey. 2005. *Changing Citizenship: Democracy and Inclusion in Education*. Maidenhead: Open University Press.

Parekh, B. 2000a. Defining British National Identity. *The Political Quarterly* 71: 4–14.

Parekh, B. 2000b. *The Future of Multi-ethnic Britain: Report of the Commission on the Future of Multi-ethnic Britain*. London: The Runnymede Trust/Profile Books.

Parekh, B. 2008. *A New Politics of Identity: Political Principles for an Interdependent World*. Basingstoke: Palgrave Macmillan.

Paul, K. 1997. *Whitewashing Britain: Race and Citizenship in the Postwar Era*. Ithaca and London: Cornell University Press.

Pearson, G. 2012. Everything Changes, Nothing Moves: The Longue Duree of Social Anxieties. In *The English Riots of 2011: A Summer of Discontent*, ed. D. Briggs. Hook: Waterside Press.

Percival, J.M. 2010. Britpop or Eng-Pop? In *Britpop and the English Music Tradition*, ed. A. Bennett and J. Stratton. Farnham: Ashgate.

Preston, J. 2003. White Trash Vocationalism? Formations of Class and Race in an Essex Further Education College. *Widening Participation and Lifelong Learning* 5: 6–17.

Renan, E. 1990. What is a Nation? In *Nation and Narration*, ed. H.K. Bhabha. Abingdon: Routledge.

Revell, L., and H. Bryan. 2016. Calibrating Fundamental British Values: How Head Teachers are Approaching Appraisal in the Light of the Teachers' Standards 2012, Prevent and the Counter-Terrorism and Security Act, 2015. *Journal of Education for Teaching* 42: 341–353.

Richardson, R. 2015. British Values and British Identity: Muddles, Mixtures, and Ways Ahead. *London Review of Education* 13: 37–48.

Rosen, M. 2014. Dear Mr Gove: What's So 'British' About Your 'British Values'? [Online]. *The Guardian*. Available: http://www.theguardian.com/education/2014/jul/01/gove-what-is-so-british-your-british-values. Accessed 04 July 2014.

Rowe, M. 2012. *Race & Crime*. London: Sage.

Rydgren, J. 2004. *The Populist Challenge: Political Protest and Ethno-Nationalist Mobilization in France*. New York: Berghahn Books.

Saeed, A., N. Blain, and D. Forbes. 1999. New Ethnic and National Questions in Scotland: Post-British Identities Among Glasgow Pakistani Teenagers. *Ethnic and Racial Studies* 22: 821–844.

Sarup, M. 2005. Home and Identity. In *Travellers' Tales: Narratives of Home and Displacement*, ed. J. Bird, B. Curtis, M. Mash, T. Putnam, G. Robertson, and L. Tickner. London: Routledge.

Scott, D.B. 2010. The Britpop Sound. In *Britpop and the English Music Tradition*, ed. A. Bennett and J. Stratton. Farnham: Ashgate.

Scourfield, J., B. Dicks, M. Drakeford, and A. Davies. 2006. *Children, Place and Identity: Nation and Locality in Middle Childhood*. Abingdon: Routledge.

Sears, A., and A. Hughes. 2006. Citizenship: Education or Indoctrination? *Citizenship Teaching and Learning* 2: 3–17.

Shore, S. 2001. Talking About Whiteness: "Adult Learning Principles" and the Invisble Norm. In *Making Space: Merging Theory and Practice in Adult Education*, ed. V. Sheared and P.A. Sissel. Westport and London: Bergin & Garvey.

Smith, A.D. 2010. *Nationalism*. Cambridge: Polity Press.

Smyth, J., and P. McInerney. 2013. Whose Side are You On? Advocacy Ethnography: Some Methodological Aspects of Narrative Portraits of Disadvantaged Young People, in Socially Critical Research. *International Journal of Qualitative Studies in Education* 26: 1–20.

Solomos, J. 2001. Race, Multi-culturalism and Difference. In *Culture and Citizenship*, ed. N. Stevenson. London: Sage.

Stahl, G., and S. Habib. 2017. Moving Beyond the Confines of the Local: Working-Class Students' Conceptualizations of Belonging and Respectability. *Young* 25 (3): 1–18.

Swann, M. 1985. Education for All: The Report of the Committee of Inquiry into the Education of Children from Ethnic Minority Groups. London: HMSO.

The Great British Bake Off. 2015. Directed by Love Productions. BBC.

The Guardian. 1999. Who Do We Think We Are? [Online]. Available: http://www.theguardian.com/theguardian/1999/jan/20/features11.g27. Accessed 20 June 2014.

The Yorkshire Post. 2014. Schools will Face Action If They Fail to Promote 'British Values' [Online]. Available: http://www.yorkshirepost.co.uk/news/main-topics/education/schools-will-face-action-if-they-fail-to-promote-british-values-1-6690092. Accessed 26 June 2014.

Thurston, M., and N. Alderman. 2014. Reading Postwar British and Irish Poetry. Oxford: Wiley Blackwell.

Vadher, K., and M. Barrett. 2009. Boundaries of Britishness in British Indian and Pakistani Young Adults. Journal of Community & Applied Social Psychology 19: 442–458.

Vasta, E. 2013. Do We Need Social Cohesion in the 21st Century? Multiple Languages of Belonging in the Metropolis. Journal of Intercultural Studies 34: 196–213.

Vertovec, S., and R. Cohen (eds.). 2002. Conceiving Cosmopolitanism: Theory, Context and Practice. Oxford: Oxford University Press.

Wagg, S. 2015. The London Olympics of 2012: Politics, Promises and Legacy. Basingstoke: Palgrave Macmillan.

Walford, C. 2012. 'We Need Community Cohesion': Ministers' Pledge to End Era of Multiculturalism by Appealing to 'Sense of British identity' [Online]. Mail Online. Available: http://www.dailymail.co.uk/news/article-2104049/Eric-Pickles-signals-end-multiculturalism-says-Tories-stand-majority.html. Accessed 10 July 2014.

Ward, P. 2004. Britishness Since 1870. London: Routledge.

Ward, P. 2009. The end of Britishness? A Historical Perspective. British Politics Review: Journal of the British Politics Society 4: 3.

Ware, V. 2009. Chasing Britishness: A Post-colonial Project. British Politics Review: Journal of the British Politics Society 4: 8.

Watson, S., and A. Saha. 2012. Suburban Drifts: Mundane Multiculturalism in Outer London. Ethnic and Racial Studies 36: 2016–2034.

Watson, V.T. 2013. The Souls of White Folk: African American Writers Theorize Whiteness. Jackson: University Press of Mississippi.

Weedon, C. 2004. Identity And Culture: Narratives of Difference And Belonging: Narratives of Difference and Belonging. Maidenhead: Open University Press.

Wemyss, G. 2009. The Invisible Empire: White Discourse, Tolerance and Belonging. Farnham: Ashgate.

Werbner, P. 2013. Everyday Multiculturalism: Theorising the Difference Between 'Intersectionality' and 'Multiple Identities'. *Ethnicities* 13: 401–419.

Whiteley, S. 2010. Trainspotting: The Gendered History of Britpop. In *Britpop and the English Music Tradition*, ed. A. Bennett and J. Stratton. Farnham: Ashgate.

Wright, M., and I. Bloemraad. 2012. Is There a Trade-off Between Multiculturalism and Socio-Political Integration? Policy Regimes and Immigrant Incorporation in Comparative Perspective. *Perspectives on Politics* 10: 77–95.

Yancy, G. (ed.). 2005. *White on White/Black on Black*. Lanham: Rowman & Littlefield Publishers.

Yousuf, Z. 2007. Unravelling Identities: Citizenship and Legitimacy in a Multicultural Britain. *European Journal of Cultural Studies* 10: 360–373.

Yuval-Davis, N., F. Anthias, and E. Kofman. 2005. Secure Borders and Safe Haven and the Gendered Politics of Belonging: Beyond Social Cohesion. *Ethnic and Racial Studies* 28: 513–535.

Žarkov, D. 2015. Reflecting on Faith and Feminism. *European Journal of Women's Studies* 22: 3–6.

Zinn, H. 2013. *A Power Governments Cannot Suppress*. San Francisco: City Lights Books.

CHAPTER 2

Researching Education
in Multicultural London

Abstract This chapter outlines features of educational, urban and critical ethnography, arts-based educational research (ABER), as well as critical race methodology (CRM) and critical pedagogy that influenced my research on the teaching and learning of Britishness. These methodological approaches value participant voice and empowerment, and encourage social justice and social change. The empirical data presented in this book was collected from two separate research studies involving two educational settings and mixed methods: (i) a questionnaire survey of trainee teachers of Art in an Educational Studies department at a London university who reflected upon the Fundamental British Values teaching requirement, and (ii) an ethnographic arts-based educational research in a London school with Art teachers and two GCSE classes who explored Britishness.

Keywords Educational research · Critical research · Research methodology · Research tools · Participant voice

RESEARCHING BRITISHNESS AND FUNDAMENTAL BRITISH VALUES (FBV)

By describing and supporting critical pedagogical approaches to exploring identities, this book aims to understand the pedagogies involved in teaching and learning about Britishness and Fundamental British Values (FBV).

Emphasis on student voice, respectful and caring dialogue, and collaborative communication is shown as the vision chosen by trainee teachers and teachers required to teach Britishness, leading to meaningful and engaged individual and collective critical reflections regarding students' stories of Britishness. The empirical data in this book was collected from two separate research studies involving two educational settings and mixed methods. Chapter 4 reports on a questionnaire survey of trainee teachers of Art in an Educational Studies department at a London university regarding FBV (2016–2017). Chapters 5, 6 and 7 detail ethnographic arts-based educational research in a London school with Art teachers and two GCSE classes who explored Britishness (2007–2008). Knowing teachers often "embrace the political as a positive means to develop critical consciousness" (Yokley 1999: 24), I present the ways (trainee) teachers negotiate political demands about Britishness and FBV teaching.

Trainee Teachers on FBV

Recent research conducted in 2016–2017 with a cohort of Art trainee teachers enrolled on a one-year Postgraduate Certificate in Education (PGCE) course at a London university is outlined in Chap. 4. The empirical data collected towards the end of the first semester of the course, and again before they commenced their second teaching placement, concerns 25 trainee teachers of ages ranging from early twenties to late thirties. I had informed the trainee teachers about the purposes of collecting the data and publishing the findings and analysis. I sought their consent, as well as that of their PGCE tutor. Some gave me their email addresses on their questionnaires so I could contact them for further information if needed. There were 19 female and 6 male respondents, mostly of White British ethnicity. I have used pseudonyms but have provided information about age, gender, nationality, ethnicity and religion exactly as they stipulated.

Teaching and Learning Britishness

Britishness teaching in schools is now a requirement (Department for Education 2014), but once was merely a proposal (BBC News 2007). This book describes two classes of London students from diverse backgrounds and their teachers, in 2007–2008, exploring constructs of Britishness and practising *pedagogies of identity*. The field work was conducted with Art teachers who *chose* to bring Britishness into the classroom. Situated in a traditionally White working-class community in London, the school caters for students from the ages of 11 to 19, where approximately 40% of students are classed as non-White. Many students are multilingual: 19% 11–16, 24% post 16. Traditionally, the students did not embark into further or higher education, but now half the students in the sixth form were progressing to university.[1] There were 34 students in total (aged 14–15), 16 students in one class and 18 students in the other class.

INTEGRATING ARTS-BASED RESEARCH WITH CRITICAL URBAN EDUCATIONAL ETHNOGRAPHIES

Ethnographers often seek to (re)present the social worlds of those frequently ignored and marginalised in academia, media and political debates (Goodall 2000). Following Clifford (1986) and Edgeworth (2014), I recognise data is partial and contextual, thus maintaining awareness of the implications of power and positionality is imperative when doing research with young people. Important to an ethical stance is the underlying principle that "to listen to counterstories within the educational system can be an important pedagogical practice for teachers and students as well as an important methodological practice for educational researchers" (Bernal 2002: 116). Avoidance of harm, while doing good, is paramount (Mitchell 2011) in educational research.

Critical Urban Educational Ethnography

Educational ethnography, important in researching social justice and cultural diversity through listening to students' stories (Gregory 2005), is well suited to researching multicultural British identities. An ethnographic approach also suits teacher research (Denscombe 2008), enabling educational ethnographers to "describe, interpret, analyse and represent the lived experiences of schools, classrooms and workplaces" (O'Toole and Beckett 2013: 48). Empirical data from small-scale 'real world' settings (Hammersley 1994) is valuable when conducting educational ethnography. Though problematic to define schools as *natural* settings, and often impossible for most to gain long-term familiarity with the setting (Wolcott 2002), the rich descriptive account using a contextualised and holistic approach based on familiarity with setting can be "flexible and adaptive" and "idiosyncratic and individualistic", permitting a researcher to select appropriate ethnographic techniques appropriate (Wolcott 2002: 33). At the ethnographic heart lies exploration of social/cultural context and participant experience (Hitchcock and Hughes 1995; Atkinson et al. 2007). Ethnography can elucidate meaningful moments in the lives of school students; urban educational ethnographies can (re)present school students' fluid identities in urban contexts.

Grounded in the works of critical pedagogues like Freire, Giroux and Shor (Brown and Dobrin 2012), critical ethnography understands teaching must "engage students…in the dialogic work of understanding their social location and developing cultural action appropriate to that location" (Brooke and Hogg 2012: 116). Critical ethnographic research questions how knowledge is received in a society where prevailing social relations and dominant social structures oppress certain social groups because of class, gender and racial differences, or through imperial, national or colonial oppression (Harvey 1990; Bhavnani et al. 2014). Moving beyond description and analysis, critical research galvanises "change, contradictions, struggle, and practice in order to counter dominant interests and advance the well-being of the world's majority" (Bhavnani et al. 2014: 176). Emancipatory educational research similarly tackles social injustice, powerlessness and oppression through political means to help disadvantaged communities (Babbie 2012; McColl et al. 2013). Others mobilise through transformative activist research reflecting upon "self, place and community" (Guajardo et al. 2008: 3).

Arts-Based Educational Research, Critical Pedagogy and Critical Race Methodology

To research pedagogies of Britishness and elevate student voice, an integrative approach that combines features of critical urban educational ethnography with principles of arts-based educational research (ABER) and critical pedagogy (CP), as well as critical race methodology (CRM), can be a useful way for working with young people on identity exploration. In the last thirty years, researchers have developed visual data collection and analysis to understand social experience (Mitchell 2011) through poetry, prose, drama, painting, photography, multimedia, sculpture and performing arts (Barone and Eisner 2006; Chilton and Leavy 2014; Kara 2015). Arts-based projects are useful in "honouring, eliciting and expressing cultural ways of knowing" and "exploring sensitive topics" (Kara 2015: 24). Examining race and racism, alongside intersections with religion, class and gender, CRM exposes oppressions and challenges dominant ideologies by providing social justice approaches for researchers (Solórzano and Yosso 2002). Ethnography shares phenomenological similarities with art; both emphasise creative and complex social realities, reflexive observation and positionality (Denscombe 2008). ABER harmonises well with critical pedagogy, as both elevate critical questioning. The "resistive capabilities of the arts" can permit contestation of dominant ideologies and social norms (Chilton and Leavy 2014: 403). ABER pursues "novel, ethical and noncoercive ways" to encourage "hopeful dialogue" and "critical consciousness", leading to "social change" (Chilton and Leavy 2014: 407). Thus ABER, like critical pedagogy, leads on issues of social justice, equity and ethics.

THE ARTWORK, INTERVIEWS AND QUESTIONNAIRES

Ethnographers do not tend to only employ one research method, and to the surprise of some traditionalists might incorporate questionnaires as an additional research tool (Wolcott 1997). My mixed methods approach provides scope for a 'complete understanding': questionnaire survey of the two Art classes, as well as the trainee Art teachers, allows for a 'general understanding' of Britishness, while semi-structured interviews with Art students and teachers provide 'detailed understanding' (Creswell and Clark 2011) of Britishness and the experiences of teaching and learning Britishness. The students, individually and collectively, explored Britishness, producing artwork which would eventually be submitted as GCSE coursework. I was motivated by the potential for visual methods to enable collaborative, reflexive and ethically considerate interdisciplinary research (Pink 2003, 2004), particularly recommended when studying communities (Back 2009).

Giving the participants creative spaces, and respecting their voices of experience on identity issues, developed their confidence to be open and honest. Teachers used critical pedagogy strategies, such as promotion of individual reflection, student voice, dialogue and collaboration, to elicit powerful and personal artwork. Some experiences are better presented through the visual (Pink 2004); planning and producing artwork proved to be an excellent medium for young people to begin to explore and discuss their identities. Painting and drawing have long been used in "encountering and expressing oneself" (Pink 2004: 7). The social justice approach of educulturalism through art and narrative can nurture "balanced, creative, informed, and open-minded citizens, who are able to fully participate in democratic society" (Lea and Sims 2008: 15).

The act of young people creating artwork privileged moments of student autonomy and empowerment. This project gave voices to young people to become "the producers and not just the objects or the consumers of research" (Mitchell 2011: 16), acquiring knowledge about "the self in society" through the construction of personal artwork (Yokley 1999: 23). Analysing young people's artwork by making assumptions about their identities would not be in the spirit of social justice and social change. To rigidly impose my personal interpretations on the artwork was never my intention. There is no single meaning of an image that can be argued, but multiple meanings, interpretations and readings (Hall 1997). Therefore, I decided to use the artwork alongside questionnaire and interview data to inform the research in multiple ways: as a crucial process for young people and their teachers to interrogate Britishness creatively, and as visual stimulus to include in the paired interviews with the students.

Directly asking about Britishness may yield limited data due to the inhibitions and self-consciousness of research participants; other times, participants may bring up issues of Britishness and Englishness themselves even when not asked (Fenton 2007; Garner 2012). Through paired interviews, I sought to empower the students to shape the interview together (Heyl 2001); with the Art teachers, I conducted individual interviews. Semi-structured interviews permitted flexibility, minimising potential research bias as questions emerged organically. Not controlling topics resulted in dismantling of traditional power relations between interviewer and interviewee (Lankshear and Knobel 2004); "listening carefully and respectfully", I let research participants "'name' the world in their own terms" (Heyl 2001: 375). I was a *privileged listener* (Siegel 1988: 30). They "understood, trusted and respected my motives in doing the study" speaking with honesty and openness (Tuettemann 2003: 18). The students and teachers were comfortable to the extent that when the allocated time slot was over, they still wanted to talk.

Educational researchers develop amicable relations to initially gain access, but later to maintain rapport with diverse participants: "Good ethnographic practice, data collection and analyses rely upon genuine empathy, trust and participation" (Coffey 1999: 47). In the interviews with the students, their voices dominated, which was a "productive" strategy; they would often enthusiastically and probingly "prompt one another" (Hammersley and Atkinson 2007: 112) and raise matters pertinent to them (Lankshear and Knobel 2004). In pairs, students were more "forthcoming", finding the interview "less threatening" (Hammersley and Atkinson 2007: 111). I found myself sometimes becoming a peripheral listener, protecting the integrity of the data by asking minimal questions. Respectful listening, awareness of my role as a researcher in co-constructing the interview with the researched and understanding "that dialogue is discovery and only partial knowledge will ever be attained" (Heyl 2001: 370) guided my interviewing.

The Art trainee teachers completed the first questionnaire (December 2016) about their thoughts and experiences of FBV, and then a second questionnaire (January 2017) developing their ideas after structured and reflective small group and whole class discussions with their peers (which I facilitated and observed) where they critically examined FBV policy. The trainees also learned about research I had previously conducted on Britishness with Art classes in a London school (detailed in Chaps. 5–7). Two classes of GCSE Art students completed questionnaires at the beginning and end of the Art project on Britishness (2007–2008). The questionnaires provided biographical information about gender, family, religion, place of birth, as well as insight into their artwork. I did not provide closed categories on the questionnaires, as I wanted participants to have the opportunity to self-define.

NOTE

1. GCSE results in 1992 were 7% (5 A*-C), but had vastly improved to 72% (5 A*-C) in 2005.

REFERENCES

Atkinson, P., S. Delamont, A. Coffey, J. Lofland, and L. Lofland (eds.). 2007. *Handbook of Ethnography*. London: Sage.

Babbie, E. 2012. *The Practice of Social Research*. California: Cengage Learning.

Back, L. 2009. Researching Community and Its Moral Projects. *Twenty-First Century Society* 4: 201–214.

Barone, T., and E. Eisner. 2006. Arts-Based Educational Research. In *Handbook of Complementary Methods in Education Research*, ed. J.L. Green, G. Camilli, and P.B. Elmore. Mahwah, NJ: Lawrence Erlbaum.

BBC News. 2007. *Schools 'Must Teach Britishness'* [Online]. Available: http://news.bbc.co.uk/1/hi/education/6294643.stm.

Bernal, D.D. 2002. Critical Race Theory, Latino Critical Theory, and Critical Raced-Gendered Epistemologies: Recognizing Students of Color as Holders and Creators of Knowledge. *Qualitative Inquiry* 8: 105–126.

Bhavnani, K.-K., P. Chua, and D. Collins. 2014. Critical Approaches to Qualitative Research. In *The Oxford Handbook of Qualitative Research*, ed. P. Leavy. Oxford: Oxford University Press.

Brooke, R., and C. Hogg. 2012. Open to Change: Ethos, Identification and Critical Ethnography in Composition Studies. In *Ethnography Unbound: From Theory Shock to Critical Praxis*, ed. S.G. Brown and S.I. Dobrin. Albany: State University of New York Press.

Brown, S.G., and S.I. Dobrin (eds.). 2012. *Ethnography Unbound: From Theory Shock to Critical Praxis*. Albany: State University of New York Press.

Chilton, G., and P. Leavy. 2014. Arts-Based Research Practice: Merging Social Research and the Creative Arts. In *The Oxford Handbook of Qualitative Research*, ed. P. Leavy. Oxford: Oxford University Press.

Clifford, J. 1986. Introduction: Partial Truths. In *Writing Culture: The Poetics and Politics of Ethnography*, ed. J. Clifford and G.E. Marcus. Berkeley: University of California Press.

Coffey, A. 1999. *The Ethnographic Self: Fieldwork and the Representation of Identity*. London: Sage.

Creswell, J.W., and V.L.P. Clark. 2011. *Designing and Conducting Mixed Methods Research*. California: Sage.

Denscombe, M. 2008. Affinity with Ethnography. In *Research in Art & Design Education: Issues and Exemplars*, ed. R. Hickman. Bristol: Intellect.

Department for Education. 2014. Promoting Fundamental British Values as Part of SMSC in Schools, ed. D.F. Education. DFE-00679-2014 ed.

Edgeworth, K. 2014. Unsettling Truths: Post-structural Ethnography as a Tool to Trouble Schooling Exclusions. In *Methodologies for Researching Cultural Diversity in Education: International Perspectives*, ed. G. Smyth and N. Santoro. London: Institute of Education Press.

Fenton, S. 2007. Indifference Towards National Identity: What Young Adults Think About Being English and British*. *Nations and Nationalism* 13: 321–339.

Garner, S. 2012. A Moral Economy of Whiteness: Behaviours, Belonging and Britishness. *Ethnicities* 12: 445–464.

Goodall, H.L. 2000. *Writing the New Ethnography*. Walnut Creek: Rowman & Littlefield.

Gregory, E. 2005. Introduction: Tracing the Steps. In *On Writing Educational Ethnographies: The Art of Collusion*, ed. J. Conteh, E. Gregory, C. Kearney, and A. Mor-Sommerfeld. Stoke on Trent: Trentham Books.

Guajardo, M., F. Guajardo, and E. Del Carmen Casaperalta. 2008. Transformative Education: Chronicling a Pedagogy for Social Change. *Anthropology & Education Quarterly* 39: 3–22.

Hall, S. 1997. Introduction. In *Representation: Cultural Representations and Signifying Practices*, ed. S. Hall. London: Sage.

Hammersley, M. 1994. Introducing Ethnography. In *Researching Language and Literacy in Social Context: A Reader*, ed. D. Graddol, J. Maybin, and B. Stierer. Avon: Multilingual Matters.

Hammersley, M., and P. Atkinson. 2007. *Ethnography: Principles in Practice*. New York: Routledge.

Harvey, L. 1990. *Critical Social Research*. London: Unwim Hyman.

Heyl, B.S. 2001. Ethnographic Interviewing. In *Handbook of Ethnography*, ed. P. Atkinson, A. Coffey, S. Delamont, J. Lofland, and L. Lofland. London: Sage.

Hitchcock, G., and D. Hughes. 1995. *Research and the Teacher: A Qualitative Introduction to School-Based Research*. London: Routledge.

Kara, H. 2015. *Creative Research Methods in the Social Sciences: A Practical Guide*. Bristol: Policy Press.

Lankshear, C., and M. Knobel. 2004. *A Handbook for Teacher Research: From Design to Implementation*. Maidenhead: Open University Press.

Lea, V., and E.J. Sims. 2008. Undoing Whiteness in the Classroom: Different Origins, Shared Commitment. In *Undoing Whiteness in the Classroom: Critical Educultural Teaching Approaches for Social Justice Activism*, ed. V. Lea and E.J. Sims. New York: Peter Lang.

McColl, M.A., W. Adair, S. Davey, and N. Kates. 2013. The Learning Collaborative: An Approach to Emancipatory Research in Disability Studies. *Canadian Journal of Disability Studies* 2: 23.

Mitchell, C. 2011. *Doing Visual Research*. London: Sage.

O'Toole, J., and D. Beckett. 2013. *Educational Research: Creative Thinking and Doing*. South Melbourne, VIC: OUP Australia & New Zealand.

Pink, S. 2003. Interdisciplinary Agendas in Visual Research: Re-situating Visual Anthropology. *Visual Studies* 18: 179–192.

Pink, S. 2004. Introduction: Situating Visual Research. In *Working Images: Visual Research and Representation in Ethnography*, ed. A.I. Alfonso, L. Kurti, and S. Pink. London: Routledge.

Siegel, B.S. 1988. *Love, Medicine and Miracles*. London: Arrow Books.

Solórzano, D.G., and T.J. Yosso. 2002. Critical Race Methodology: Counter-Storytelling as an Analytical Framework for Education Research. *Qualitative Inquiry* 8: 23–44.

Tuettemann, E. 2003. Grounded Theory Illuminates Interpersonal Relationships. In *Qualitative Educational Research in Action: Doing and Reflecting*, ed. T. O'Donoghue and K. Punch. Abingdon: Routledge.

Wolcott, H.F. 1997. Ethnographic research in education. Complementary methods for research in education.

Wolcott, H.F. 2002. Ethnography? Or Educational Travel Writing? In *Ethnography and Schools: Qualitative Approaches to the Study of Education*, ed. Y. Zou and E. Trueba. Maryland: Rowman & Littlefield.

Yokley, S.H. 1999. Embracing a Critical Pedagogy in Art Education. *Art Education* 52: 18.

CHAPTER 3

The Pedagogical Is Political

Abstract This chapter outlines key features of critical pedagogy such as reflection and critical consciousness. I argue that teachers and students wanting to explore identities, social experiences and belongings would benefit from using critical pedagogy approaches in the classroom. I show that critical pedagogy complements the research methodologies discussed in Chap. 2, and that critical pedagogy is especially important in neoliberal times when the emphasis is on the individual. Education should not be about creating subservient automatons unwilling to rise up to transform the social injustices pervading local, national and globalised spaces. Education needs to inspire and enable students to grow in confidence to critique the oppressive social order. Critical pedagogy can counter-neoliberal ideologies and promote collaboration, collective action, social justice and social change.

Keywords Critical pedagogy · Critical consciousness · Social justice Education · Neoliberalism

What Is Critical Pedagogy?

Paulo Freire, often cited as one of the original critical pedagogues, argued for a progressive pedagogy of *possibility*, with its basis in education for *liberation*: traditional *banking* methods of education where teachers-held knowledge which they routinely and uninspiringly transferred to students

S. Habib, *Learning and Teaching British Values*,
DOI 10.1007/978-3-319-60381-0_3

were seen as shackling student knowledge and hindering liberation (1985a, b, 2000, 2001; Freire and Freire 2004). *Problem-posing* education which prizes respectful and caring *dialogue*, praxis (moving beyond theoretical reflection and critical dialogue into reflective action) and *conscientizacao* (critical reflection about oppression) was perceived by Freire as necessary to educate and free marginalised communities. Critiquing the social world—through education—was advocated to transform lives and society. To empower students to respond to social injustices, teachers can use key critical pedagogy principles that support:

i.   student participation and critical consciousness;
ii. the language of hope and possibility;
iii. problem-posing pedagogy where students formulate questions and solutions; and
iv. the belief that teachers, students and citizens can engage in reflective action for social justice/change (Freire 2000; Brett 2007).

Teachers might embrace strategies from diverse educational models to promote *dialogue, praxis* and *conscientizacao.* Two approaches that work harmoniously with critical pedagogy by elevating students' cultural experiences and knowledge are 'critical educulturalism' and 'culturally responsive teaching'. Culturally relevant pedagogy emphasises academic success, cultural competence and critical consciousness (Ladson-Billings 1995). Educulturalism is "an activist learning process" utilising "visual and performing arts, narrative, oral history, and critical dialogue" (Lea and Sims 2008: 15) to enable "critical thinking about social and cultural issues" through "social justice-oriented, culturally responsive, critical, and creative curricula" (Lea and Sims 2008: 1). Educulturalism with Maori students, for example, involves working on classroom relationships, caring and unity (Macfarlane et al. 2007). Culturally responsive teaching serves to enhance student engagement and achievement through knowledge about cultural diversity, culturally diverse curricula and pedagogies and learning communities that value caring and communication (Gay 2002).

CRITICAL PEDAGOGY TO COUNTER NEOLIBERAL EDUCATION

Growing neoliberal education philosophies are responsible for producing non-autonomous state subjects, rather than critical citizens (Di Leo et al. 2014). This is an affront to critical pedagogues, an indignity to the teaching profession. Teachers and students witness education become "a subsector of the economy, designed to create cybercitizens within a teledemocracy of fast-moving images, representations and lifestyle choices" (McLaren 2000: 16). Neoliberal perspectives of learning embrace "individualist and competitive aspects of education", popularising supposed 'useful knowledge'" (Gadotti 2009: 32). How might teachers and students respond to neoliberal policies and practices that suppress and stifle identities? In this book, I call for radical change when it comes to exploring identities. Schools can seek to enhance our philosophies and practices of education with "an enobling, imaginative vision" (Giroux 2013: 5). When exploring British identities, critical pedagogy can help to produce this ennobling and imaginative space of creative collaboration. Critical pedagogues know it is "ethically responsible to scrutinize, challenge, and oppose people, structures, and systems that oppress and dehumanize" (Kirylo 2013: xix) using critical tools to reflect and act upon social struggles in specific contexts with communities and students who inhabit local places (Giroux 2013). For educational researchers, like myself, critical pedagogy—as a theory—also helps ask necessary questions needed to better understand the social world (Kincheloe and McLaren 2002).

Neoliberal ideas about multicultural citizenship and national identity marginalise experiences of oppressed groups (Sleeter 2014), "stifling critical thought, reducing citizenship to the act of consuming, defining certain marginal populations as contaminated and disposable, and removing the discourse of democracy from any vestige of pedagogy" (Giroux 2013: 8). The pedagogical is political. Through the National Curriculum government can "exert direct control over what is taught in schools and how" (Coffey 2001: 43), and teacher education is often impacted upon by government ideology (Arnot and Barton 1992). Knowledge produced and disseminated to students through schooling is "cultural capital that comes from somewhere" imparting the "beliefs of powerful segments of our social collectivity" (Apple 2013: 25). Pedagogy is political, for it is "inherently productive and directive practice rather than neutral or objective" (Giroux 2013: 6).

Following Freirean philosophies, I call for pedagogies that guide students to "question answers rather than merely answer questions" (Brett 2007: 4). By applying critical multicultural and critical pedagogical perspectives, I argue education can expose and disrupt "monovocals, master narratives, standard stories, or majoritarian stories" (that privilege the White male political elite) by contributing and elevating counter-narratives (Solórzano and Yosso 2002: 28). Steinberg (2009) and Vavrus (2015) endorse critical multiculturalism for exploration of race, class, power, privilege, social inequalities, knowledge and resistance. Schools have long been spaces to challenge racist ideas that White skin is required to belong to Britain (Swann 1985), making it all the more concerning then that schools still struggle with vague definitions of Britishness invoking a "desire to keep Britain White" (Maylor 2010: 245). Critical multiculturalism can interrogate pernicious and persistent examples of White supremacy and racial oppression. Critical pedagogy and critical multiculturalism are necessary tools at a time when school teachers and students observe racism post-Brexit and post-Trump[1] as no longer concealed or clandestine, but becoming barefaced and brash.

Social Inequalities and Injustices

Policymakers—increasingly in neoliberal times—favour educational developments that conflict with critical pedagogical ideas about student voice and social justice. Critical pedagogues see social inequalities and injustices as impacting upon ordinary communities, who need hope and possibility to fight oppression. Structural inequalities perpetuated through neoliberal policies can have far-reaching consequences on social identities. Political choices impact in devastating ways upon the lives and identities of the nation's citizens:

> A radical break with the principles of the Welfare State coincided politically with a move towards competitive individualism (Tomlinson 2008b), and a growing belief in the need to safeguard and protect the British national identity (and white majority) from the 'enemy within'. (Gilroy 1987)" (Garratt 2011: 29).

Critical pedagogy "represents a transformational educational response to institutional and ideological domination, especially under capitalism" (Gruenewald 2003: 4). Schools reproduce conforming teachers and passive students (Apple 2013; Giroux 2013), but other times these are sites where complex modes of agency and resistance challenge hegemonic practices (Giroux 2001; Anyon 2011). Critiquing curriculum and pedagogy disrupts the "invisibility... of subjugated knowledges" (Edgeworth 2014: 38); education expands as "a site for resistance to bourgeois hegemony", challenging cultural production and reproduction (Au and Apple 2009: 87).

Alarmingly, "we rarely hear from those folks whom official discourse classifies as Other, about *their* fears" as they struggle to belong to social spaces where they experience hostility, hate, poverty and discrimination (Sandercock 2005: 232). One such example is the summer 2011 riots in English cities that begun as community demonstrations against institutional discrimination and state violence—sparked by the killing of north Londoner Mark Duggan by the police—but the narrative quickly became about 'disenfranchised' youth looting and rioting. The media and politicians whipped up a frenzied moral panic about "gangs", "problem youth", "dysfunctional families" and a "feral underclass" (Briggs 2012: 27). In contrast, academics countered the damaging accusations with more balanced and nuanced analysis about "social mobility, racism, discrimination and aggressive policing" (Briggs 2012: 12).

To empathise with marginalised and disenfranchised young citizens, "repositioning" allows teachers to observe "the world through the eyes of the dispossessed and act against the ideological and institutional processes that reproduce oppressive conditions" (Apple et al. 2009: 3). Engaging in critical practices is necessary for social justice and social change; criticality can be promoted through: examining and exposing ideological educational policies; revealing contradictions, contestations and "spaces of possible action" for resistance and radicalism; redefining research and using academic privilege by providing "thick descriptions of critically democratic school practices" and of "transformative reforms", and; solidarity and collaboration with social movements (Apple et al. 2009: 4). "Productive pedagogies" such as connectedness, supportiveness, recognising and valuing difference and diversity and intellectually demanding schooling—alongside redistributive policies and funding—enable social justice in education and society (Lingard and Keddie 2013). Critical pedagogy needs to be relevant and exciting for students to critically interrogate existing social structures and values, and seek social justice.

CRITICAL PEDAGOGY, CRITICAL RACE APPROACHES AND THE ARTS

The arts can animate "critical awareness of injustice and oppression in participatory and action-oriented ways" (Chilton and Leavy 2014: 407), thus, the arts are conducive to critical pedagogy. Visual arts education is able to draw upon critical pedagogy's frameworks (Eglinton 2008), while the 'resistive capabilities' of the arts (Chilton and Leavy 2014), support critical pedagogues, in opposing prevailing ideologies, subverting the status quo, transforming social injustices and resisting hegemonic practices. If critical pedagogues emphasise how schools can "become sites of resistance and democratic possibility through concerted efforts among teachers and students" (Kincheloe and McLaren 2002: 89), then the arts can assist pedagogies of resistance and possibility.

Inspired by Braidotti, Kincheloe, McLaren, Giroux and others, Tourinho and Martins (2008: 65) argue visual arts critical pedagogy should include:

i.   "nomadic consciousness" embracing multiple and unfixed identities/
     attachments;
ii. "radical qualitative perspective" towards pedagogies and research,
     where asking questions about the world and seeking multiple
     voices, is the norm; and
iii. "favouring the public sphere", emphasising "collaborative char-
     acter of knowledge, the constructive dimension of understand-
     ing and the participatory condition of human development and
     transformation".

Arts-based educational research and critical pedagogy, therefore, share many commonalities, particularly the pursuit of social justice, desire to challenge the status quo and hope for transformation (Chilton and Leavy 2014). Visual arts critical pedagogues advocate "a radical qualitative" approach to research, teaching and learning, having faith this "expands the expressive possibilities of language in that it recognizes multiple voices and seeks for more contingent, circumstantial and poetic ways to narrate and reflect on what is and is not done, thought and felt in schools" (Tourinho and Martins 2008: 65).

Critical pedagogy and critical race methodology (CRM) can together reject racist legacies of colonialism and empire. CRM recognises "race and racism are endemic, permanent", intersecting with other social inequalities, thus CRM questions traditional research methodologies that neglect the 'experiential knowledge' of marginalised communities (Solórzano and Yosso 2002: 25). CRM also critiques prevailing ideologies that profess "objectivity, meritocracy, colorblindness, race neutrality, and equal opportunity" of curriculum/schooling by researching and emphasising the voices and social experiences of students who are otherwise silenced by the White supremacist master narratives of the political status quo (Solórzano and Yosso 2002: 26). Critical race approaches reveal Black students' "histories, experiences, cultures, and languages are devalued, misinterpreted, or omitted within formal educational settings" (Bernal 2002: 106). CRM researchers focus on exposing, resisting or eliminating social injustices and inequalities and empowering marginalised groups (Solórzano and Yosso 2002). CRM also shares similarities with ethnographic approaches to research. For example, by emphasising the value of "experiential knowledge" of minorities, CRM researchers utilise methods that allow for research participants to tell their stories (Solórzano and Yosso 2002: 26), always questioning "Whose stories are privileged in educational contexts and whose stories are distorted and silenced?" (Solórzano and Yosso 2002: 36).

Schools Need Critical Pedagogy

This chapter examined concepts relevant to exploring identities with young people in neoliberal times, foregrounding the importance of schools questioning the status quo, interrogating prevailing ideologies that privilege the elite and challenging media and political narratives that perpetuate hegemony and inequalities.[2] Education should not be about creating subservient automatons unwilling to rise up to transform the social injustices pervading local, national and globalised spaces. Education needs to inspire and enable students to grow in confidence to critique the oppressive social order. Young people who reflect upon *race* and *place* (See Chapter Seven) are provided with welcome opportunities to carefully interrogate concepts of belonging to Britain often for the first time in their lives. It is my hope they keep on questioning notions of race and social class, and act upon injustices and inequalities as they eventually move on from school into adult life. Students who explicitly explore their situationality through the problem-posing education, advocated by Freire (2000), will develop critical consciousness to better grasp how social institutions control communities and thus will be in a better position to keep questioning and resisting.[3]

Trainee teachers, Chapter Four confirms, are facing new educational policy challenges. Expected to teach Fundamental British Values, trainee teachers are problematising this requirement. Student teachers who are reflecting upon pedagogies with their peers and teacher educators, observing existing teachers in school placements and embarking upon new practices of teaching are very well placed to gain knowledge about ways to critical pedagogies in classroom activities. Research high-lights that trainee teachers are generally able to "combine a critical stance with a willingness to teach *about* complex issues, while generally refusing to promote simple or simplistic messages on behalf of politicians" (Jerome and Clemitshaw 2012: 39). In the next chapter, I draw attention to student teachers who are keen to promote multicultural Britishness. The most comprehensive study on trainee teachers' attitudes towards Britishness found they were "overwhelmingly sceptical" about "being asked to deliver what they considered to be propaganda-like messages through their teaching" (Jerome and Clemitshaw 2012: 38). Nevertheless, the next chapter shows trainee teachers are willing to teach Britishness through a framework about inclusive, diverse and multiple identities (Jerome and Clemitshaw 2012).

Notes

1. Donald Trump was inaugurated President of the USA in January 2017.
2. There is a critique that critical pedagogy is not neutral. However, it does not purport to neutrality as it concerns the lives, struggles and oppressions of those treated unjustly by social structures, seeking social justice with passion and determination, not with objective neutrality (Kincheloe 2008).
3. Some critics argue Freirean philosophies provide insufficient guidance on how to "move from critical thought to critical practice", but this can be a strength as Freire "urged his readers to reinvent him in the context of their local struggles" (McLaren 2000: 13).

References

Anyon, J. 2011. *Marx and Education*. New York: Routledge.

Apple, M.W. 2013. *Knowledge, Power, and Education: The Selected Works of Michael W. Apple*. New York: Routledge.

Apple, M.W., W. Au, and L.A. Gandin. 2009. Mapping Critical Education. In *The Routledge International Handbook of Critical Education*, ed. M.W. Apple, W. Au, and L.A. Gandin. New York: Routledge.

Arnot, M., and L. Barton. 1992. Introduction. In *Voicing Concerns: Sociological Perspectives on Contemporary Education Reforms*, ed. M. Arnot and L. Barton. Wallingford: Triangle Books.

Au, W., and M.W. Apple. 2009. Rethinking Reproduction: Neo-Marxism in Critical Education Theory. In *The Routledge International Handbook of Critical Education*, ed. M.W. Apple, W. Au, and L.A. Gandin. New York: Routledge.

Bernal, D.D. 2002. Critical Race Theory, Latino Critical Theory, and Critical Raced-Gendered Epistemologies: Recognizing Students of Color as Holders and Creators of Knowledge. *Qualitative Inquiry* 8: 105–126.

Brett, P. 2007. *Endowing Participation with Meaning: Citizenship Education, Paolo Freire and Educating Young People as Change-Makers.* http://www.citized. info/pdf/commarticles/Endowing%20Participation%20Peter%20Brett.pdf.

Briggs, D. (ed.). 2012. *The English Riots of 2011: A Summer of Discontent.* Hook: Waterside Press.

Chilton, G. and P. Leavy. 2014. Arts-Based Research Practice: Merging Social Research and the Creative Arts. In *The Oxford Handbook of Qualitative Research.*Leavy, ed. P. Leavy. Oxford: Oxford University Press.

Coffey, A. 2001. *Education and Social Change.* Buckingham: Open University Press.

Di Leo, J.R., H.A. Giroux, S.A. McClennen, and K.J. Saltman. 2014. *Neoliberalism, Education, Terrorism: Contemporary Dialogues.* Colorado: Paradigm Publishers.

Edgeworth, K. 2014. Unsettling Truths: Post-structural Ethnography as a Tool to Trouble Schooling Exclusions. In *Methodologies for Researching Cultural Diversity in Education: International Perspectives*, ed. G. Smyth and N. Santoro. London: Institute of Education Press.

Eglinton, K.A. 2008. Using Participatory Visual Ethnography to Explore Young People's Use of Visual Material Culture in Place and Space. In *Research in Art & Design Education: Issues and Exemplars*, ed. R. Hickman. Bristol: Intellect.

Freire, P. 1985a. *The Politics of Education: Culture, Power and Liberation*, Connecticut: Bergin & Garvey.

Freire, P. 1985b. Reading the World and Reading the Word: An Interview with Paulo Freire. *Language Arts* 62: 15–21.

Freire, P. 2000. *Pedagogy of the Oppressed.* New York: Bloomsbury Publishing.

Freire, P. 2001. *Pedagogy of Freedom: Ethics, Democracy, and Civic Courage.* Maryland: Rowman & Littlefield Publishers.

Freire, P., and A.M.A Freire. 2004. *Pedagogy of Hope: Reliving Pedagogy of the Oppressed.* London and New York: Continuum.

Gadotti, M. 2009. Adult Education and Competence Development: From a Critical Thinking Perspective. In *International Perspectives on Competence Development: Developing Skills and Capabilities*, ed. K. Illeris. Abingdon: Routledge.

Garratt, D. 2011. Equality, Difference and the Absent Presence of 'Race' in Citizenship Education in the UK. *London Review of Education* 9: 27–39.

Gay, G. 2002. Preparing for Culturally Responsive Teaching. *Journal of Teacher Education* 53: 106–116.

Giroux, H.A. 2001. *Theory and Resistance in Education: Towards a Pedagogy for the Opposition.* Westport, CT: Bergin & Garvey.

Giroux, H.A. 2013. *On Critical Pedagogy*. New York and London: Bloomsbury Academic.

Gruenewald, D.A. 2003. The Best of Both Worlds: A Critical Pedagogy of Place. *Educational Researcher* 32: 3–12.

Jerome, L., and G. Clemitshaw. 2012. Teaching (About) Britishness? An Investigation into Trainee Teachers' Understanding of Britishness in Relation to Citizenship and the Discourse of Civic Nationalism. *Curriculum Journal* 23: 19–41.

Kincheloe, J.L. 2008. *Critical Pedagogy Primer*. New York: Peter Lang.

Kincheloe, J.L., and P. McLaren. 2002. Rethinking Critical Theory and Qualitative Research. In *Ethnography and Schools: Qualitative Approaches to the Study of Education*, ed. Y. Zou and E. Trueba. Maryland: Rowman & Littlefield.

Kirylo, J.D. (ed.). 2013. *A Critical Pedagogy of Resistance: 34 Pedagogues We Need to Know*. Rotterdam: Sense Publishers.

Ladson-Billings, G. 1995. But That's Just Good Teaching! The Case for Culturally Relevant Pedagogy. *Theory into Practice* 34: 159–165.

Lea, V., and E.J. Sims. 2008. Undoing Whiteness in the Classroom: Different Origins, Shared Commitment. In *Undoing Whiteness in the Classroom: Critical Educultural Teaching Approaches for Social Justice Activism*, ed. V. Lea and E.J. Sims. New York: Peter Lang.

Lingard, B., and A. Keddie. 2013. Redistribution, Recognition and Representation: Working Against Pedagogies of Indifference. *Pedagogy, Culture & Society* 21: 427–447.

Macfarlane, A., T. Glynn, T. Cavanagh, and S. Bateman. 2007. Creating Culturally-Safe Schools for Māori Students. *The Australian Journal of Indigenous Education* 36: 65–76.

Maylor, U. 2010. Notions of Diversity, British Identities and Citizenship Belonging. *Race Ethnicity and Education* 13: 233–252.

McLaren, P. 2000. Paulo Freire's Pedagogy of Possibility. In *Freireian Pedagogy, Praxis, and Possibilities: Projects for the New Millennium*, ed. S.F. Steiner, H.M. Krank, R.E. Bahruth, and P. Mclaren. New York: Falmer Press.

Sandercock, L. 2005. Difference, Fear and Habitus: A Political Economy of Urban Fears. In *Habitus: A Sense of Place*, 2nd ed, ed. J. Hillier and E. Rooksby. Aldershot: Ashgate.

Sleeter, C.E. 2014. Multiculturalism and Education for Citizenship in a Context of Neoliberalism. *Intercultural Education* 25: 1–10.

Solórzano, D.G., and T.J. Yosso. 2002. Critical Race Methodology: Counter-Storytelling as an Analytical Framework for Education Research. *Qualitative Inquiry* 8: 23–44.

Steinberg, S.R. (ed.). 2009. *Diversity and Multiculturalism: A Reader*. New York: Peter Lang.

Swann, M. 1985. Education for All: The Report of the Committee of Inquiry into the Education of Children From Ethnic Minority Groups. HMSO.

Tourinho, I., and R. Martins. 2008. Controversies: Proposals for a Visual Arts Critical Pedagogy. In *International Dialogues About Visual Culture, Education and Art*, ed. R. Mason and T. Eça. Bristol: Intellect.

Vavrus, M. 2015. *Diversity and Education: A Critical Multicultural Approach*. New York: Teachers College Press.

CHAPTER 4

Trainee Teachers "Unravel, Criticise and Re-imagine" British Values

Abstract This chapter relays trainee teachers' conceptions of Fundamental British Values (FBVs) and their attitudes towards an educational policy on FBV. My research at a London teacher training institution reveals future teachers wary of promoting patriotic agendas about a notion that they perceive as ambiguous and debatable. I show how the trainee Art teachers were mystified on personal and professional levels by FBV. Finding it difficult to define Britishness and FBV, they resorted to recalling common stereotypes about British identities. Rejecting reification and homogeneity, the trainee teachers viewed FBV as problematic and contentious. The trainee teachers emphasised the need to explore multicultural Britishness and universal values, and called for more guidance, support and training.

Keywords Teacher training · Teacher education · Teachers' standards Fundamental British values · Universal values

TEACHING BRITISHNESS AND FUNDAMENTAL BRITISH VALUES

There are currently no empirical studies on trainee Art teachers' experiences of Britishness teaching or Fundamental British Values (FBV), however, we can benefit from research conducted about teaching Britishness in school subjects other than Art. For example, Jerome and Clemitshaw (2012: 31) found Citizenship and History trainee teachers had "a strong notion of the

© The Author(s) 2018
S. Habib, *Learning and Teaching British Values*,
DOI 10.1007/978-3-319-60381-0_4

democratic classroom, but one which sits uneasily alongside the more simplistic exhortations of politicians for the promotion of identity and democratic responsibilities through the curriculum". Jerome and Clemitshaw (2012) observed student teachers are often cynical about governmental agendas, but they are confidently willing to teach Britishness through a framework about inclusive, diverse and multiple identities. Empirical research, with Year Nine students (aged 13–14), and Citizenship and History teachers, in London schools, also highlights schools should neither ignore, encourage or discourage patriotism, but should "adopt a stance of neutrality and teach the topic as a controversial issue" (Hand and Pearce 2009: 454).

Government sees Citizenship Education as moulding responsible young citizens to feel a sense of belonging, opportunity and fairness in a cohesive society (DFE 2010), but Britishness has been taught superficially, focusing mainly on stereotypes, while Citizenship Education has been generally ignored or misunderstood (OFSTED 2010). Research has also shown that often teachers are misinformed that subjects like Maths or Science "do not allow for discussion about the world and local and national contexts" (Maylor et al. 2007: 5). Breslin et al. (2006: 13) recommend Citizenship teachers should adopt "a carefully measured approach that recognises the complexity" of Britishness, for it is "a contested concept, for some specific, others dynamic, and others nebulous". If Britishness is contested, schools must ensure identities of all students are explored with "sensitivity" through a curriculum that "enables pupils (particularly the majority population) to appreciate their own identities within a wider British diversity" (Maylor 2010: 248).

As a result of "current global conditions, postmodern identities and political economies" new educational policies emerge, necessitating teacher training to be updated to account for new times (Freedman 2008: 47). Student teachers' understanding of diversity, race and inclusion is under researched (Bhopal and Rhamie 2013), and trainee teachers are still not guided on how to handle everyday incidents of racism, or on how to deal with structural racism confidently by challenging the Eurocentric curriculum (Lander 2014). Worse yet hostile racial examples like "It's our country meant for white people" or "paki" continue to feature in young people's discourses of belonging (Sanderson and Thomas 2014: 8). Bhopal and Rhamie (2013: 18) show student teachers are aware that, though identity is fluid and malleable, "visible markers of difference" of Whiteness and Blackness will inevitably "impact upon the teaching and learning experience". Student teachers require training on how to handle these markers or racial and ethnic difference, especially at a time when they are encouraged to promote British Values, with their classed and racialised connotations.

TEACHER TRAINING

We hope times have moved on since a teacher referred to an ethnic minority student as a *wog* (Anwar 2002), yet today "new racisms" have resulted in young people branded as "terrorists" by their teachers (Shammas and Evans 2015; Revesz 2016; Pettifor 2016). Teacher training and school professional development courses, in the UK, fail to give issues of multiculturalism and diversity due time and attention (Carrington et al. 2000; Maylor et al. 2006a; Pearce 2012; Stokes and Nea 2013; Bhopal and Rhamie 2013; Lander 2014). Teachers in the USA and Australia similarly complain about key challenges that impact upon their profession, such as decreased funding, educational attainment of ethnic minority students, increase in racial and hate crime, lack of training on diversity and challenging monocultural and Eurocentric curricula, and political rhetoric that demonises ethnic minorities (Howard 2006). Teachers in the USA have also witnessed increasing calls for schools to teach patriotism (Banks 2010), and since 9/11 an "intensified nationalist superpatriotism" prevails (Zinn 2013).

Government acknowledges diversity training is necessary to teach in British schools (Home Office 2001), but teachers, in the UK, receive insufficient support on teaching citizenship education in a multicultural society, and schools are unsure on how to deliver it through the curriculum (Faulks 2006). Similarly, teachers are not well trained or guided on how to approach FBV (Elton-Chalcraft et al. 2017). In Citizenship Education lessons, topics like race, racism and Britishness are frequently misrepresented and essentialised, the topic of racism is not adequately handled, and Britishness is equated with Whiteness by teachers (Chadderton 2009). As racism is "a notoriously difficult concept to define", and complex too for "there is no one monolithic racism but numerous historically situated racisms" (Back 1996: 9), teachers need support in how to tackle racism, Britishness and Whiteness. Moreover, as there are many conceptions of citizenship experienced by young Britons—multicultural, European, and global—teachers require guidance in responding to "multiple identities and allegiances" (Heater 2004: 195).

Educationalists tackling racism, by interrogating Whiteness and White privilege, are frequently subjected to startlingly negative responses from students, the media or wider society (Lund and Carr 2010; Smith and Lander 2012). Teachers, sincere in dismantling racist structures with their students, need to be reflexive about race, racism and Britishness. Yet when it comes to implementing FBV policy—branded as divisive, racist and Islamophobic by many academics and unions—teachers are not in a position to contest FBV and its "insidious racializing implications" (Elton-Chalcraft et al. 2017: 29). Critical deconstruction of Whiteness might be more effective if teachers are not overwhelmed by blame and guilt for White privilege and power (Howard 2006; Lea and Sims 2008; Lund and Carr 2010); teachers not grasping cultural diversity leads to misconceptions about students, damages students' confidence and hinders educational progress. Teacher education in the USA, for instance, is critiqued for promoting *majoritarian stories* or *monovocals* "to explain educational inequity through a cultural deficit model and thereby pass on beliefs that students of color are culturally deprived" (Solórzano and Yosso 2002: 31). Then there will be teachers who students perceive to be racist (Gillborn 1995).

When it comes to teaching Britishness more specifically, there is more to consider. Firstly, social inequalities can be reflected in schools, adversely affecting inter-ethnic relations in the classroom; working out ways of promoting inter-ethnic classroom harmony in school is not always easy (Verma et al. 1994). Some schools have high "levels of racial harassment" (Carrington et al. 2000: 20); teaching Britishness in such schools will be challenging. Secondly, Citizenship and History teachers, familiar with teaching controversial topics, regard patriotism as a sensitive, divisive and difficult topic to teach (Hand and Pearce 2009). Teachers are "suspicious of using history to promote any sense of British identity" because of its legacy of colonialism and empire (Husbands et al. 2010: 153). Thirdly, primary schools teachers especially need guidance on citizenship teaching (Maylor et al. 2007), as national identity is complex to comprehend and explain to younger students (Carrington and Short 1995). Finally, overseas-trained teachers with no experience of teaching London students from ethnically diverse backgrounds may be new to promoting London-specific diversity (Maylor et al. 2006b), and thus they may require cultural awareness training about multilingual, multifaith and multi-ethnic British identities.

Racism prevalent in schools is highlighted by head teachers as a problem that needs addressing (Maylor 2010). Gaine (2005: 114) describes a class watching a video briefly featuring an Asian teacher, to which a White student responds: "My mum says if I had a Paki teacher she'd send me to another school". To combat racism, teachers require "knowledge and confidence" to explore multicultural Britishness (Maylor 2010: 249). Of concern is the insufficient numbers of ethnic minority teachers in our schools (Anwar 2002), not reflective of the general population and neglectful of the opportunity to provide positive role models and educational change-makers in schools, and also raising questions about whether institutional racism in the education system impacts upon ethnic minority teacher recruitment and retention.

Students, even those in "monocultural" schools, appreciate teachers who permit controversial discussions expanding understanding of diverse perspectives (Hess 2009). Trainee teachers who receive some appropriate training still believe their educational institutions "could and should do more to equip students with greater skills to deal with incidents of racism and prejudice as well as with a focused understanding of these issues" (Bhopal and Rhamie 2013: 18). White teachers in multicultural schools will not be able to easily "behave in ways that are inconsistent with their own life experiences, socialization patterns, worldviews, and levels of racial identity development" (Howard 2006: 6).

It is not only White trainee teachers who require diversity training (Bhopal and Rhamie 2013), but also trainee teachers from diverse ethnic backgrounds (Maylor et al. 2006a; Howard 2006). Jerome and Clemitshaw (2012: 31) found though trainee teachers perceived racism, and other prejudices, as "undesirable", they were uncertain about how to handle racism in the school. For a long time, knowledge and understanding about diversity in schools and teacher training programmes has been problematic (Maylor et al. 2007); thus, more research on identity and diversity is necessary, particularly as when diverse identities are addressed in teacher training curriculums, they are sometimes peripheral and superficial (Bhopal and Rhamie 2013). As it stands to be a teacher "involves far more complex bodies of knowledge and conceptual insights" than is often recognised in teacher training (Kincheloe 2007: 12).

A 2003–2006 on-line educational project *Multiverse* urged trainee teachers to become more aware of race, religious diversity, ethnicity, multilingualism and social class, as well as importantly to critically examine their own cultural affiliations, prejudices, biases and positionality (Maylor et al. 2006a: 42). Such a concerted effort in criticality is necessary for teachers "to recognise prejudice and their role in reinforcing stereotypes, and confront any assumptions they may make about those considered 'different' and develop antiracist/inclusive practice (James 2001)" (Maylor et al. 2006a: 42). Bhopal and Rhamie (2013), while highlighting examples of positive practice of diversity training, raise concerns about teacher training that does not address racism, barriers to achievement, and teacher expectations, resulting in overwhelmed teachers unable to challenge racism. Recent work on the ways initial teacher education responds to issues of race and ethnicity calls for more training for teachers on how to move classroom conversations beyond media stereotypes about ethnic minorities (Lander 2014). Multicultural diversity and anti-racism implementation do not solely involve teachers' reflections upon personal identity and cultural identifications. Teachers must also come to understand and challenge White supremacy and privilege (Howard 2006), otherwise the act of upholding a "dysconscious racism" (King 1991) results in White teachers not comprehending their "social dominance" (Howard 2006: 8).

The 1960s and 1970s "immigration" assimilation policies continued well into the 1990s (Troyna and Carrington 2012), and FBV policy shows the extent to which assimilationist rhetoric remains present today. Unsurprisingly, there are teaching staff who commit to the government's vision of assimilation. Keddie (2013: 6) conducted empirical research in a large multifaith and multicultural London school where teaching staff echoed public and political "anxieties": "a concern articulated by over half of the staff interviewed related to students' lack of connectedness or affiliation with 'British' culture" (Keddie 2013: 9). Although Keddie (2013) emphasises teachers are generally advocates of social integration rather than assimilation, strikingly some teaching staff she interviewed believed students from ethnic minority communities who associated with their ethnic/cultural identities were *alienated* from Britishness:

> ... that students' constructions of their identities as 'first and foremost' Indian, Afghani or Pakistani are incompatible or incommensurable with their affiliation with British identity—as Ms L says students affiliate with these identities despite being born in Britain. (Keddie 2013: 11)

Similarly, Elton-Chalcraft et al. (2017) refer to trainee teachers viewing Britishness through an assimilationist approach, perhaps influenced by media and political discourses about migrants and multiculturalism. Cultural assimilation is promoted by those educationalists who assume "a successful student of color is an assimilated student of color" (Solórzano and Yosso 2002: 31). Teachers, like the aforementioned Ms L, can be guilty of transmitting an ideology of assimilation to their students, insensitively diminishing the everyday significance of multiple, fluid and evolving identities and attachments. The "message" received here by ethnic minority students is "forget the culture of your parents, discard any affiliation to your ethnic background and blend in" (Troyna and Carrington 2012: 2).

Critical multiculturalism is a useful approach for teachers who recognise cultural and linguistic diversity is not threatening to the nation's culture, and need not be diluted (Vavrus 2015). Trainee teachers who are keen to project a multicultural notion of Britishness (Jerome and Clemitshaw 2012) could apply critical multiculturalism principles in the classroom when exploring British identities. Recognising that schools with diverse curriculums tend to give precedence to global diversity rather than British diversity (Maylor et al. 2007), throughout this chapter, I will show how trainee teachers are keen to move away from restrictive and narrow conceptions of British diversity, seeking instead to reflect upon universal values and global identities. I will firstly relay how the trainee teachers describe Britishness, and experience FBV policy requirements in relation to Teachers' Standards and classroom practice. Next, I will go on to present some of the possible problems and benefits of exploring FBV as highlighted by the trainees, as well as how they might approach identity investigation through their subject of Art.

TRAINEE ART TEACHERS CRITICALLY REFLECTING UPON FUNDAMENTAL BRITISH VALUES

This research conducted at a London teacher training institution reveals future teachers are wary about promoting patriotic agendas about a notion that they perceive as ambiguous and debatable. The literature presents student teachers as critical but also willing "to teach *about* complex issues, while generally refusing to promote simple or simplistic messages on behalf of politicians" (Jerome and Clemitshaw 2012: 39).

When exploring Britishness, the trainee teachers, teachers and students I encountered were sensitive to identities as unfixed and difficult to capture concretely or definitively in their Art lessons. Knowing "identities are never completed, never finished; that they are always as subjectivity itself is, in process" (Hall 1991: 47) has profound implications for how we might teach FBV or explore British identities with young people.

The Meanings of Britishness

The trainee Art teachers struggled to articulate personal meanings of Britishness, resorting to popular stereotypes like silence on the tube, queueing, the Queen, corgis, Sunday dinner, pork pie, having tea and biscuits, afternoon tea, fish and chips on a Friday or at the beach, and even curry! They portrayed Britishness as being reserved, complaining, being patriotic, being smug, waiting for a bus, the Union Jack, or even the British flag hanging out of the window. Trainee teacher Pete's vision of Britishness was reminiscent of Conservative Prime Minister, John Major, who in 1993, described his exclusionary Anglo-centric romanticised Britain: "long shadows on county (cricket) grounds, warm beer, invincible green shrubs, dog lovers..." (Bratberg and Haugevik 2009; Kearney 2012). Pete moved beyond the pastoral to what he recounted as stock images of Britishness: "Rolling hills, quaint villages, stiff upper lip, sarcasm, political systems, structure, tweed, a sense of history of time and place, a reserve...".

Rarely dwelling upon whether they accepted or rejected these stereotypes, the trainees observed these were ways Britishness was commonly perceived. Other interesting responses alluded to freedom of speech or self-expression, fairness, respect, democracy, tolerance and self-deprecating comedy. Some trainee teachers might be uncritical of Britishness, while other trainees are aware of the necessity of examining the nuances of Britishness (Elton-Chalcraft et al. 2017). Teacher educators might find trainee teachers would benefit from engaging in deeply reflexive opportunities to better know their personal positionality on Britishness and FBV. If teachers are expected to teach FBV to young people, would it not make sense for teachers to first critically reflect upon their own meanings and experiences of Britishness?

When trainees were dismissive of formulaic "Britishness", they cited contemporary Britishness should concern diversity and multiculturalism. Britishness in London was seen as unique:

Rebecca: ...London has a feeling of diversity whereas the rest of the country feels very patriotic. London has a completely different attitude to Britishness, being more open to other cultures... the rest of the country seems more closed-minded.

The "cultural and spatial mosaics of societies" that alter due to diasporic influences (Ehrkamp 2008: 118) inevitably come to impact upon how Britishness changes throughout time. The East End of London, for example, has evolved over centuries as the Huguenots, the Irish, the Jews, and the Bangladeshis sought sanctuary and better lives (Wemyss 2009). Carrie, a Welsh trainee, believed Britishness exploration in a multicultural capital city would be a very different experience than in the rest of the UK. Gareth was "ambivalent" about teaching FBV: "I think you will get very different answers depending on who you ask and where you ask". Julia, reflecting upon her northern English roots, argued FBV teaching would be influenced by where the school was geographically situated; she thought it would be more "difficult" to teach FBV in the north of England, than in "diverse" London. However, Lilia, a Portuguese trainee, claimed the multicultural nature of the UK, and particularly London, would mean FBV teaching was inappropriate. London, as epitomising multicultural Britishness, was a common theme, perhaps because of the recent referendum, in June 2016, exposing geographical divisions within Britain about remaining within or leaving the European Union.

Trainee teachers expressed concerns about FBV teaching leading to racism, recognising it was important that schools should support anti-racist education in a post-Brexit Britain.[1] Peyton—an American—felt Britishness was synonymous with Brexit, while Elena—a Romanian—troubled that Britishness teaching was about promoting "exclusion" raised post-Brexit racism as a worry: "It seems the message is you have to be British, not that Britishness is about inclusion". Britishness and FBV were viewed as complex, therefore difficult to define and teach. Eve summarised how her peers felt about the nebulous and changeable nature of Britishness, noting that it is "influenced and defined by ethnicity, geography, age, gender and the make-up of the communities in which we live". Teaching Britishness was therefore often rejected for its connotations of segregation and exclusion. Kenny, for example, admitted FBV might be "positive in theory" but worried it was "misappropriated by parties for selfish gains".

Lucy preferred the concept of "world citizen", repudiating Britishness for it connoted separateness. Gwen felt Britishness was overwhelming in its implications of "patriotism". An Irish trainee teacher from Belfast, Gwen stated "I am not British". She declared FBV as no different from general fundamental values (FV) of "respecting each other" and practising "inclusion of all faiths/beliefs". Carrie, a Welsh trainee teacher, also critiqued FBV: "I don't like that it's labelled as being British... it's just FV. Inclusion. Acceptance. Tolerance. Respect". Gwen insisted schools should not teach FBV, for it was imposing a policy of "exclusion". Both personally and pedagogically, she was highly critical of enforcing teachers to fulfil duties around FBV:

Gwen: An impossible task for me to do as I am Irish, and very much reject Britishness. Growing up in Northern Ireland, I had to fight to be Irish, and always had to prove my Irishness. I think that children may feel the same and don't want to be pigeon-holed.

Wary about *teaching* FBV, concerned about racism, Gwen explained she would rather *critically interrogate* British identities with students. After Gwen had explored some ways to examine Britishness[2] with her peers, she highlighted FBV was a "complex" topic, requiring extensive discussion in the classroom. Gwen observed the potential for "open and honest dialogues between teachers and pupils", arguing "children need to explore multiple identities".

Janine was "uncomfortable" about teaching Britishness: "I'm not too sure what it means". Janine condemned FBV as problematic ideology about "democracy and tolerance", particularly as government "condones war and has such a bloody past". Reflecting upon "the history of the British empire being built from slavery, corruption, colonisation... far from being 'great'", Julia felt "guilt" when critically reflecting upon Britishness. As Britain consists of richly diverse identities, Julia proposed teaching about "human values" rather than FBV. Androula also preferred the term "universal values" over FBV: "When I think of Britishness, I think of colonialism. And how after colonialism, being a Brit and proud is more apparent".

Teachers are working against a backdrop where advocates of nationalism, through politics and education, frequently grant "a weak concession" to cosmopolitanism, instead promoting nation as more important than world citizenship (Nussbaum 1996: 5). Liberal multiculturalism also seems to focus on "the boundaries of the nation", ignoring "the wider global picture" (Osler 2008: 16). The trainee teachers, I surveyed, tended to elevate respect, tolerance, human rights and diversity as key values schools should teach (Jerome and Clemitshaw 2012), acknowledging that these themes of cosmopolitan citizenship allow for exploration of "shared global problems" (Stevenson 2003: 332).

Kenny was not only "apprehensive", but also "indifferent" from a personal perspective as a Singaporean, about teaching FBV. Acknowledging values in the FBV policy were positive ones to impart to young people in order to build societal and national cohesion, he was, nevertheless, concerned about how FBV had been framed, and its potential to be "misconstrued". His indifference and apprehension perhaps stemmed from his not feeling "British". Kenny felt "confused and worried" as he pondered over the extent to which he was obliged to submit to FBV and whether there was room for critical analysis of FBV. Multiple and global attachments as the norm (Vertovec and Cohen 2002; Osler and Starkey 2003) is a notion that trainee teachers must examine before they can explore multiple identities and belongings with their students. Not all teachers find it easy to embrace diversity, difference, and global or multiple identities (Carrington et al. 2000; Maylor et al. 2006a; Pearce 2012; Stokes and Nea 2013; Bhopal and Rhamie 2013; Lander 2014). Kenny, for example, lacked confidence in how to embrace his Singaporean identity while simultaneously teaching FBV critically.

Universal Values, not British Values

The trainee teachers, I was observing, tended to follow the view that when teaching Britishness, we can take the chance to "make hegemonic forms of subjectivity and identity strange" by "problematizing and relativizing them" (Weedon 2004: 4). Such an approach might help teacher educators to motivate trainee teachers to explore young people's narratives on identities and belongings through critical reflection. The trainee teachers saw themselves as facilitators of debate and discussion about identity in an open, safe and respectful classroom environment, rather than teachers of FBV. They understood the importance of teaching about identities in schools, but struggled with using terms like "Britishness" or "FBV". They were demonstrating awareness about the complexities of notions of national identity that they felt could connote privilege and cause exclusion. For example, if nations necessitate communal obligations between co-nationals, then the idea that it is only co-nationals who deserve justice impacts upon those with transnational attachments (Young 2000).

Contemporary Britishness is often critiqued for evoking "a particular narrative of British history" (Croft 2012: 167), one that serves to "distort the character and history" (Parekh 1999: 323) of the British nation as unique, special and worthy of celebration. Politicians create "rhetorical frames through which to define how the public sees policy issues", and who is a friend or enemy, or who are outsiders or insiders (Grube 2011: 628). The promotion of Britishness—a social phenomenon—has been critiqued as a means for the powerful elite to perpetuate "officially constructed patriotism" (Colley 1992: 145). I learned that trainee teachers were concerned that the FBV set out in educational policy were "exclusionary" if championed as uniquely British. Helena declared FBVs were values held by most people regardless of whether they were British or not:

Helena: As teachers we should teach our students to be kind, respectful and uphold the law. However I don't think these should be called British values... It is debateable whether British society upholds these values.

James also highlighted the 'oxymoronic' nature of calling for FBV when this needed to include respect for the beliefs of others. Lucy argued "law, 'tolerance', and liberty" are important but should not be taught under the banner of FBV; she posed the question of whether Britain was tolerant enough.

Carrie believed FV mattered more than FBV particularly to "develop well-rounded students ready for life after school". Pete would be happier teaching FV, "rather than making them exclusively British", concluding values should be imparted in schools but it was problematic if government was "anchoring" them to Britain. Gareth wondered "what is British?" He perceived this lack of clarity to be a major obstacle teachers would face when implementing FBV policy. Rebecca similarly critiqued FBV as tricky and slippery:

Rebecca: How many people are British? Are British Values still relevant to today's society? I don't feel comfortable because "FBV" are so different from what the majority of the UK actually think. Will students agree with the FBV?

Rebecca concluded she would happily teach FV, not FBV. Androula, argued "Britishness" had "harsh or awkward connotations", thus she would also rather refer to universal values. She worried about students feeling "shy or apprehensive" about sharing views on British identities, and also that FBV teaching could cause offence if students were not respectful in discussions, or that there would even be a rise in racism. Androula advocated getting to know the students well before exploring identities.

Fundamental British Values: School Policies & Practices

There were not many detailed examples of policies and practices regarding FBV encountered by the research participants in their teaching placements. One trainee, Natalie, stated she had never "been exposed to" FBV policy or practice. Some had observed group discussions in pastoral time about elections/referendums or debates about Trump[3]/Brexit. Others had seen displays about FBV in their placement schools. Pete critiqued a project entitled "It's Great to be British" in his placement school which superficially focused on "high tea, cakes, biscuits". FBV in PSHE lessons, or a PSHE lessons on LGBT rights where British values of tolerance and acceptance were taught were mentioned too. Some cited school policies—on behaviour, equal opportunities or Prevent[4]—that referenced FBV. Eve had experienced an OFSTED[5] inspection "specifically addressing evidence of FBV in the Art curriculum".

The trainees regarded FBV teaching as insufficient or redundant in contemporary British schools, instead placing emphasis upon anti-racist and multicultural education:

Keeley: I have seen schools try and teach FBV, however that only hit superficial elements of high tea and the Queen. The school also had to deal with racial incidents around the same time because of this.

James reasoned "education is the most powerful tool against intolerance", that through FBV students can learn about "tolerance and acceptance" of other cultures. He was, nevertheless, uneasy about introducing Britishness if it might lead to awkwardness, social divisions and racism. Jusna insisted schools should promote multicultural education, rather than FBV, as young people inhabited multicultural social locations. Lucy felt as "not all people are British", the policy could be divisive. Rachel was sceptical about FBV teaching, finding it "offensive" and "insulting to students", and as potentially "creating barriers" between young people: "good citizenship matters...but labelling them as 'FBV' implies other nationalities do not hold these same beliefs. They do".

Kayley understood FBV could enhance student "wellbeing" and create a sense of "school community" where diverse young people "need to get along"; she was approving of the notion of "mutual respect" as "pupils must feel safe at school", that this would prepare the young people for life beyond school. Yet Kayley still felt "quite confused" about any significance of Britishness to her personally, concluding it was more appropriate to encourage debate within the classroom about the nature, features and critiques of FBV. Samantha viewed FBV teaching as "awkward". She saw the values politicians considered to be "British" as "contentious", "stagnant" and "limiting". Samantha maintained schools should teach notions of respect, tolerance and inclusion, which she felt were "crucial for a functioning and well developed" society; she was firm these should not be taught under the "branding" of FBV. Arguing FBV requirements were "common sense", particularly in preventing prejudices, Samantha was reluctant to deem these British.

Gareth admitted FBVs were "good principles for life", however—before discussion with peers—he saw no perceived benefits to teaching FBV; later, he recognised students might open up and study self, the other and society critically. Nevertheless, he was still conscious of the difficulties in "creating the environment where students feel at ease sharing their views and opinions openly". Eve felt FBV policy was "problematic":

Eve: I am unsure about the aim of teaching FBV. I assume this drive towards tolerance/democracy is to counter extremism... I do question why they are called FBV. They are broad generic values that can be identified as fundamental human values.

FBV teaching might cause "discrimination and alienation" if young people identify with cultures not specifically British, Eve speculated; she admitted that exploring FBV could become a space for "opening up discussions around agency" which might in turn "activate critical and political thinking in young people". Karl believed schools should promote tolerance and respect, values "essential for a functioning society, especially in a multicultural society". Pete was concerned about lack of time to tackle issues arising when discussing "emotive" topics like Britishness. Keeley argued FBV policies exclude students not considered British, students who do not identify as British, and dual nationals. Thus, she stated that she could not teach FBV. Instead she would work with students on how to become ethical and active citizens who "contribute to their ever changing community".

Teachers' Standards & Fundamental British Values

Critiquing the language employed in the FBV policy, Terry felt FBV was "political propaganda". He felt challenged by the policy as it is "difficult to define Britishness"; he dismissed the Teachers' Standards requirement, not to *undermine fundamental British values* (Department for Education 2011), as government "trying to micro manage schools". Like Terry, teacher educators argue trainee teachers who are frustrated to find their future careers are increasingly politicised by government rhetoric regarding FBV (Elton-Chalcraft et al. 2017). Carrie questioned, "How do you promote something you don't agree with?" Kayley worried about FBV authorising spaces for students to express "extremist views" and "racism, sexism, class discrimination". Jusna rationalised that the government was attempting to maintain social control and social order by insisting teachers "respect" FBV and act as role models for students. Teacher educators must introduce this Standard to trainee teachers from diverse cultural backgrounds while coming to terms with their own personal perspectives and experiences of British values (Maylor 2016). What about teachers who do not feel affiliated to Britishness or British values? What becomes of those who critique the way the government defines FBV? Can Teacher's Standards be implemented in a way that gives trainee teachers the confidence to challenge stereotypes, racism and narrow conceptions of Britishness, and the courage to promote a critical consciousness (Maylor 2016)?

Rachel interrogated the language used in the Teachers' Standards as dictatorial and alienating; it needed to be positively expressed, to get teachers on board. Insisting "teachers should not have to specifically teach" FBV, Gareth asserted that the responsibility for the transmission of FBV should relate to school ethos, and more so "it should be the responsibility of society". Keeley felt Teachers' Standards on FBV were farcical, a ruse for government "to come across as inclusive and appease people". Helena accepted values should be taught in school, but not in ways that "exclude or alienate non-British teachers or students". Peyton felt "uneasy" about teaching FBV, stating "I am American"; thus "questioning their legitimacy" was important, as was "teaching students to be better more respectful humans". Lilia also declared her "unBritishness":

Lilia: I don't think teaching FBV or including it in my teaching will make me a better teacher. I am not British. Obviously I am part of this country, but I still have my own values, as Portuguese and as an individual.

If FBVs, for example, are "White" values (Maylor 2016), then the requirement to not undermine FBV—as required of the Teachers' Standards - might result in teachers feeling unable to speak out against the racist and Islamophobic undercurrents of FBV narratives.

Sarah—a Black trainee teacher born in Britain and who had lived here all her life—stated "I don't consider myself to be British". She admitted FBV teaching might promote unity and respect for the law, community and society, nevertheless, she confessed: "I need to get my head around what Britishness or FBV is". Sarah wanted to know about how FBV fit into a framework that celebrated distinctive ethno-religious communities, the Commonwealth and anti-colonial movements. Britishness, therefore, with its "systematic, largely unspoken, racial connotations" (Parekh 2000: 38), can be perceived as just as problematic as Englishness (McGuigan 2010), with ethnic minority young people often finding British identity is not inclusive (Phoenix 1998; Barrett 2002; Phillips and Ganesh 2007).

Art in Safe Spaces Honours Difference and Diversity

Celebrating the creative and experimental potential of using Art to explore cultures and belongings through innovative and imaginative ways was central to the trainee Art teachers' professional identities. Kenny was eager to use "political art" to explore identities with his students.

Initially, Jusna could not think of how to incorporate FBV in her lessons; after collective reflection with peers, Jusna pondered over seeking students' definitions and experiences of FBV and Britishness. The discussion with peers gave Jusna confidence to want to speak about FBV teaching with colleagues and friends, and the desire to explore Britishness through "open-ended" conversations in the classroom where students expressed their personal opinions about identities. Lucy too believed young people should form their opinions, rather than follow governmental definitions; she proposed establishing "basic rules" in the classroom about respect and encouraging students to "be open-minded and hear out the full argument".

Androula cited passion for "dialogic learning" and "theories of Paolo Freire"; she believed critical pedagogy was important when exploring identities with young people. Wanting to combine Freirean pedagogies with "political art" and "current real world news affairs" within her practice of art education, she was enthusiastic about developing students' critical consciousness for life beyond the classroom. Helena explained she would steer away from a canonical or Eurocentric approach by teaching about British artists from diverse cultural, religious and ethnic backgrounds. Dismissing FBV, Lilia's motto was "Art is about difference"; she called for a pedagogy of Art that gives students insight into cultural diversity.

Karl and Gareth emphasised getting to know students before embarking on a project about identities. Karl envisioned teachers "creating a safe environment in which students are able to talk openly about issues with tolerance and respect", while Janine wanted a "safe environment with clear rules". Natalie too felt helping students to "feel as comfortable and safe as possible" was crucial for students to "express themselves freely". Gareth added he would need to build "an environment based on trust". Only if all these factors were properly established, Gareth explained, would he explore identities. Karl echoed Gareth: "Knowing the context of your school, and the students in your class, and what kind of issues might arise" were foundational requirements. FBV was sometimes forced into the curriculum "merely to tick a box", thus Pete called for stricter planning and delivery:

Pete: It's a difficult subject to broach in Art... it needs to be taught in a relevant way. Not just drawing Union Jacks and Rich Tea biscuits. It needs to be taught with the students' own experiences in mind.

Gwen thought a "difficult subject to tackle" would be best done through, for example, an Art debate club in a "forward thinking school that is open to exploring these issues". Debate in the classroom should be lively, engaging, reflective and collaborative. Yet since FBV policies came into play, students today are not offered the same opportunities to debate controversial issues, as teachers encounter "the fault lines of tension, fear and ambiguity that exits between policy and practice" (Maylor 2016: 278).

OFSTED insists "inspectors will evaluate the extent to which leaders, managers and governors 'actively promote British values'" (Revell and Bryan 2016: 342), resulting in hastily compiled displays of British—often London-centric—iconography (flags, images of red buses, pillar boxes, cups of tea and the Queen) in school hallways and classrooms to welcome OFSTED inspectors to a school apparently bursting with pride about its Britishness. The trainee teachers I surveyed were aware of this "tick-box exercise" and wary of conforming to superficial saluting of FBV. Distinguishing between Britishness and FBV, Rachel emphasised "I would want to explore Britishness not FBV", as Britain's "interesting history" would "make appropriate and interesting subject matter" to "explore social, emotional and cultural issues". Karl also wanted to teach values by encouraging students to "explore their own cultural identities", and how these might connect with FBV. Eve concluded exploring British identities through Art could be "most exciting" if students were given structured and creative opportunities to "unravel, criticise, re-imagine" Britishness and FBV.

Supporting Trainee Teachers to Explore Identities

Outlining my research in London with GCSE Art students and teachers[6] to these trainee teachers later helped them to collectively reflect upon how they might approach (national) identity exploration. James had initially felt FBV was exclusionary, but after learning more about my research, he explained he was "much more open" to teaching Britishness, and sensed potential for critical reflection about identities. Lucy had originally felt "frustrated" about ways "Britishness can be perceived and how it can be used negatively and exclusively"; later, Lucy still felt Britishness was "limiting and exclusive", but was reassured that "like-minded people… some of them my peers" will be teaching FBV critically. Lucy emphasised "how we interpret" Britishness matters: "I feel more confident about deconstructing Britishness, but not about teaching 'British' values".

Samantha believed there were no benefits to teaching FBV, but advocated teaching universal "common sense" values of a cohesive and progressive society, and required training on exploring FBV neutrally. Before the discussion, Samantha had felt FBV teaching was "boring, frustrating and problematic": "I thought I was never going to freely approach it". Discussion with peers resulted in Samantha still "hesitant to tackle it", but "less daunted and angered" about FBV, viewing it "as a platform for discussion". Still unconfident about teaching Britishness—"my issue with the labelling of FBV is still a problem"—she anticipated her future classroom practices with students to revolve around identities, not FBV. Janine was heartened to explore teaching about identities "in a much more open way": "focusing on the interpretation of the pupils and letting this create discussion". Janine's initial dismissal of FBV evolved into viewing Britishness projects as having potential through the wider concept of identities: "rather than feeling like you have to prescriptively teach" FBV, sharing ideas was paramount, to empower students to "gain a greater sense of self". Androula also found peers' views useful in providing ideas of how to explore identities through "discussion" and "anti-racism education", a "way to get to know and bond with the class".

Some students, like Terry, remained unconvinced about teaching FBV, concerned it would lead to stereotyping, confrontation and racism: "I would still find it challenging to teach". Carrie stated her ideas remained unchanged, but she was relieved to observe peers raising similar concerns about the exclusive and divisive nature of FBV. Before the discussion, Gareth had felt "ambivalent" about FBV teaching, unsure "how to approach such a complex subject". However, this opportunity to critically reflect upon how to explore Britishness with young students felt promising for Gareth. Sensing scope to do work with young people who would "probably be quite engaged as they are possibly torn between their own ideas of belonging", Gareth was more confident about teaching Britishness, but he would prefer to introduce Britishness more broadly "as an idea within a project regarding identity".

Terry could see that if reflection was encouraged, deeper thinking would develop; he would particularly emphasise critical questioning and developing empathy. Lucy welcomed training on incorporating FBV critically through pastoral care; Rachel believed training was required for new teachers on British history/cultures, active citizenship, social movements and anti-racist education. Pete called for "a clear definition of what exactly are FBVs or what is deemed as 'Britishness'".

Eve also argued "more clarity" was required regarding about defining FBV, as well as an "open forum" for teachers to discuss FBV policies and practices. Keeley had been "very apprehensive", but after discussion with peers, Keeley's outlook "slightly changed", with a better understanding of how to explore Britishness through Art. Nevertheless, she still stated she was "not fully confident", and would need to engage in extensive lesson planning and preparation to do this well.

Current definitions of FBVs were seen as insufficient and controversial by the trainees. There was confusion too with one trainee even stating FBV referred to "fish and chips...the British flag... being reserved". Trainees, like Rachel, advocated a "critical approach" whereby teachers should ask students "about what they understand as Britishness" and use students' ideas as the foundations to draw upon wider issues of "identity and respect". Before the peer discussion, Karl had been "very confused" about teaching the "problematic" and "loaded" term "Britishness" with its ties to the BNP and EDL. After the reflective session, Karl was more contemplative about "moving the focus from teacher-led learning of FBV to allowing students to lead". Still wary about teaching Britishness, he would prefer to unpack and critically analyse notions such as "respect" and "tolerance" in student-led discussions. Pete focused upon the pedagogies of Art, pondering over assessment criteria and the possible outcome if he was to explore identities with students, while Julia, Natalie, Androula and Elena called for support on critical questioning skills. Kenny reflected upon how this critical discussion with peers was "empowering", inspiring confidence about exploring FBV with his students through examining identities more generally; he would encourage students to create a space characterised by "negotiating and understanding".

BRITISHNESS, RESPECT AND DIVERSITY

Schools are fast becoming "an ideological battleground for competing versions of 'Britishness'" causing teaching staff to be "increasingly positioned on the frontline of the 'war on terror' at home, with an emphasis on the surveillance and control of BME students rather than their education" (Alexander et al. 2015: 4). Trainee teachers choose to reject indoctrinating or undemocratic pedagogies preferring instead that students become independent learners (Jerome and Clemitshaw 2012). Yet this chapter has revealed that trainee teachers are disconcerted about having to negotiate politicised FBV. New teachers are often thrust in compromising and uncomfortable positions. Often they find themselves increasingly "pilloried by the media" as well as subjected to "ill-informed, poorly conceptualized and damaging policies developed by politicians" (Smyth and McInerney 2007: 6).

The FBV policy and the "Teachers' Standards" require teachers not to *undermine fundamental British values* (Department for Education 2011), raising questions about teachers unfortunately and unexpectedly implicated in enacting racist and Islamophobic policies, serving as "instruments of the state" (Lander 2016: 275):

> Respect for the rule of law is announced in the Standards as a fundamental British value. Where does that leave a history teacher's approach to the suffragette movement, say, or the anti-apartheid struggle? What of any discussion of tuition fees or the Occupy movement, of the Arab spring or Palestine? What, too, of the requirement that these standards apply as much to a teacher's life beyond the school gates as to anything that might happen in the classroom? (Turvey et al. 2012: 38)

Teachers naturally feel uneasy personally, professionally and pedagogically about the contradictions and injustices surrounding the promotion of FBV, as well as about being coerced into institutionally racist behaviour through monitoring, surveilling and reporting on students who are seen as dissenting or as resisting hegemonic societal attitudes, expectations and ideologies (Lander 2016; Farrell 2016; Smith 2016; Panjwani 2016; Maylor 2016). The trainee teachers, I have written about in this chapter, voiced "fundamental disagreements" with political and policy narratives "about the nature of citizenship, belonging and what it means to be 'British'" (Sales 2012: 34). The trainee teachers were expecting they would continue to encounter such disagreements about Britishness and FBV when working with Art classes; primarily they expressed preference to explore universal human values and identity more broadly with their students, as FBV was limiting and exclusionary.

A major critique of FBV is that the FBV guidance does not root from education policy, but from Home Office documents on "extremism" (Richardson 2015). Extremism is defined by the government as "vocal or active opposition to fundamental British values..." (HM Government 2015: 2). Britishness discourses initially emerged from political elite's anxieties about Scotland and Wales seeking independence, but by 2011 "unintegrated" ethnic minorities, particularly Muslims, became the target of FBV policies (Maylor 2016). Rather than preparing teachers to work with ethnically, racially and culturally diverse student demographics, teacher educators find themselves negotiating a securitisation and surveillance driven agenda attached to "upholding" FBV (Lander 2016). Teacher educators and trainee teachers are conscious that critical thinking flourishes when an "open mind" is encouraged (hooks 2010: 10). Teacher-facilitated open discussion in order to promote respect and diversity, therefore, is the desired practice among those teacher educators and trainee teachers who are brave and confident about tackling Britishness through critical pedagogy approaches.

As "diversity" will inevitably arise in discussions on nation and identity (Kedourie 1993), teacher educators can interrogate the roles and responsibilities of FBV teaching in multicultural society with trainees. The trainee teachers I had the privilege of learning from saw the potential for critical engaged pedagogy's focus on student voice and independent thinking in "empowering" students (hooks 2010: 21). The notion of "engaged pedagogy", however, has become difficult for teachers to experiment with in British schools. Educational policy has evolved to include statutory obligations upon teachers to monitor and counter radicalisation through the FBV duty. The ways such policies are interpreted by teachers—and students—and enacted at the classroom level need to be investigated. Panjwani's research with Muslim teachers, for example, shows they do not find British and Islamic values to be incompatible, but argue FBV duty is flawed and problematic: "the lack of clarity, irrelevance, inadequate choice of values, conflict between proclaimed values and state practices or simply a facade to hide the 'real' British values" (2016: 333).

The potentially narrow, insular and racist approaches to FBV policy and practice are brought to light by the Teachers' Standards that implicate teachers in monitoring and reporting students' sense of Britishness, and also in enforcing an assimilatory vision upon young (Muslim) people:

> Though not stated, the instruction teachers will be bound by (that is not to undermine British values) suggests that teachers instead will through their teaching impose British values on students and by doing this downplay the value of minority ethnic cultures and the values that inform minority ethnic cultures. (Maylor 2016: 319)

Teacher educators have commented upon how the inclusion of stipulation to not "undermine FBV" in the Teachers' Standards has been unchallenged by the media, schools and even teacher education organisations; yet, a "wider debate" about this requirement is urgently needed (Elton-Chalcraft et al. 2017). Student teachers would benefit from exploring how this standard impacts upon their personal and professional identities with teacher educators and with their peers. Trainee teachers can perhaps explore cultures and identities by compiling reflective written autobiographies to be used by teacher trainers developing culturally responsive pedagogies with the student teachers (Gunn et al. 2013). Through critical reflection trainees might strengthen their critical pedagogies, becoming "culturally responsive teachers" who "know how to determine the multicultural strengths and weaknesses of curriculum designs and instructional materials and make the changes necessary to improve their overall quality" (Gay 2002: 108).

Teachers from diverse backgrounds with distinctive perceptions and experiences of Britishness are expected to adhere to a government narrative on FBV, but are voices of teachers who find the sociopolitical nature of FBV to be conflicting, contradictory and contested being heard? An open and honest debate necessitates teachers and students to express their concerns and fears about the implications and consequences of FBV policies and practices. In the next three chapters, I describe the learning and teaching of Britishness in the classroom. Working with two Art classes and their teachers, before the duty to promote FBV, the project sought to value the contributions of students and teachers through encouraging engaged pedagogies when exploring identities. By presenting teachers and students doing identity work collectively, individually and critically, the remaining chapters in this book seek to inform the current FBV work expected by schools. Critical pedagogy, I show, can encourage teachers to explore difficult notions of belongings and identities with their students. Critical awareness about Britishness and belonging develops through pedagogical practices promoting dialogue, collaboration, reflection and action.

NOTES

1. Brexit refers to the process and act of Britain exiting the European Union as result of the UK referendum in June 2016.
2. The trainee teachers critically and collaboratively reflected upon ways to incorporate British identity exploration in their lessons. Throughout this paper, I make reference to how this collective discussion might have helped their views evolve.
3. Donald Trump won the US General Election in November 2016 after a campaign which many political and social commentators lambasted as racist.

4. The Prevent duty is the duty in the Counter-Terrorism and Security Act 2015 on public sector workers like teachers and doctors to prevent people from being drawn into terrorism (HM Government 2015).
5. OFSTED (Office for Standards in Education) is the governmental department responsible for inspecting and regulating schools, colleges and teacher education. Since 2007 it has been known as the Office for Standards in Education, Children's Services and Skills.
6. See Chaps. 5, 6 and 7.

References

Alexander, C., D. Bernard-Weekes, and J. Arday. 2015. *The Runnymede School Report: Race, Education and Inequality in Contemporary Britain*. London: The Runnymede Trust.

Anwar, M. 2002. *Between Cultures: Continuity and Change in the Lives of Young Asians*. London: Routledge.

Back, L. 1996. *New Ethnicities and Urban Culture: Racisms and Multiculture in Young Lives*. London: Routledge.

Banks, J.A. 2010. Approaches to Multicultural Curriculum Reform. In *Multicultural Education: Issues and Perspectives*, ed. J.A. Banks and C.A.M. Banks. Hoboken, NJ: Wiley.

Barrett, M. 2002. Children's Views of Britain and Britishness in 2001: Some Initial Findings from the Developmental Psychology Section Centenary Project. Annual Conference of the Developmental Psychology. University of Sussex, British Psychological Society.

Bhopal, K., and J. Rhamie. 2013. Initial Teacher Training: Understanding 'Race,' Diversity and Inclusion. *Race Ethnicity and Education* 17: 304–325.

Bratberg, O., and K. Haugevik. 2009. Identity in an Age of Uncertainty. *British Politics Review: Journal of the British Politics Society* 4: 2.

Breslin, T., D. Rowe, and A. Thornton. 2006. Citizenship Education: Current State of Play and Recommendations (Memorandum of Submission to the Education Select Committee). Citizenship Foundation.

Carrington, B., A. Bonnett, A. Nayak, C. Skelton, F. Smith, R. Tomlin, G. Short, and J. Demaine. 2000. The Recruitment of New Teachers from Minority Ethnic Groups. *International Studies in Sociology of Education* 10: 3–22.

Carrington, B., and G. Short. 1995. What Makes a Person British? Children's Conceptions of their National Culture and Identity. *Educational Studies* 21: 217–238.

Chadderton, C. 2009. Citizenship Education in the UK: An Increasingly Dangerous Space for Minority Ethnic Young People. *BERA*. Manchester University.

Colley, L. 1992. *Britons: Forging the Nation, 1707–1837.* New Haven: Yale University Press.

Croft, S. 2012. *Securitizing Islam: Identity and the Search for Security.* Cambridge: Cambridge University Press.

Department for Education. 2011. Teachers' Standards: Guidance for School Leaders, School Staff and Governing Bodies.

DFE. 2010. Young People and Community Cohesion: Analysis from the Longitudinal Study of Young People in England (LSYPE). https://www.gov.uk/government/uploads/system/uploads/attachment_data/file/181542/DFE-RR033.pdf.

Ehrkamp, P. 2008. Risking Publicity: Masculinities and the Racialization of Public Neighborhood Space. *Social and Cultural Geography* 9: 117–133.

Elton-Chalcraft, S., V. Lander, L. Revell, D. Warner, and L. Whitworth. 2017. To Promote, or not to Promote Fundamental British Values?—Teachers' Standards, Diversity and Teacher Education. *British Educational Research Journal* 43: 29–48.

Farrell, F. 2016. 'Why All of a Sudden Do We Need to Teach Fundamental British Values?' A Critical Investigation of Religious Education Student Teacher Positioning Within a Policy Discourse of Discipline and Control. *Journal of Education for Teaching* 42: 280–297.

Faulks, K. 2006. Rethinking Citizenship Education in England: Some Lessons from Contemporary Social and Political Theory. *Education, Citizenship and Social Justice* 1: 123–140.

Freedman, K. 2008. Leading Creativity: Responding to Policy in Art Education. In *International Dialogues about Visual Culture, Education and Art,* ed. R. Mason and T. Eça. Bristol: Intellect.

Gaine, C. 2005. *We're All White, Thanks: The Persisting Myth About 'White' Schools.* Stoke on Trent: Trentham Books Limited.

Gay, G. 2002. Preparing for Culturally Responsive Teaching. *Journal of Teacher Education* 53: 106–116.

Gillborn, D. 1995. *Racism and Antiracism in Real Schools: Theory, Policy, Practice.* Buckingham: Open University Press.

Grube, D. 2011. How Can 'Britishness' Be Re-made? *The Political Quarterly* 82: 628–635.

Gunn, A., S. Bennett, L. Shuford Evans, B.J. Peterson, & J.L. Welsh. 2013. Autobiographies in Preservice Teacher Education: A Snapshot Tool for Building a Culturally Responsive Pedagogy. *International Journal of Multicultural Education,* 15.

Hall, S. 1991. Old and New Identities, Old and New Ethnicities. In *Culture, Globalization and the World-System,* ed. A.D. King. Minneapolis: University of Minnesota Press.

Hand, M., and J. Pearce. 2009. Patriotism in British Schools: Principles, Practices and Press Hysteria. *Educational Philosophy and Theory* 41: 453–465.

Heater, D. 2004. *A Brief History of Citizenship.* Edinburgh: Edinburgh University Press.

Hess, D.E. 2009. *Controversy in the Classroom: The Democratic Power of Discussion.* New York: Routledge.

HM Government. March 2015. *Revised Prevent Duty Guidance: For England and Wales.*

Home Office. 2001. *Community Cohesion: A Report of the Independent Review Team,* Chaired by Ted Cantle. London: HMSO.

hooks, b. 2010. *Teaching Critical Thinking: Practical Wisdom.* New York and London: Routledge.

Howard, G. 2006. *We Can't Teach What We Don't Know: White Teachers, Multiracial Schools.* New York and London: Teachers College Press.

Husbands, C., A. Kitson, and S. Steward. 2010. *Teaching History 11–18: Understanding the Past 11–18.* Maidenhead: Open University Press.

Jerome, L., and G. Clemitshaw. 2012. Teaching (about) Britishness? An Investigation into Trainee Teachers' Understanding of Britishness in Relation to Citizenship and the Discourse of Civic Nationalism. *Curriculum Journal* 23: 19–41.

Kearney, H. 2012. *The British Isles: A History of Four Nations.* Cambridge: Cambridge University Press.

Keddie, A. 2013. The Politics of Britishness: Multiculturalism, Schooling and Social Cohesion. *British Educational Research Journal* 40: 539–554.

Kedourie, E. 1993. *Nationalism.* Oxford: Blackwell.

Kincheloe, J.L. 2007. Critical Pedagogy in the Twenty-First Century. In *Critical Pedagogy: Where are We Now?* ed. P. Mclaren and J.L. Kincheloe. New York: Peter Lang.

King, J.E. 1991. Dysconscious Racism: Ideology, Identity, and the Miseducation of Teachers. *Journal of Negro Education* 60: 133–146.

Lander, V. 2014. Initial Teacher Education: The Practice of Whiteness. In *Advancing Race and Ethnicity in Education,* ed. R. Race and V. Lander. Basingstoke: Palgrave Macmillan.

Lander, V. 2016. Introduction to Fundamental British Values. *Journal of Education for Teaching* 42: 274–279.

Lea, V., and E.J. Sims. 2008. Undoing Whiteness in the Classroom: Different Origins, Shared Commitment. In *Undoing Whiteness in the Classroom: Critical Educultural Teaching Approaches for Social Justice Activism,* ed. V. Lea and E.J. Sims. New York: Peter Lang.

Lund, D.E., and P.R. Carr. 2010. Exposing Privilege and Racism in the Great White North: Tackling Whiteness and Identity Issues in Canadian Education. *Multicultural Perspectives* 12: 229–234.

Maylor, U. 2010. Notions of Diversity, British Identities and Citizenship Belonging. *Race Ethnicity and Education* 13: 233–252.

Maylor, U. 2016. 'I'd Worry about How to Teach It': British Values in English Classrooms. *Journal of Education for Teaching* 42: 314–328.

Maylor, U., B. Read, H. Mendick, A. Ross, and N. Rollock. 2007. *Diversity and Citizenship in the Curriculum: Research Review* (Research Report 819). London: The Institute for Policy Studies in Education, London Metropolitan University.

Maylor, U., A. Ross, and N. Rollock. 2006a. 'It is a Way of Life'—Notions of Good Multicultural Practice in Initial Teacher Education and Curriculum Delivery in England. In *Citizenship Education: Europe and the World*, ed. A. Ross. London: CiCe.

Maylor, U., A. Ross, N. Rollock, and K. Williams. 2006b. *Black Teachers in London*. London: Greater London Authority.

McGuigan, J. 2010. *Cultural Analysis*. London: Sage.

Nussbaum, M.C. 1996. *For Love of Country?* Boston: Beacon Press.

OFSTED. 2010. *Citizenship Established? Citizenship in schools 2006/09*. London: OFSTED.

Osler, A. 2008. Citizenship Education and the Ajegbo Report: Re-imagining a Cosmopolitan Nation. *London Review of Education* 6: 11–25.

Osler, A., and H. Starkey. 2003. Learning for Cosmopolitan Citizenship: Theoretical Debates and Young People's Experiences. *Educational Review* 55: 243–254.

Panjwani, F. 2016. Towards an Overlapping Consensus: Muslim Teachers' Views on Fundamental British Values. *Journal of Education for Teaching* 42: 329–340.

Parekh, B. 1999. The Incoherence of Nationalism. In *Theorizing Nationalism*, ed. R. Beiner. New York: State University of New York Press.

Parekh, B. 2000. *The Future of Multi-ethnic Britain: Report of the Commission on the Future of Multi-ethnic Britain*. London: The Runnymede Trust/Profile Books.

Pearce, S. 2012. Confronting Dominant Whiteness in the Primary Classroom: Progressive Student Teachers' Dilemmas and Constraints. *Oxford Review of Education* 38: 455–472.

Pettifor, T. 2016. Teacher Sacked 'For Calling Muslim Schoolboy Terrorist After He Complained about Detention'. *The Mirror*, January 28.

Phillips, A., and G. Ganesh. 2007. *Young People and British Identity*. Ipsos MORI/Camelot Foundation.

Phoenix, A. 1998. 'Multicultures', 'Multiracisms' and Young People, Contradictory Legacies of 'Windrush'. *Soundings* 10: 86–96.

Revell, L., and H. Bryan. 2016. Calibrating Fundamental British Values: How Head Teachers are Approaching Appraisal in the Light of the Teachers' Standards 2012, Prevent and the Counter-Terrorism and Security Act, 2015. *Journal of Education for Teaching* 42: 341–353.

Revesz, R. 2016. Teacher Calls 12-Year-Old Muslim Pupil a 'Terrorist' as He Laughs Watching 'Bend It Like Beckham'. *The Independent*, April 03.

Richardson, R. 2015. British Values and British Identity: Muddles, Mixtures, and Ways Ahead. *London Review of Education* 13: 37–48.

Sales, R. 2012. Britain and Britishness: Place, Belonging and Exclusion. In *Muslims in Britain: Making Social and Political Space*, ed. W. Ahmad and Z. Sardar. Abingdon: Routledge.

Sanderson, P., and P. Thomas. 2014. Troubling Identities: Race, Place and Positionality among Young People in Two Towns in Northern England. *Journal of Youth Studies* 17: 1–19.

Shammas, J., and T. Evans. 2015. Muslim Student Claims Teacher Told Him: 'Stop Talking, You Terrorist' as Council Launches Investigation. *The Mirror*, December 08.

Smith, H.J. 2016. Britishness as Racist Nativism: A Case of the Unnamed 'Other'. *Journal of Education for Teaching* 42: 298–313.

Smith, H.J., and V. Lander. 2012. Collusion or Collision: Effects of Teacher Ethnicity in the Teaching of Critical Whiteness. *Race Ethnicity and Education* 15: 331–351.

Smyth, J., and P. McInerney. 2007. *Teachers in the Middle: Reclaiming the Wasteland of the Adolescent Years of Schooling*. New York: Peter Lang.

Solórzano, D.G., and T.J. Yosso. 2002. Critical Race Methodology: Counter-Storytelling as an Analytical Framework for Education Research. *Qualitative Inquiry* 8: 23–44.

Stevenson, N. 2003. Cultural Citizenship in the 'Cultural' Society: A Cosmopolitan Approach. *Citizenship Studies* 7: 331–348.

Stokes, E., and B. Nea. 2013. Shaping the Future: Getting the Best for Black, Asian and Minority Ethnic Children and Young People Race on the Agenda.

Troyna, B., and B. Carrington. 2012. *Education, Racism and Reform*. London: Routledge.

Turvey, A., J. Yandell, and L. Ali. 2012. English as a Site of Cultural Negotiation and Contestation. *English Teaching: Practice and Critique* 11: 26–44.

Vavrus, M. 2015. *Diversity and Education: A Critical Multicultural Approach*. New York: Teachers College Press.

Verma, G.K., P. Zec, and G. Skinner. 1994. *The Ethnic Crucible: Harmony and Hostility in Multi-ethnic Schools*. London: Falmer Press.

Vertovec, S., and R. Cohen (eds.). 2002. *Conceiving Cosmopolitanism: Theory, Context and Practice*. Oxford: Oxford University Press.

Weedon, C. 2004. *Identity and Culture: Narratives of Difference and Belonging: Narratives of Difference and Belonging*. Maidenhead: Open University Press.

Wemyss, G. 2009. *The Invisible Empire: White Discourse, Tolerance and Belonging*. Farnham: Ashgate.

Young, I.M. 2000. *Inclusion and Democracy*. Oxford: Oxford University Press.

Zinn, H. 2013. *A Power Governments Cannot Suppress*. San Francisco: City Lights Books.

CHAPTER 5

Learning and Teaching About Britishness

Abstract This chapter presents South East London school teachers and students exploring Britishness through Art. I describe the personal nature of the project on identity and belonging as impacting positively upon teacher–student relations. Students responded eagerly to interest in their frustrations and concerns, as well as their dreams and ambitions, thereby strengthening relationships with teachers and peers. I argue that because both Art teachers in my research were keen to validate their students' stories, interests and cultural experiences of family, community and belonging, the levels of student involvement were consistently high. This chapter—and the chapters that follow—attest to the benefits of using critical pedagogies when examining Britishness and belonging, and while engaging with differences and diversities regarding Britishness.

Keywords Critical pedagogy · Art education · Racism · Patriotism Diversity

DIVERSITY, IDENTITY AND PEDAGOGY

In this chapter, I present South-East London school teachers and students exploring Britishness through Art. The personal nature of the project on identity and belonging impacted positively upon teacher–student relations. Students tended to respond eagerly to interest in their frustrations

© The Author(s) 2018
S. Habib, *Learning and Teaching British Values*,
DOI 10.1007/978-3-319-60381-0_5

and concerns, as well as their dreams and ambitions, thereby strengthening relationships with teachers and peers. This chapter—and the following chapters—attest to the benefits of using critical pedagogies when examining Britishness and belonging, and while engaging with differences and diversities regarding Britishness. This message is particularly crucial if schools are failing to explore "what is meant by 'diversity', the type of diversity messages they would like to promote, and how they want such diversity messages to be received and understood" (Maylor 2010: 248).

The evidences presented in this book about the value of critical pedagogy are also important at a time when confusion and lack of training on how to approach Britishness and FBV teaching (Elton-Chalcraft et al. 2017) overshadow pedagogies of possibility and hope. Pedagogies of possibility and hope that identity exploration could bring for schools, students and teachers. Recognising that the close relationship between identity, diversity and achievement can enhance teaching and learning philosophies and practices (Knowles and Lander 2011), teachers might opt to practise apply culturally responsive teaching to benefit students who otherwise struggle to succeed if a remote and unfamiliar middle-class Eurocentric curriculum is all they know (Gay 2010). Turvey et al. (2012: 33), for example, refer to a school student, who is disengaged from learning, until the teacher "recognises the complexity of the relationship" between "identity" and "learning". I argue, in this chapter, that because both Art teachers were keen to validate the students' stories, interests and cultural experiences of family, community and belonging, the levels of student involvement were consistently high.

The little research conducted about Britishness teaching reveals the nervousness and reluctance of teachers to debate a topic perceived as controversial. It is a worry that schools are often guilty for not tackling the issue of diversity in Britain effectively (Maylor 2010), for how then will they be able to explore multicultural Britishness? Concerns about how Britishness and FBV teaching intersect with multicultural and anti-racist education need addressing. For example, in mainly White communities "active support of minority ethnic identities" can become necessary through "education of white children about cultural diversity" (Scourfield et al. 2005: 222), and sometimes teachers are in danger of "underestimating" their White students' understanding and experience of diversity in Britain (Maylor 2010). Moreover, schools only tend to equate diversity with students from minority ethnic backgrounds, thereby neglecting White British and dual heritage experiences

(Maylor 2010), whose only "experience of identity issues in the curriculum is that they have a deficit or residual British/English identity" (Maylor et al. 2007: 8). Some schools neglect teaching about diversity in Britain, assuming White students "are unlikely to engage in ethnically diverse communities" (Maylor 2010: 241), yet statistically "virtually no secondary schools" are all-White (Gillborn and Mirza 2000: 6).

Presumptions made in multi-ethnic schools, that the teaching of diversity in Britain is not needed as students already "do diversity" daily and that minority ethnic students are innately knowledgeable about diversity (Maylor 2010), disclose the British education system's deficiencies in not supporting schools to value evolving and complex multicultural British identities. The complexities of choices available to young people, as well as the consequences of these choices, can impact upon how ethnic minority youth position themselves[1] in relation to, for example, their "Asianness" or "Britishness" (Hall 2000). Mixed heritage students also find their identity needs are insufficiently addressed or incorrectly diagnosed as lacking and problematic.[2] Stereotyped as coming from "fragmented homes" and having "confused identities", mixed heritage students can become "…invisible at policy level with no guidance in place about terminology or monitoring of achievement" (Fuller 2013: 142).

RACISM IN SCHOOLS

The 2016 European Union Referendum revealed mainstream British politicians employing the aggressive rhetoric of Othering and exclusion when peddling Britishness. In the backdrop to Britishness promotion, politicians have rendered race invisible by underemphasising, even ignoring, institutional racism and racial inequalities in social policy initiatives and public discourses and debates (Gillborn 1995; Ratcliffe 2011; Craig and O'Neill 2013). This neglect has seeped into professional practice with new teachers oblivious to race and racism (Solomon et al. 2005; Pearce 2012; Lander 2014). Whiteness dominates conversations on Britishness in education, polity and the media. A major challenge for anti-racist activism then is how to ensure principles of critical White studies[3] are incorporated into the pedagogies, policies and practices encountered by teachers and students.[4]

I argue throughout this book that race, racism and racial inequalities urgently need examining in schools (Maylor et al. 2006) particularly by using the tools offered by critical race theory and critical pedagogy.

Now more than ever society should "understand the reality and experiences of racism while acknowledging that race is a socially constructed concept, and that racialisation connects with other socially constructed discourses in the processes of 'othering'", leading to "stigma, exclusion, disadvantage and humiliation" (Craig and O'Neill 2013: 94). Examples of the "downgrading of the 'race' agenda" include political rhetoric, loss of funding for regional Black and Minority Ethnic (BME) networks, the EHRC's responsibilities being decreased, and the Government Equalities Office having its budget almost halved (Gillborn 1995; Craig and O'Neill 2013). Institutional racism and racial inequalities are deemed insignificant. Yet "Britain cannot get over its past and racism holds the society hostage" (Back 2009: 205).

Critical race theorists argue that "when the ideology of racism is examined and racist injuries are named, victims of racism can find their voice"; they can share solidarity with similarly demonised or oppressed peoples and become empowered in a collective story-sharing experience, "hearing their own stories and the stories of others, listening to how the arguments against them are framed, and learning to make the arguments to defend themselves" (Solórzano and Yosso 2002: 27). Schools must interrogate not only "personal prejudice and ignorance", but also institutional racisms (Gillborn 1995: 36), and "new racisms" that reveal sociocultural targeting of the Other (Back 1996); schools must deconstruct racism and racial injustices, both old and new. Regarding new and growing forms of racism like Islamophobia, British society has long been warned by academics to be wary about "debates led by politicians and the media" that "quickly become the norm and end up fuelling racism" against Muslims who are racialised and blamed for not integrating in British society (Bhavnani et al. 2005: 49).

The Ajegbo, Crick and Cantle Reports have been criticised for focusing on "diversity" rather than directing critical attention to structural racism, societal and global inequalities, youth voice or experience of education and human rights (Osler 2008; Ratcliffe 2011; Osler 2015): "the re-incarnation of citizenship education through the Crick Report (QCA 1998)" included "only two paragraphs on multicultural issues (Tomlinson 2008a), and, significantly, no mention at all of racism" (Garratt 2011: 30). Osler (2008: 13) further denounces The Crick Report for astonishingly it almost "reflects, rather than challenges, the institutionalised racism of British society" through pejorative language and stereotypical representations of ethnic minority communities.

Nandi and Platt (2014) argue the "failure" of multicultural policies in creating social cohesion is often cited in relation to Muslim communities, while other minority groups and the White majority are rarely investigated. Yet some ethnic minority communities have strong affiliations to British identity (Manning and Georgiadis 2012), "stronger in fact than the White majority" (Nandi and Platt 2014: 41).

PROBLEMATIC PATRIOTISM

For some politicians, patriotism is a prized value to be instilled in the nation. Osler (2009: 89), investigating political speeches, concludes Gordon Brown's vision of Britishness was patriotic and "progressive": endorsing symbols such as the union flag and a national day, Brown argued that these "must be reclaimed from far right and racist political parties, and adopted as a symbol of unity, tolerance and inclusion". In the USA, "arrogant nationalism" reverberates through indoctrination of young Americans to support the powerful elite in society, while racial and religious groups are ostracised and even violently harmed: "... that devotion to a flag, an anthem, a boundary, so fierce it engenders mass murder ...along with racism and religious hatred" (Zinn 2013: n.p.). Research in the UK reveals students and teachers often affirm neutrality of approach towards patriotism "in the context of open discussion" (Hand and Pearce 2009: 453); interestingly, Hand and Pearce (2009: 461) reported teachers and students felt it was "a good thing for people to be patriotic", but overall there was support for a neutral stance on patriotism, and some even argued it should be avoided.

Surveys in the 1990s stated European identity would overtake national identifications (Kershen 1998). Yet in Europe, the rise of ugly nationalism (Bhambra 2014), through "aggressive political demagoguery, targeting minorities, immigrants and democracy itself" no longer remains the sole domain of far right extremists but is witnessed in "mainstream political forces" (Amin 2012: 119). The Brexit[5] campaign brought forth a rise in nationalism and racism in parts of the UK, while some Britons battled to retain their European affiliation. The relationship between ugly nationalism and persistent (state) racism has long been troublesome for ethnic minority communities in the UK and in Europe. The way the French and German states, for example, view their minorities as "problems", are "reflections of how these states run themselves, run their schools, and run the curricula" (Baumann 1999: 151).

The 2008 Green Paper, *The Path to Citizenship*, a Home Office document, depicts immigrants as a criminal threat to Britain's stability: "Negative messages about newcomers are contrasted with 'British values'... the document gives the impression that Britain is a country under siege by certain unspecified newcomers unlikely to subscribe fully to such values" (Osler 2011: 196). Berke (1998: 43) perceives nationalism as "narcissism" that obsesses over size and shape through boundaries and borders, as well as about the inner and the exterior, through ideas of racial purity and prestige. This narcissism features heavily in political and media posturing about multicultural Britain. Even seemingly innocent census data can, for example, be "used by the media to feed xenophobia, and by politicians as grounds for *reducing* services" (Sebba 2017: 8).

The education system, through the National Curriculum, may attempt to encourage students—and teachers—to be proud of their national identity, and target ethnic minority students in a programme of assimilation. Yet, there will continue to be teachers and students who resist jingoistic doctrine. For example, they will not be keen "to endorse the use of national symbols, such as the flag, in school contexts" (Osler and Starkey 2005: 12). Instead, students and teachers prefer open classroom discussion about patriotism; others express wariness about promoting patriotism as it is potentially "socially divisive" in excluding non-British students, as one teacher explains, "patriotism about being British in my experience tends to be a white preserve" (Hand and Pearce 2009: 460). In solely championing British history, values and identity, diverse students' ethnic and cultural heritages are viewed as marginal, insignificant and worthless.

Writers on nation have emphasised the problematic nature of claiming an exclusive nation by proclaiming racial or linguistic superiority:

> Such exaggerations enclose one within a specific culture, considered as national; one limits oneself, one hems oneself in. One leaves the heady air that one breathes in the vast field of humanity in order to enclose oneself in a conventicle with one's compatriots. Nothing could be worse for the mind; nothing could be more disturbing for civilization. (Renan 1990: 17)

Pride in the nation is perpetuated at the expense of acknowledging the shameful histories of Britain's colonial aggressions (Fortier 2005; Zembylas 2008). In the USA, teachers who openly critique colonial aggression and the political status quo are also vulnerable to neoliberal hard-lined practices and neoconservative ideologies destroying their teaching career and livelihood (Groenke and Hatch 2009; Gabbard 2009).

EXPLORING BRITISHNESS THROUGH ART

The students in the London school where I conducted my research on learning and teaching Britishness came to know diverse and multiple ways of reading and comprehending nuanced British identities through creating powerful self-portraits and engaging in structured collective discussions in the classroom. This book shows Art teachers are no strangers to dissecting sociopolitical commentary to enhance students' "critical consciousness" (Yokley 1999: 24), just like teachers of English who can provide students with the "shared experience of the class novel" to better critically reflect upon the "socio-historical and socio-political contexts" that might, for example, cause displacement and create refugees (Habib 2008: 45). Recognising the classroom can be a place where hegemony is resisted and cultural reproduction challenged (Au and Apple 2009), Art teachers are well placed in "revealing conditions of the past, illuminating present politics and forecasting possible futures" (Grierson 2008: 22), similar to teachers of English (Habib 2008). Education that is liberating is a core concern for critical pedagogues like the Art teachers I had the honour of observing (Freire 1985, 2000; hooks 1994). The analysis, in the following chapters, reveals two reflective teachers practising *critical consciousness* and generating *dialogue* (Freire 2000), without explicitly employing critical pedagogy terminology.

Teachers and students were collaboratively participating in critical reflection and dialogue. Such "critical praxis" develops better schools and societies (Kincheloe 2008). The Art teachers treated students with respect and care as together they created knowledge about everyday lived experiences of British identities. Critical pedagogy, we will see, is a prism through which we can observe complex relationships between teaching and learning, and between teachers and learners; the prism brings to light sociopolitical, socio-economic and sociocultural aspects of our present and our past (Wink 2005). The Art teachers' approaches would eventually inspire confidence and independence, as students individually and collectively reflected upon Britishness in personal artwork and class discussions. Critical pedagogy excellently champions "changing how people think about themselves and their relationship to others and the world", significantly "energizing students and others to engage in those struggles that further possibilities for living in a more just society" (Giroux 2004: 64). Moving beyond critical pedagogy, Ladson-Billings (1995: 160) argues for "culturally relevant teaching as a pedagogy of opposition (1992c) not unlike critical pedagogy but specifically committed to collective, not merely individual, empowerment".

Rather than treating viewpoints of teachers and students as distinct categories, I have intentionally chosen to interweave their experiences together, for critical pedagogues see teaching and learning as inseparable (Freire 2000, 2001). I also wanted to highlight collaboration and collectivity. Teachers both teach and learn, and students both learn and teach. Such is the nature of progressive pedagogical encounters. The Art teachers, we will learn in this chapter, wanted to educate, not indoctrinate. They recognised "liberating education consists in acts of cognition, not transferrals of information" (Freire 2000: 79). The Art teachers were engaging in *culturally responsive teaching*, as though they seemed to understand that "caring" is "a moral imperative, a social responsibility, and a pedagogical necessity" (Gay 2002: 109). Valuing student autonomy and criticality resulted in fluidity and focus; students became emotionally engaged, confident and independent, while re-learning about learning, about identities and histories, and about multicultural Britain. I will now discuss the teachers' intentions and motivations for the project, before examining how critical pedagogies employed in the classroom enabled students and teachers to reflect upon identity issues with growing confidence.

BEGINNING BRITISHNESS TEACHING IN THE CLASSROOM

Multicultural Britishness: Diversity and Difference

Head of Art, Ms Anderson, designed the coursework module enthusiastically, but cautiously, explaining she anticipated wide ranging experiences of belonging to Britain. Students often encounter varied viewpoints in school, far more than at home, as their classmates come from diverse backgrounds (Hess 2009). If students come to our classrooms with diverse backgrounds and influences, promoting inclusion and equality by recognising difference is necessary (Knowles and Lander 2011). Ms Anderson was uneasy that Britishness teaching "potentially inflames some... deep felt emotions about how people have been treated in Britain". She mulled over possible controversies, "particularly if their families come from other countries... or if they've been impacted upon in any way by you know an influx of refugees and feel hard done by". Ms Anderson knew refugees are scapegoated in public discourses, leading to prejudices and distortions against those seeking sanctuary. Young people, my teaching and research have previously shown, are inevitably impacted upon by this negative rhetoric against refugees and asylum seekers (Habib 2008). When I read Benjamin Zephaniah's Refugee Boy with young Londoners, I made a "shocking and disturbing discovery": they thought refugees and asylum seekers were to blame for the 7/7 and 9/11 bombings, thus "the often misused terms 'terrorist' and 'refugee' had become one entity" (Habib 2008: 48). My experiences and Ms Anderson's concerns are not unique, but an indictment of British societal attitudes towards refugees. Rutter (2005: 133), for example, observed a lesson where students expressed tabloid news "crude stereotypes", branding refugees as "money-grabbing terrorists". A critical race theory approach can give students the space to deconstruct "normalised" racist caricatures of social groups (Taylor 2016) like refugees. Teachers can facilitate classroom discussion of controversial topics by challenging stereotypes and enabling multiple perspectives to emerge for debate (Hess 2009).

Chris, one of the Art students, recalled mocking reactions towards new non-English speaking arrivals during primary school. He argued young children should explore belonging to multicultural British society. His peer, Ellie, recognised younger students may lack emotional maturity to sensitively address multicultural belongings. Reflecting upon diversity and difference (Knowles and Lander 2011), Art teacher, Mr Martin was also initially "apprehensive", and "expecting all sorts of different outcomes really because it was quite open". The Art teachers' concerns are unsurprising, as teachers frequently find themselves labouring to "reconcile the increasingly complex agendas that come into classrooms with young lives" alongside providing "an authentic, relevant, fulfilling and meaningful educational experience" (Smyth and McInerney 2007: 7).

This educational experience is arrived at through pedagogies that "connect with students' narratives, needs, experiences and communities" in multicultural and globalised societies (Stuhr et al. 2008: 83). Critical pedagogues actively work to develop a curriculum "responsible to the lives, aspirations, and cultures of young people" (Smyth et al. 2013: 317). The philosophy that there is "no teaching without learning" (Freire 2001: 31) comes alive when teachers learn about their diverse students' cultures and identities; additionally improving student engagement and achievement (Knowles and Lander 2011), while nurturing creativity and collaborative learning in the classroom.

Mr Martin "worried" students may have "inherited" parental prejudices; nevertheless, he encouraged students to discuss Britishness with family to gain a broad understanding, which he found they enjoyed. Students, like Joe, displayed affective attachments to Britishness that may have felt very personal, but simultaneously were not his alone. Far right rhetoric seeps into speeches of mainstream politicians "trying to appease national majorities that have been destabilized by growing economic and welfare insecurity, cultural and ethnic mixity, and future uncertainty" (Amin 2012: 119); young people may internalise political and public discourses, family talk and media rhetoric on multiculturalism (Wetherell 2012).

Beyond the Banking Method: Teachers, Students and Knowledge Production

Focus on school standards and improvement in educational policies results in less time and opportunities for examining identities (Turvey et al. 2012). Teachers cannot merely function as robotic clerks to maintain standards, practising what Freire (2000) refers to as the *banking* approach by acting as depositors of items of "knowledge" (officially sanctioned "correct" deposits) into students (the depositories). Some students have only known years of schooling characterised by uninspiring pedagogies and uncritical curriculums, often pushed by dull and regimented educational policies that restrict teachers' time, potential, ambitions, creativity and scope. Though sometimes students may not realise their oppressed positions, I follow Giroux and Shor's views that students are not "dupes of dominant ideology", but are "fighting for their humanity", at times "without quite realizing how they might reclaim it" (George 2001: 96).

Banking education does not give students space to develop a critical consciousness (*conscientizacao*), but instead it arrests "our curiosity, our inquisitive spirit, and ourcreativity" (Freire 1985: 2). When teaching about Britishness, teachers must remember that the official curriculum "is never simply a neutral assemblage of knowledge, somehow appearing in the texts and the classrooms of a nation", but "always part of a *selective tradition*, someone's selection, someone's group vision of legitimate knowledge" (Apple 1993: 222). Increasingly, young people seem to have become "subjects, to whom the curriculum is delivered", which is contrary to the ideals of youth voice emphasised in the 1989 UN Convention on the Rights of the Children (Gamman 2004: 149). Students come of age in a context where they are treated as passive automata:

> ...the objects of government policies, testing regimes, curriculum frameworks... that they might have something important to say about curriculum, pedagogy and school organization or that they have the knowledge and skills to shape their own learning has not found much favor with policy makers. (Smyth and McInerney 2007: 39)

Critical pedagogues witness suppression of youth voice, as "'free spaces' within the institution of schooling where young people can express themselves and do their identity work are being severely eroded" (Smyth and McInerney 2013: 3). Critical pedagogues strive to re-define 'knowledge', less about the teacher, more about students asking questions and posing problems (Shor 1996).

Freedom granted to students resulted in some students worrying about what the teacher thought, wanted and knew; both Art teachers worked to challenge hegemonic representations of Britishness by encouraging students to become more autonomous in expressing and valuing their own voices. Traditional *banking* methods of teaching elevate teacher knowledge at the expense of student knowledge (Freire 2000). The Art students, I learned, needed gentle steering away from such limiting authoritarianism. They were guided towards "engaged pedagogy" for "we learn best when there is an interactive relationship between student and teacher" (hooks 2010: 19). Though the Art teachers were facilitating, not dictating, their knowledge was still perceived as more valuable, with some students finding it difficult to escape traditional attitudes of "teacher knows best". Traditional *banking* methods of schooling assume teachers hold "knowledge", which they transfer to students with the aim of making them knowledgeable (Freire 2000). Mr Martin, rejecting a traditional *banking* style of teaching, was adapting his teaching to re-emphasise to students the project was not about "his perspective":

> Mr Martin: ...they were waiting for me to say "You can't do that! It has to have a flag in it... or it has to have some bit of culture in it...".... I moved in my approach and I sort of said "You do it. There's a reason why you are doing it"...

Students are often not used to developing criticality and conversation. Teachers might become "discouraged" when students struggle with critical thought (hooks 2010: 10). Historically, systems of schooling have firmly established an "anti-conversation model of education" in the pedagogical frameworks of students and teachers: "The teacher speaks according to a set curriculum which must be ingested by the student. The teacher distributes handouts... The students listen, read and take notes" (Batsleer 2008: 7).

To quash disappointment or frustration, exploring Britishness took careful thought and flexibility for teachers and students. Being granted pedagogical freedom was novel, unexpected, and disconcerting for students often socialised, through standard schooling practices and rigid traditional pedagogies, into believing the teacher's knowledge is the only knowledge. Good teaching recognises "knowledge and understanding are waiting to be created rather than existing in some a priori dimension beyond human intervention" (Brookfield 2009: 38); the Art teachers took great lengths to emphasise idea this in their classrooms. Mr Martin believed students wanted him to tell them, for instance, to "draw a portrait of themselves with a Union Jack in the background... a nice cup of tea... and a nice red phone box". Mr Martin adapted lessons to challenge students, reminding them, sometimes to their frustration, this was not about *his* knowledge, but about *their* knowledge. Even in critical pedagogy practices, tensions about the authenticity of "democratic" teaching and learning practices emerge as teachers have the power to shift the course of the teaching and learning, more so than the students. Mr Martin observed critical thinking is difficult for students; especially, if they have become "comfortable with learning that allows them to remain passive" (hooks 2010: 10). Both teachers were negotiating traditional power relations between teachers and students, searching and re-searching with their students (Freire 2001), encouraging students to venture out of curriculum comfort zones through exciting and interpretative pedagogies.

Research participant Chris recalled classmates challenging conventional ideas about Britishness, believing "they should represent where they are coming from, like where their parents are from". The idea of "shared values" is a problematic and partial understanding of British identity, with some students not convinced about belonging to mythical narratives (Young 2000; Faulks 2006). Some students, like Kadisha and Ellie, grasped moments of flexibility and freedom to express unique attachments to transnational or local belongings, rather than nation alone. The Art students gradually acquired the understanding of the value of their own experiences and voices, coming to appreciate their own and their peers' discourses on identities. Ellie observed classmates disrupting superficial and stereotypical notions of Britishness: "I think British colours are just colours on a flag. And that's not what anyone really did their work about. Everyone did it about something that was kind a personal to them". Approaching identity work through "independence of thought and developing skills of reflection, enquiry and debate" (Gamman 2004: 154) was challenging but yielded student participation and engagement.

Mr Martin explained he challenged very simplistic notions of Britishness for which students sought teacher approval. To ensure students understood about multiple identities, teacher and students developed knowledge together about the diversity within the classroom. Mr Martin required students to reflect upon multilingual Britain, for example. His students had discussed Britishness with their families, finding holding a passport and speaking the English language[6] as key to Britishness.[7] Mr Martin challenged students' monocultural acceptance by discussing multilingual students, schools and cities. Young people are growing up in a society where official discourses repress the expression of the multilingual diversities encountered in Britain, hindering the efforts of progressive pedagogues. On the last UK census (Office for National Statistics 2011), Question 18 asked "What is your main language?" with the possible responses requiring you to choose between English or the Other language you chose to specify. Thus, the census neglected to ask Britons about bilingualism or multilingualism (Fuller 2013: 144). This "emphasis on English *only* displays an ideology of monolingualism which devalues bilingualism and linguistic diversity, leading to a 'blind spot' where 'main language' becomes 'only language'" (Sebba 2017: 3).

The teachers wanted students to analyse national identity as more than merely a practical concept manifested through a passport or birth certificate. National identity might relay the story of belonging to a place (Byrne 2006). The Art teachers recognised that narratives of belonging, in all their muddling and enthralling contradictions, would differ depending on students' sociocultural experiences. The project laid bare diverse identities. Things hitherto unknown were revealed, sometimes to the surprise of students and teachers. For Mr Martin, the project was "an uncovering" to foster thinking beyond simple stereotypes.

The "political" may need to be embraced when helping students to "develop critical consciousness" (Yokley 1999: 24) was evident to both teachers. Studying national cultural identity entails "political" entanglements: "national culture which is primarily political is the site where cultural beliefs and values are formed, sanctioned, and/or penalized" (Stuhr et al. 2008: 86). Both Art teachers embraced the "political", accepting it was inevitable and necessary when exploring Britishness.

Britishness: Education, not Indoctrination

Political and media rhetoric on Britishness informed both teachers' pedagogical approaches. Mr Martin had heard suggestions on news programmes of British school students pledging national allegiance. Teaching Britishness, teachers know, can become jingoistic (Hand and Pearce 2009, 2011; Jerome and Clemitshaw 2012). Mr Martin feared American-style pedagogies seeping into British education, patriotic acts like "saluting the flag" which dominated a "corner of the classroom". Proposals "for schools to have flags and other national (and nationalist) symbols and ceremonies to celebrate Britishness" (Peterson et al. 2016: 112) are not unheard of. Mr Martin argued this was "indoctrination". While in America it might be the norm to openly demonstrate patriotism (Johnston 2007; Banks 2010; Zinn 2013), where school policy, curriculum and textbooks inculcate students with the meaning of "good" patriotic citizenship (Stratton 2016), both Art teachers I worked with were receptive to students resisting patriotic notions of national identity.

Critical pedagogy emphasises both student and teacher knowledge as important. Both Art teachers valued and sought student knowledge, which students responded to with enthusiasm and engagement. Increasing student participation and engagement necessitates discussion about the reasons for studying the topic and its relevance to local and cultural diversity (Gamman 2004). Four *interests* held by students are "natural resources, the uninvested capital, upon the exercise of which depends on the active growth of the child" (Dewey 1900: 45):

1. conversation/communication;
2. inquiry/finding out;
3. interest in construction/creating; and
4. interest in artistic expression.

Dewey (1900: 46) reflects upon how to increase the potential of these interests in our students: "...are we to ignore it, or just excite and draw it out? Or shall we get hold of it and direct it to something ahead, something better?" By promoting critical questioning, which is "the epistemic stance of critical learners and citizens" (Shor 1996: 54), the Art teachers developed students' independent exploration of multicultural British identities.

Teaching Britishness to critically educate, not uncritically indoctrinate, was important. Mr Martin wanted to deconstruct patriotism, but "worried about not having the tools to do that as a teacher". He anticipated being "confronted by students who... want to do quite deep investigations... but I'm not able to support them". Patriotism can easily become "dangerous nationalism" (Carrington and Short 1998: 150), which concerned both teachers. They began the project with care and forethought, aware possible controversies and conflicts might arise. Both teachers cited anxiety about teaching Britishness to students from diverse ethnicities and cultures. Maylor (2010) also found teachers had concerns about teaching diverse students; teachers often require guidance on exploring "multiple identities and allegiances" (Heater 2004: 195).

Pedagogies of liberation (Shor and Freire 1987) were evident in the teachers' strategies. Ms Anderson endorsed student freedom, autonomy and criticality when exploring identity. Mr Martin valued "individual thought and belief" and "freedom of thought and freedom of information", which he perceived as significant when teaching Britishness. There were three typical student responses to the pedagogies practised, Ms Anderson explained:

1. students who scratched the superficial surface of Britishness as they were "a bit flummoxed", lacking personal attachment to Britishness, perhaps finding the project too complex;
2. students who enjoyed exploring what Britishness meant to them providing "...some quite fun responses, like to do with their leisure time"; and
3. students who grappled with personal attachments or detachments to Britishness who delved "deeper into who they were and their identity, and found it quite cathartic to actually say something quite deep about themselves".

Teaching and learning about Britishness, even approached through pedagogies of freedom, autonomy and criticality would therefore yield a range
of responses, with some students more intensely engaged than others.

If students become accustomed to pedagogical practices prohibiting
self-reflection and social criticism, they may come to believe there is only
one version of truth, to be gleaned from the omniscient teacher's oracle
of "knowledge". Currently, the FBV policies and practices are authoritar-
ian, singular and lacking in possibilities; often taught through a banking
style of education, where political rhetoric about values is deposited into
students by unhappy teachers.

To challenge a depressing and dystopian educational landscape, school
students and teachers can actively engage in pedagogies that enable a
hopeful and progressive future. Critical pedagogy approaches encourage students to become responsible and active participants and citizens,
willing them to become unafraid to seek social transformation and social
justice. Exploring Britishness critically—by valuing young people's voices
and experiences—validates and permits production of new knowledge
about nation, citizenship and belonging. Pedagogies of hope and possibility bring new ways of understanding belonging and identities.

NOTES

1. Language and music are two social sites where London youth may come
   together sharing urban multicultural ways of doing Britishness through
   contesting racisms (Back 1996).
2. There is "a failure to reflect Mixed heritage experience and identities in the
   curriculum and school" (Fuller 2013: 142).
3. Critical White Studies concerns White people "and their sense of self, their
   interests and concerns" (Cole 2016: 5).
4. If White people are (un)witting members of "a club that enrols certain
   people at birth, without their consent, and brings them up according to its
   rules", whether politicians, policymakers or teachers, then if they "question
   the rules, the officers are quick to remind them of all they owe to the club,
   and warn them of the dangers they will face if they leave it" (Ignatiev and
   Garvey 1996: 10).
5. The 2016 referendum on whether Britain should remain or exit the
   European Union.
6. Speaking the English language seems to be regarded as a core characteristic of British citizenship (Sebba 2017).
7. See Park et al. (2014) for similar findings in the British Social Attitudes
   survey.

References

Amin, A. 2012. *Land of Strangers*. Cambridge: Polity Press.

Apple, M.W. 1993. The Politics of Official Knowledge: Does a National Curriculum Make Sense? *Teachers College Record* 95 (2): 222–241.

Au, W., and M.W. Apple. 2009. Rethinking Reproduction: Neo-Marxism in Critical Education Theory. In *The Routledge International Handbook of Critical Education*, ed. M.W. Apple, W. Au, and L.A. Gandin. New York: Routledge.

Back, L. 1996. *New Ethnicities and Urban Culture: Racisms and Multiculture in Young Lives*. London: Routledge.

Back, L. 2009. Researching Community and Its Moral Projects. *Twenty-First Century Society* 4: 201–214.

Banks, J.A. 2010. Approaches to Multicultural Curriculum Reform. In *Multicultural Education: Issues and Perspectives*, ed. J.A. Banks and C.A.M. Banks. Hoboken, NJ: Wiley.

Batsleer, J.R. 2008. *Informal Learning in Youth Work*. London: Sage.

Baumann, G. 1999. *The Multicultural Riddle: Rethinking National, Ethnic and Religious Identities*. New York and London: Routledge.

Berke, J. 1998. Malice and Fascism. In *Hate Thy Neighbour: The Dividing Lines of Race and Culture*, ed. S. Greenberg. London: Camden Press.

Bhambra, G.K. 2014. *Connected Sociologies*. London: Bloomsbury Academic.

Bhavnani, R., H.S. Mirza, V. Meetoo, and J.R. Foundation. 2005. *Tackling the Roots of Racism: Lessons for Success*. Bristol: The Policy Press.

Brookfield, S.D. 2009. The Concept of Critically Reflective Practice. In *Handbook of Adult and Continuing Education*, ed. A.L. Wilson and E.R. Hayes. San Francisco: Wiley.

Byrne, B. 2006. *White Lives: The Interplay of 'Race', Class and Gender in Everyday Life*. Abingdon: Routledge.

Carrington, B., and G. Short. 1998. Adolescent Discourse on National Identity: Voices of Care and Justice? *Educational Studies* 24: 133–152.

Cole, Mike. 2016. *Racism: A Critical Analysis*. London: Pluto Press.

Craig, G., and M. O'Neill. 2013. The Official 'Invisibilisation' of Minority Ethnic Disadvantage. In *Social Policy Review 25: Analysis and Debate in Social Policy, 2013*, ed. G. Ramia, K. Farnsworth, and Z. Irving. Bristol: The Policy Press.

Dewey, J. 1900. *The School and Society*. Chicago: The University of Chicago Press.

Elton-Chalcraft, S., V. Lander, L. Revell, D. Warner, and L. Whitworth. 2017. To Promote, or Not to Promote Fundamental British Values?—Teachers' Standards, Diversity and Teacher Education. *British Educational Research Journal* 43: 29–48.

Faulks, K. 2006. Rethinking Citizenship Education in England: Some Lessons from Contemporary Social and Political Theory. *Education, Citizenship and Social Justice* 1: 123–140.

Fortier, A.-M. 2005. Pride Politics and Multiculturalist Citizenship. *Ethnic and Racial Studies* 28: 559–578.

Freire, P. 1985. *The Politics of Education: Culture, Power and Liberation.* Westport, CT: Bergin & Garvey.

Freire, P. 2000. *Pedagogy of the Oppressed.* New York: Bloomsbury Publishing.

Freire, P. 2001. *Pedagogy of Freedom: Ethics, Democracy, and Civic Courage.* Lanham, MD: Rowman & Littlefield Publishers.

Fuller, K. 2013. *Gender.* London: Identity and Educational Leadership.

Gabbard, D. 2009. Anarchist Movement and Education. In *Handbook of Social Justice in Education*, ed. W. Ayers, T.M. Quinn, and D. Stovall. New York: Routledge.

Gamman, R. 2004. Children and the Curriculum. In *Children at the Margins: Supporting Children, Supporting Schools*, ed. T. Billington and M. Pomerantz. Stoke on Trent: Trentham Books.

Garratt, D. 2011. Equality, Difference and the Absent Presence of 'Race' in Citizenship Education in the UK. *London Review of Education* 9: 27–39.

Gay, G. 2002. Preparing for Culturally Responsive Teaching. *Journal of Teacher Education* 53: 106–116.

Gay, G. 2010. *Culturally Responsive Teaching: Theory, Research, and Practice.* New York: Teachers College Press.

George, A. 2001. Critical Pedagogy: Dreaming of Democracy. In *A Guide to Composition Pedagogies*, ed. G. Tate, A. Rupiper, and K. Schick. Oxford: Oxford University Press.

Gillborn, D. 1995. *Racism and Antiracism In Real Schools: Theory, Policy, Practice.* Buckingham: Open University Press.

Gillborn, D., and H.S. Mirza. 2000. *Mapping Race, Class and Gender. Educational Inequality.* London: Ofsted.

Giroux, H.A. 2004. Cultural Studies, Public Pedagogy, and the Responsibility of Intellectuals. *Communication and Critical/Cultural Studies* 1 (1): 59–79.

Grierson, E. 2008. Creativity and Culture: Redefining Knowledge Through the Arts in Education for the Local in a Globalized World. In *International Dialogues about Visual Culture, Education and Art*, ed. R. Mason and T. Eça. Bristol: Intellect.

Groenke, S.L., and J.A. Hatch (eds.). 2009. *Critical Pedagogy and Teacher Education in the Neoliberal Era: Small Openings.* New York: Springer.

Habib, S. 2008. Refugee Boy: The Social and Emotional Impact of the Shared Experience of a Contemporary Class Novel. *Changing English* 15 (1): 41–52.

Hall, S. 2000. A Question of Identity (II). *The Observer*, 15 October.

Hand, M., and J. Pearce. 2009. Patriotism in British Schools: Principles, Practices and Press Hysteria. *Educational Philosophy and Theory* 41: 453–465.

Hand, M. & J. Pearce. 2011. Patriotism in British Schools: Teachers' and Students' Perspectives. *Educational Studies* 37: 405–418.

Heater, D. 2004. *A Brief History of Citizenship*. Edinburgh: Edinburgh University Press.

Hess, D.E. 2009. *Controversy in the Classroom: The Democratic Power of Discussion*. New York and London: Routledge.

hooks, b. 1994. *Teaching to Transgress: Education as the Practice of Freedom*. New York and London: Routledge.

hooks, b. 2010. *Teaching Critical Thinking: Practical Wisdom*. New York and London: Routledge.

Ignatiev, N., and J. Garvey (eds.). 1996. *Race Traitor*. New York and London: Routledge.

Jerome, L., and G. Clemitshaw. 2012. Teaching (About) Britishness? An Investigation into Trainee Teachers' Understanding of Britishness in Relation to Citizenship and the Discourse of Civic Nationalism. *Curriculum Journal* 23: 19–41.

Johnston, S. 2007. *The Truth About Patriotism*. Durham and London: Duke University Press.

Kershen, A.J. (ed.). 1998. *A Question of Identity*. Aldershot: Ashgate.

Kincheloe, J.L. 2008. *Critical Pedagogy Primer*. New York: Peter Lang.

Knowles, G., and V. Lander. 2011. *Diversity, Equality and Achievement in Education*. London: Sage.

Ladson-Billings, G. 1995. But That's Just Good Teaching! The Case for Culturally Relevant Pedagogy. *Theory into Practice* 34: 159–165.

Lander, V. 2014. Initial Teacher Education: The Practice of Whiteness. In *Advancing Race and Ethnicity in Education*, ed. R. Race and V. Lander. Basingstoke: Palgrave Macmillan.

Manning, A., and A. Georgiadis. 2012. Cultural Integration in the United Kingdom. In *Cultural Integration of Immigrants in Europe*, ed. Y. Algan, A. Bisin, A. Manning, and T. Verdier. Oxford: Oxford University Press.

Maylor, U. 2010. Notions of Diversity, British Identities and Citizenship Belonging. *Race Ethnicity and Education* 13: 233–252.

Maylor, U., A. Ross, N. Rollock, and K. Williams. 2006. *Black Teachers in London*. London: Greater London Authority.

Maylor, U., B. Read, H. Mendick, A. Ross, and N. Rollock. 2007. Diversity and Citizenship in the Curriculum: Research Review. Research Report 819. London: The Institute for Policy Studies in Education, London Metropolitan University.

Nandi, A., and L. Platt. 2014. *Britishness and Identity Assimilation Among the UK's Minority and Majority Ethnic Groups* [Online]. ISER Working Paper Series, No. 2014-01. Available: https://www.econstor.eu/dspace/bit-stream/10419/91705/1/776496069.pdf. Accessed 8 July 2014.

Office for National Statistics. 2011. Census [Online]. Available: https://www.ons.gov.uk/census/2011census. Accessed 31 March 2016.

Osler, A. 2008. Citizenship Education and the Ajegbo Report: Re-imagining a Cosmopolitan Nation. *London Review of Education* 6: 11–25.

Osler, A. 2009. Patriotism, Multiculturalism and Belonging: Political Discourse and the Teaching of History. *Educational Review* 61: 85–100.

Osler, A. 2011. Education Policy, Social Cohesion and Citizenship. In *Promoting Social Cohesion: Implications for Policy and Evaluation*, ed. P. Ratcliffe. Bristol: The Policy Press.

Osler, A. 2015. The Stories We Tell: Exploring Narrative in Education for Justice and Equality in Multicultural Contexts. *Multicultural Education Review* 7: 12–25.

Osler, A., and H. Starkey. 2005. *Changing Citizenship: Democracy and Inclusion in Education*. Maidenhead: Open University Press.

Park, A., C. Bryson, and J. Curtice. 2014. *British Social Attitudes: The 31st Report*. London: NatCen Social Research.

Pearce, S. 2012. Confronting Dominant Whiteness in the Primary Classroom: Progressive Student Teachers' Dilemmas and Constraints. *Oxford Review of Education* 38: 455–472.

Peterson, A., I. Davies, K.M. Chong, T. Epstein, C.L. Peck, A. Ross, A. Sears, M.A. Schmidt, and D. Sonu. 2016. *Education, Globalization and the Nation*. Basingstoke: Palgrave Macmillan.

Ratcliffe, P. 2011. From Community to Social Cohesion: Interrogating a Policy Paradigm. In *Promoting Social Cohesion: Implications for Policy and Evaluation*, ed. P. Ratcliffe and I. Newman. Bristol: The Policy Press.

Renan, E. 1990. What is a Nation? In *Nation and Narration*, ed. H.K. Bhabha. Abingdon: Routledge.

Rutter, J. 2005. Understanding the Alien in Our Midst: Using Citizenship Education to Challenge Popular Discourses About Refugees. In *Teachers, Human Rights and Diversity: Educating Citizens in Multicultural* Societies, ed. A. Osler. Stoke on Trent: Trentham Books.

Scourfield, J., J. Evans, W. Shah, and H. Beynon. 2005. The Negotiation of Minority Ethnic Identities in Virtually All-White Communities: Research with Children and Their Families in the South Wales Valleys. *Children and Society* 19: 211–224.

Sebba, M. 2017. 'English a Foreign Tongue': The 2011 Census in England and the Misunderstanding of Multilingualism. *Journal of Language and Politics* 16 (2): 264–284.

Shor, I. 1996. *When Students Have Power: Negotiating Authority in a Critical Pedagogy*. Chicago: University of Chicago Press.

Shor, I., & P. Freire. 1987. *A Pedagogy for Liberation: Dialogues on Transforming Education*. Westport: Bergin & Garvey Publishers.

Smyth, J., and P. McInerney. 2007. *Teachers in the Middle: Reclaiming the Wasteland of the Adolescent Years of Schooling*. New York: Peter Lang.

Smyth, J., and P. McInerney. 2013. Whose Side are You On? Advocacy Ethnography: Some Methodological Aspects of Narrative Portraits of Disadvantaged Young People, in Socially Critical Research. *International Journal of Qualitative Studies in Education* 26: 1–20.

Solomon, R.P., J.P. Portelli, B.-J. Daniel, and A. Campbell. 2005. The Discourse of Denial: How White Teacher Candidates Construct Race, Racism and 'White Privilege'. *Race Ethnicity and Education* 8: 147–169.

Solórzano, D.G., and T.J. Yosso. 2002. Critical Race Methodology: Counter-Storytelling as an Analytical Framework for Education Research. *Qualitative Inquiry* 8: 23–44.

Stratton, C. 2016. *Education for Empire: American Schools, Race, and the Paths of Good Citizenship*. California: University of California Press.

Stuhr, P., C. Ballengee-Morris, and V.A. Daniel. 2008. Social Justice Through Curriculum: Investigating Issues of Diversity. In *International Dialogues about Visual Culture, Education and Art*, ed. R. Mason and T. Eça. Bristol: Intellect.

Taylor, E. 2016. The Foundations of Critical Race Theory in Education. In *Foundations of Critical Race Theory in Education*, ed. E. Taylor, D. Gillborn, and G. Ladson-Billings. New York and London: Routledge.

Turvey, A., J. Yandell, and L. Ali. 2012. English as a Site of Cultural Negotiation and Contestation. *English Teaching: Practice and Critique* 11: 26–44.

Wetherell, M. 2012. *Affect and Emotion: A New Social Science Understanding*. London: Sage.

Wink, J. 2005. *Critical Pedagogy: Notes from the Real World*. Boston: Pearson/Allyn & Bacon.

Yokley, S.H. 1999. Embracing a Critical Pedagogy in Art Education. *Art Education* 52: 18.

Young, I.M. 2000. *Inclusion and Democracy*. Oxford: Oxford University Press.

Zembylas, M. 2008. The Politics of Shame in Intercultural Education. *Education, Citizenship and Social Justice* 3: 263–280.

Zinn, H. 2013. *A Power Governments Cannot Suppress*. San Francisco: City Lights Books.

CHAPTER 6

Students and Teachers Need Critical Pedagogy

Abstract This chapter builds upon the last chapter by revealing that when students are encouraged to be creative and responsible in how they approach the exploration of Britishness, this helps young people who are grappling with defining the self and contesting imposed classed and racialised labels. In this chapter, I present students who are increasingly becoming confident in expressing their identities and owning their knowledge. I stress that the association of Britishness with Whiteness in students' discourses necessitates the examination of race and racism in multicultural Britain. This chapter also demonstrates the benefits of healing and therapeutic pedagogies. The creative journey the students undertook with energy and zeal resulted in astounding artistic and verbal expressions on the importance of identity issues.

Keywords Whiteness · Racism · Student voice · Creativity
Critical pedagogy

Student Independence and Emotional Engagement

Young people, compelled to attend school, may not feel they belong in a classroom environment. Schools have great potential to respond sensitively to these students by carefully creating culturally diverse spaces where notions of belongings with regard to school, locality and nation

© The Author(s) 2018
S. Habib, *Learning and Teaching British Values*,
DOI 10.1007/978-3-319-60381-0_6

can be critically assessed and collaboratively negotiated. The critical pedagogies employed by the Art teachers in the London school gave students a chance to respond with emotional intelligence to the complexities of belongings and identities. Young people can benefit from culturally diverse spaces to discuss controversial topics through openly inclusive curriculums and with reflective teachers (Hess 2009). Both teachers found the project on identity was cathartic and meaningful for some students who used the opportunity to reveal something significant about their sense of self and their understanding of the Other. In student Ellie's case, the revelation concerned an unfair imposition of a stereotype causing her anger and frustration, while another student, Kadisha, though reluctant to claim a British identity, used the space to resist and contest traditional schooling she felt was exclusionary in its homogeneity.

Too often it might be the case that schools are under pressure to focus on examination results and associated targets. This pressure shifts upon teachers and students who are not allowed the spaces needed to engage in imaginative and creative pedagogies. Schools then— "through uninspiring pedagogy"—can repress "individuality" and "creativity" (Smyth and McInerney 2007: 59). Rejecting humdrum pedagogy and resisting a banking style education, teachers can seek to promote key elements of creativity including "using one's own voice", "trusting one's own judgement and "sustaining inner atmosphere of exploration" (Booth 2015: 56); the teachers in my research encouraged such creativity. Students were encouraged to be creative and responsible in how they approached Britishness, which helped those who were grappling with defining the self; it was also beneficial to the students learning about contesting imposed classed and racialised labels. In this chapter, I present students becoming confident in expressing their identities and owning their knowledge about Britishness. I stress that the association of Britishness with Whiteness in students' discourses necessitates the examination of contemporary and historical notions of race and racism in multicultural Britain. This chapter also demonstrates the benefits of healing and therapeutic pedagogies. The creative journey the students undertook with energy and zeal, at times by themselves, at times along with their peers and teachers and at time as well with me—the researcher, resulted in extraordinary artistic and verbal expressions on the importance of identity issues.

Responsible and Creative Freedom

Ms Anderson explained to students they were in a safe and open environment, free to express themselves without fear of judgement, but reminded them opinions should be presented respectfully, sensitively and empathetically. This was risky and brave, but obtained and maintained students' trust and interest. Creative art can aid student "autonomy" and "awareness" (Chilton and Leavy 2014: 403), leading to responsible freedom within boundaries of acceptability. Students need to work hard to negotiate these boundaries of acceptability and configure ways of expressing their frustrations and disappointments. Art can successfully contribute to students' perceptions of the self and society, bolstering ways of "seeing and thinking differently" (Chilton and Leavy 2014: 403). Students may come to learn about the fluid, evolving and contextual constructs of Britishness, and become aware that "fluidity of identity does not mean that there is no coherence, but rather that this has to be continually reproduced to ensure fixity" (Edensor 2002: 29). To achieve this transformation of self requires freedom of expression within the boundaries of what is deemed appropriately inclusive and socially just.

In order to establish an open classroom where students are able to *rethink* self and society, the Art teachers needed to develop open relationships and good rapport with their students. Creativity involves not just "pleasure in creating, inquiring, and reflecting", but also "trying on multiple points of view", and "working with others" (Booth 2015: 58). Students were encouraged to move forward in their investigations into Britishness in a meaningful and sensitive manner to acquire knowledge about culture and identity. Art projects are conducive to sensitive and respectful cultural knowledge acquisition (Kara 2015). Creativity in the classroom—intending to illuminate students' interests and experiences— also enables students to gain "deep, cultural knowledge about the power of art and their power to communicate through it" (Freedman 2008: 46). Arts-based pedagogues advocate the need for "cultural literacy and intercultural studies in every single school... in order to be able to read and build a multicultural world which guarantees cultural rights, together" (Baron Cohen and Souza 2008: 79). Visual arts critical pedagogues argue "paradoxes" of contemporary lives such as "global/local, private/public, identity/difference, knowledge/feelings, etc." necessitate sustained "critical theorization in order to help us articulate teaching practices together with the social, political and cultural issues that constitute, design and could transform them" (Tourinho and Martins 2008: 63).

A flexible and participatory curriculum will often account for "local social or cultural variation", leading students to increase their sociopolitical awareness, and to become more active participants in their local communities (Gamman 2004: 151). The Art students tended to situate themselves in their localities when discussing Britishness. Ms Anderson explained it was "very personal which direction they chose to take... we gave them a lot of freedom to take it off in their own direction and so what happened happened". When exploring Britishness, students often seem to be principally concerned with locality and local attachments and belongings (Scourfield et al. 2006; Phillips and Ganesh 2007; Maylor 2010; Stahl and Habib 2017), which Ms Anderson noted about her students too. She consciously did not deter students from traversing their "own direction". National identity exploration, therefore, cannot ignore local or international place-based identities (Back 1996; Gilroy 2002; Scourfield et al. 2006; Phillips and Ganesh 2007; Maylor 2010), as both Art teachers observed and appreciated in their exploration of Britishness with young people.

Creativity, through art, is for *all* students if practised in supportive environments (Booth 2015). Both teachers advocated "freedom" in the classroom, facilitating students to pursue creativity through individual and collective journeys, exploring multiple viewpoints about identity. Students came to know the self and society better through art. As students enjoyed independent pursuit of their personal exploration of identity, Ms Anderson noticed they seemed more focused, especially the usually "easily distracted" students. Students Ellie and Chris voiced appreciation for the freedom and fluidity granted by the teachers. Both students keenly discussed their peers' passionate perspectives and enthusiastic responses to multicultural Britishness. The artwork was "evoking empathy and resonance" (Chilton and Leavy 2014: 403):

> Ellie: ...so everyone's is completely different...because it's all your own idea... your own thought on Britain and how you perceive it, there's similarities in people's, but everyone's means something individually to them.

Ellie delighted in the "open" nature of the project: "we could interpret it however we wanted to". This openness allowed her to be creative and appreciate the distinctive artworks of her peers.

Creativity gave students a sense of courage to begin to trust their own voices. They began to take delight in "creating, inquiring, and reflecting" (Booth 2015: 58) on this topic of British identities. Yet, while some students became quite deeply involved with expressing meaningful aspects of their identity, for others it was not as easy to represent abstract notions or express personal voice. Mr Martin found some male students were not as keen as the majority of the class in exploring identities; as it was their first GCSE assignment, some may have found identity interrogation slightly challenging. He believed students were not used to this invitation to defy traditional banking methods and emphasise their personal voices critically. Student voice is not heard often enough in the context of schooling, and even though it is a productive pedagogical approach, sometimes collaborative communication in the classroom is not encouraged enough due to curriculum constraints (Darder et al. 2009). When flexibility and freedom are promoted by teachers, to adapt to these pedagogical practices can take time for students new to innovative pedagogies. Even in the relatively safe spaces of these Art classrooms, at times the teachers and students were chipping away at hesitancies and uncertainties about what it might mean to engage with critical pedagogies.

Cathartic Journey: Disclosing and Unburdening

The teachers observed that explorations of identity through Art could be cathartic, meaningful, healing and therapeutic for the students. Adolescence is an important time for forming identities (Mauro 1998; McGann 2006); the young people in these Art classes were able to disclose and unburden themselves. Art exploration is potentially healing and therapeutic (McNiff 1998; Chilton and Leavy 2014), as evident in Ms Anderson's recollection of her student deliberating upon social class struggles:

> Ms Anderson: ...she wanted to get some of her...angry feelings out about being seen as a chav...which is obviously in her mind not a very nice term...that people have called her...so she did this really interesting piece of work...beautifully done... of her face that is kind of chained around... with Tiffany chains and bracelets, and Lacoste logos and all the kinds of fashion labels that go with that idea of being a chav. And then a gun that was shooting Burberry bullets...at her head...and Lacoste crocodile trying to eat her...

Ellie's thoughtful and detailed portrait of wider society labelling her as a chav points towards Ellie's conscious reflection on being caricatured and demonised due to her White working-class position in British society (see Chap. 7 for more on Ellie's developing class consciousness). Ms Anderson also engaged in critical awareness when she analysed Ellie's artwork. Thus, teaching and learning come together in a Freirean encounter. Through critical pedagogical processes, Ms Anderson was learning of Ellie's experiences of social inequalities, coming to understand Ellie's positionality, realising what Ms Anderson described as Ellie's "angry feelings" at unjustly being demonised, marginalised and caricaturised in British society as a Bermondsey chav. Working-class young people will often provide counter-narratives to resist "deficit discourses regarding the pathologisation of their locale" (Stahl and Habib 2017: 3).

Freire (2000) emphasises the necessity of this type of *conscientizacao*, which we witness here in the reflections of Ellie and her teacher: consciousness and critical analysis about societal oppressions. Critical pedagogues believe myths about racialised and classed peoples "must be confronted and exposed for what they are—vicious lies" (Kincheloe 2008: 73): "Such confrontation and the plethora of insights that emerge in the process constitute what Freire labels *conscientization*—the act of coming to critical consciousness", whereby "individuals grasp the social, political, economic and cultural contradictions that subvert learning". Chapter 7 will show students interrogating these "contradictions" imposed upon them, paradoxes that might impact upon their ways of being and ways of learning. According to Freire, learning and being are entangled notions (Kincheloe 2008), and thus, their intersections must be considered holistically.

The teachers conducting this Art project also understood that learning and being were inseparable. Ms Anderson stressed the significance of giving students, like Ellie, a safe opportunity, to mull over identities in meaningful, creative and purposeful ways; Ms Anderson explained: "…I think she found it really useful because it gave her a chance to actually say something about herself… that maybe she can't actually directly say in day to day life". Ellie's development of critical consciousness about classed British identities was a proud moment for Ellie's teacher. Students from marginalised communities sometimes find critical consciousness is difficult to activate, as they have too long been repressed by powerful myths and untruths, confining them to racialised and classed existences (Freire 2000). Ellie's self-portrait was creative contestation.

It was an act of "consciousness" and "cognition" (Freire 2000). It was an act of "talking back" (hooks 2015). It was an act of "critical pedagogy".

A classroom environment that ensures "optimal learning" needs teachers to know about their students' "emotional awareness and emotional intelligence" (hooks 2010: 19). Mr Martin's students also experienced emotional release about the lived realities of London, "actually dealing with it, they are actually telling us something", demonstrating their "awareness" of urban multicultural experiences. Mr Martin saw his students were "communicating" something significant, to him and to the other students, about the interplay between social categories and lived experiences. Students found the project cathartic as they could deliberate over lived realities of classed and racialised belongings to Britain. Revelations about identities were powerfully communicated by the students independently; they not been instructed on what to put in their artwork. Instead, gentle encouragement from teachers resulted in what Mr Martin explained were "really powerful artworks that have led us to read into it more and think 'Actually that is quite a sophisticated comment you have put in there', so it's very healthy kind of letting the kids reflect on that".

STUDENT VOICE, KNOWLEDGE AND IDENTITY

Students demonstrated high levels of engagement expressing their knowledge, identities and experiences of Britishness to peers and teachers. Visual art students can develop their "self-expression, intuition and imagination", while undertaking a journey of "personal growth" (Hickman and Eglinton 2015: 146). Personalities were projected into the artwork, as students learned to be more confident in valuing their own knowledge. Student and teacher motivation increases when a rigid curriculum is replaced by emphasis on student voice and choice (Gamman 2004; Smyth and McInerney 2007). The "boredom and despair" of schooling is combated by appealing to students' interests and identities through curriculum and classroom activity (Smyth and McInerney 2007: 4). Students do not often have a chance to explore personal identity intensively in lessons, and this book keenly emphasises that young people—and their teachers—both welcome and require the opportunity. For Art students to develop creativity, not just produce meaningless artefacts, they need encouragement to project their identities into their artwork (Freedman 2008). Ms Anderson emphasised students were motivated to produce outstanding artwork because of this opportunity to (re)present the self: "...it gave them a freedom they don't often have to be able to express themselves about who they are". Mr Martin's class were also "very excited" about the project, and he surmised: "because it sort of unpicks something about their own personality and they found that really rewarding".

The students were able to project their analyses of identity into newfound knowledge about diverse meanings of Britishness. The students were "always keen" on exploring their identity, Mr Martin found, and recommended teachers "approach it from the identity angle... what are the things that make you... and then encourage them to sort of engage in some discourse". In the case of his class, he observed "it's been a sort of outpouring". This "outpouring", referred to by Mr Martin, and the "catharsis", emphasised by Ms Anderson, underline the significance of giving students opportunities to explore identity in a safe and structured manner. Mr Martin frequently stated the project provided powerfully poignant opportunities for students "to make a statement ... a communication and to make that clear and evocative". This was the ultimate outcome for him: "that's really what we wanted to do with Art". He observed a deep level of involvement with the project for some, for example he referred to the student who was "locked away in some sort of other world" as she created "strong and bold" artwork about urban realities.

The students who were *deeply engaged* with the project seemed to benefit most, the teachers found. Some delved into childhood memories, relaying personal histories. One of Mr Martin's students created artwork about the seaside in Margate: "... and you couldn't help but think that had been something...a genuine part of her life when she was younger... that she sort of unfolded and told us". The girls surprised him with their "intensity", more than the boys. The girls produced revelatory artwork about their ambitions and dreams. Mr Martin observed Amiela had explored her self-identity with profound patience, working on her portrait with deep involvement, for longer, ultimately presenting aspirations to succeed in fashion. Mr Martin was pleased by the dedication of students like Amiela, but reiterated perhaps the project was too challenging to be completed as a first GCSE project or in one term alone.

For some male students, there may have been reluctance to invest "emotion and energy" into the project, according to Mr Martin. Some boys were not as deeply involved. More time was needed for students to "unpick, uncover and discuss" identity issues (which might have particularly helped the male students), as the process was neither easy nor straightforward, but took careful reflection. When students did arrive at what they deemed important about their identity, Mr Martin explained they experienced "a real energy once they've latched onto something they felt that was really good". He observed this "maintains through the project and they got it finished... had that not had occurred... they probably would have just hit the doldrums and just been told what to do...". The exploration of identity takes time for teachers wanting to move beyond banking education models. The process the students underwent was "powerful as a learning experience", perhaps more powerful than their final outcomes, Mr Martin believed. Ellie observed her class move beyond superficial Britishness through deep self-reflection, as they were "trying to figure out" Britishness. Careful deliberation on identity resulted in Ellie creating a stunning portrait about vicious social stereotypes encountered by White working-class youth (see Chap. 7). That White British students need to explore identity alongside ethnic minority students (Ajegbo et al. 2007) was apparent throughout this research. If teachers neglect exploration of White British identities, White working-class students "undervalue their British heritage" and "feel less confident to talk about it" (Maylor 2010: 243).

OWNING BRITISHNESS THROUGH WHITENESS

The Head of Art reflected upon whether the White students felt they "owned" Britishness; they were "defiantly defensive about this area", claiming it was the "best place". Observing their loyalty to Bermondsey, she asked them, "But you haven't seen anywhere else?" Ms Anderson found the White Bermondsey students were "very much into being in London – concerned about their locality more than their nationality" (Stahl and Habib 2017). I follow Rattansi (2000: 123) on disrupting generalisations, for just as "there is no essential black British 'youthness'", we know there is no essential White British "youthness" either[1]. When it comes to Britishness, the local often commands loyalties and attachments that national identities cannot (Barrett 2002; Maylor et al. 2007; Sanderson and Thomas 2014).

Ms Anderson commented upon some of the White working-class Bermondsey boys—who moved beyond locality—painted self-portraits about Britishness from the perspective of the England football team.

However, other students brought their Britishness back to Bermondsey by focusing on the local team Millwall FC. Ms Anderson explained there was a "certain kind of political opinion"—a covert racism—underlying their expressions of the interconnections between race and football: "Some of them felt quite strongly that too many footballers these days in British football were from other countries... so it was done in a very sort of round the houses kind of way...". Some students claimed Britishness as the domain of heroic White footballers, being infiltrated by foreign footballers. Yet football can also be a uniting cultural citizenship experience, as Hussain and Bagguley (2005) found in their study of Bradford's British Pakistani community proudly supporting England during the football World Cup.

Joe, like some of the other White Bermondsey boys, demonstrated possessiveness towards Britishness. The promotion of "male military heroism", often "excluding" of others (Cooling 2013: 106), was evident in Joe's pride. While some of his male peers referenced football to present "White male heroism", Joe depicted the British army in his portrait which he entitled *Pride of Britain*: Man for Man we are the best. In the past, working-class boys were galvanised into passionate patriotism and unquestioning loyalty through motifs of empire and monarchy (Heater 2001; Ward 2004). This pride and superiority is evident in Joe's depiction of the army in his portrait. At one point, Joe dismissed Britishness exploration as only for ethnic minority students, not White students: "It's interesting if you're not British. If you're not White. If you know for sure you've got some other race in you". Yet paradoxically, he repeated his passion for the project on a number of occasions—in the lesson, in the interview and on his questionnaire—revealing "primordial attachments"—to Britishness: "Such ties are a complex mix of myth, belief, emotion, and the realities of physical existence" (Allahar 2006: 32). Media and political narrative frequently calls for minorities to scrutinise and declare their Britishness, but disregards White Britishness (Nandi and Platt 2014); Joe might have become accustomed to media and polity, questioning the Britishness of those not White.

Joe wanted to own Britishness, emphasising loyalty to Britishness; other times, he professed his stable or secure sense of White Britishness:

Joe: People... that aren't British...or that don't consider themselves to be British would search to find out about who they are... why they are here... whereas White people are like "I'm White. I'm British. That's it.

The evolving complexities of belonging to Britain reveal ethnic minorities often pronouncing more loyalty to British identity than their White counterparts (Modood 1998; Thomas 2009; Manning and Georgiadis 2012; Nandi and Platt 2014; Karlsen and Nazroo 2015). Joe, though, perceived ethnic minorities as disloyal to Britishness, as seeking mythical belonging in distant lands. Joe disregarded culture and identity exploration as for those from other cultures, yet interestingly he had embraced the Britishness project, finding a space to express his identity and local cultural history:

> Joe: I learnt about the dockers and that from my dad 'cos he used to work on the rice mills when he was fourteen... The rice mills... down Rotherhithe Street. They are still there.

Celebrating "other cultures" and understanding racisms, oppressions, White privilege and power are important aspects of multicultural and anti-racist education, as are exploring diverse White cultural experiences (Howard 2006). When I asked him to tell us more about the docks, Joe was animated about his family history, local history and British history:

> Joe: They just made boats come in with a load of rice and they like sacked it and packed it and all that... My granddad worked there his whole life. Which he told me. He worked there, his sisters, his brothers. He had like six brothers and sisters...And he said that his whole family grew up in the rice mills as a docker.

Britishness, for Joe, is represented through the army, and through the dockers and their legacy, specifically White dockers:

> Joe: I think that most dockers are British. If you've got mums and dads, or their dads that were dockers that's kinda British 'cos I don't think you could say that or that any Black person could say that.

Following in his family's footsteps, Joe might have once sought work on the docks. Since the decline of the docks though, the army had become an appealing post-education route for Joe. "Owning Britishness" for Joe—as the teachers labelled it—was (re)presenting patriotism in his artwork, as well as discussing family, locality and British history, as well as his enthusiasm for the army.

Although Joe passionately articulated his Britishness, he claimed: "I was scared that I would be too racist". Joe accepted he can be controversial. The teachers and students recognised identity work can unleash racist attitudes and perceptions. Joe also interestingly touched upon the relationship between racisms, positionality and privilege:

> Joe: I think White people are scared of being racists 'cos it upsets people. Whereas if a Black person was racist towards a White person... we don't care... (laughs) ...it really don't bother me.

Teachers need to be able to explore the socio-historical aspects of race and racism, as often students know a little but not enough. Regarding racism, Joe explained he does not "take it seriously" and is not "cautious about it": "To some people it means more and they get upset easier". Joe's statements highlight how necessary it is to bring critical race principles and pedagogies into the curriculum. It is important for students to overcome the current "colour-blindness", where White people perceive race to be only about ethnic minorities, irrelevant to their own "normal" non-racialised lives (Lewis 2004), as well as to engage in deconstructions of racial categories, privilege and power. To develop much needed anti-racist pedagogies in the classroom, we must examine the "politics at play through which white working classes are the proxy through which hegemonic notions of racialised social boundaries are being regulated" (Patel and Tyrer 2011: 43).

Critical race research reveals stories of race and racism (Solórzano and Yosso 2002), by interrogating the "specific tools used in the construction of majoritarian stories" that normalise and make neutral White power and privilege (Love 2004: 229). One of the "tools" employed to ensure master narratives remain dominant includes "invisibility", whereby "invisibility of white privilege is maintained by what is not discussed", and also "majoritarian stories are not viewed as stories at all. Rather, they are viewed as history, policies, procedures, rules, regulations, and statements of fact" (Love 2004: 229). We can observe the ways politicians seem to neglect the seriousness of racial inequalities (Ratcliffe 2011; Craig and O'Neill 2013), when it comes to majoritarian "stories" about British identities. Thus, by utilising another "tool"—"schooling as neutral and apolitical and the myth of the meritocracy"—to maintain majoritarian narratives (Love 2004), we find this inattention to racial injustices seems to have impacted upon teachers lacking guidance in dealing with issues of inequalities (Solomon et al. 2005; Pearce 2012; Lander 2014). Inevitably, as race and racism pervade society, intersecting with other social inequalities (Gillborn 1995; Solórzano and Yosso 2002), and Britishness divulges "systematic, largely unspoken, racial connotations" (Parekh 2000: 38), critical race theory becomes a recommended approach to help students to reflect and act upon realities and consequences of racialised identities.

Reading hooks (2015: 5), we learn that telling counter-stories of race and racism is "talking back"—that is, "daring to disagree" and "having an opinion". I observed critical pedagogical moments between the students where they engaged in critical dialogue and came to consciousness about stories of race and racism, and by talking back, disagreeing and sharing their opinions (see more in Chap. 7). Kadisha "talks back". She challenges Joe's ideas about Whiteness, highlighting the need to deconstruct race when analysing nation and national identity.

Joe: I consider White people as like the first race…
Kadisha: They weren't White.
Joe: Weren't they?
Kadisha: Have you not heard of how everyone originated from Africa?
Joe: No.
Kadisha: Have you never heard that? Have you Miss?

One of the foundations of critical race theory in education is a "refusal to remain silent", thereby exhibiting "strength and empowerment" (Taylor 2016: 19). In Kadisha, we see strength and empowerment. She refuses to stay silent and instead talks back eloquently and confidently throughout the project on Britishness.

National identity might connote kinship/ancestry, "those things one cannot help" (Anderson 2006: 147) in right-wing discourses. Yet the supposed "biological character of ancestry, kinship, and descent are popular fictions" (Baumann 1999: 39), needing critiquing in safe and respectful classrooms. Students benefit from examining Whiteness as fluid and historically situated.[2] More evidence of why race—as a social construct—needs exploring is evident in Kadisha and Joe's very different perceptions of school demographics. Joe stated more Black students are arriving each year: "most of the Year Sevens are Black". Kadisha contested this, arguing the school is "mixed": "Like as half Black and half White.

I don't see many Asians". Blackness is visible to Joe: "I swear there's only one Black teacher in the school. Or two Black teachers that I've seen. There's one that works upstairs outside Mr Griffith's office and Mr Mensah". Ironically, one of the "Black teachers" Joe mentions is a school administrator, not a teacher. Joe declares "the school's a bit racist", before beginning a discussion on "... a White person would hire the White person and a Black person would hire the Black person". Joe's conflicted discourses on Blackness and Whiteness necessitate a dedicated and patient teacher committed to critical race theory to help students to better interrogate multiple views on "race". On the one hand, Joe recognises the lack of diversity in the teaching staff (institutional racism) as problematic, as "a bit racist", yet he seems to see diversity among the student body as displeasing (everyday racism).

LEARNING ABOUT BRITISHNESS THROUGH CRITICAL PEDAGOGY

Why is critical pedagogy a valuable theoretical framework to apply to learning about Britishness? Teaching and learning is complex and never neutral, for it "entails judgements about what knowledge counts, legitimates specific social relations, defines agency in particular ways, and always presupposes a particular notion of the future" (Giroux 2013: 6). To understand students' experience of social relations, to count their knowledge, to encourage them to be agents of social change projecting their visions of the future of Britain and to successfully challenge the dominant ideologies[3] that serve to exclude students, we need critical pedagogy. Combatting inequalities and injustices might not be at the heart of policy decisions, especially in times of austerity (Bradley 1996), resulting in critical pedagogy not welcomed by all. It does not serve prevailing elitist interests for students and teachers to become interrogators of policy and polity. Yet ideologies—"sets of values, beliefs, myths, explanations and justifications that appear self-evidently true and morally desirable" (Brookfield 2009: 38)—can be challenged if we give students the space for critical reflection and collaboration.

Throughout this book, I argue students hearing others' stories and telling their stories is important if we want to hope, to critique and to transform injustices and inequalities of our world. Students' stories can become tools of resistance, of presenting hope and possibility and of aiding a journey of discovery of the self, the other and society, ultimately laying seeds of social change. The project demonstrated students capturing lived realities, signifying their concerns as young Londoners, and teachers observing student engagement, creativity and learning. Careful and sensitive handling of the potentially controversial elements to identity exploration by the teachers who enjoyed exploring Britishness with their classes resulted in students gaining new perspectives on individual and collective meanings of Britishness. High levels of student engagement and what the teachers deemed as successful outcomes resulted in the Art department, continuing the Britishness project with new GCSE Art classes too.

Personal positionality impacts upon teachers' pedagogies and "interacts with affect and emotion" when teaching diversity or controversial issues, as "people typically have strong emotions and much passion" (Tisdell et al. 2009: 134). The ways Art teachers situate themselves is important, as they are able to position themselves to explore the sociopolitical (Yokley 1999), open up a dialogue on British identities and multicultural society, and pursue critical pedagogies with their students to challenge stereotypes and reconceptualise belongings and identities. The Head of Art explained she would "encourage them to go deeper and think beyond the obvious..." in future, but without directing the students, as she valued student voice: "...it's a careful balance of letting them have their own ideas and introducing them to new ideas". Mr Martin explained he would like to conduct the project over a longer period of time.[4]

Uncovering identity issues enabled students to recognise their voices and views were respected and required. Students became confident and independent, and learning their personal journey was part of the story of Britishness. For some students, the experience was cathartic and poignant, especially dissecting the realities of their lives as young Londoners. Students demonstrated diverse cultural ideas about what it means to belong to a nation, with some preferring to focus upon local or global attachments. Some students were more emotionally and intellectually engaged than others, delving deep into abstract concepts of identity. For others, the project was demanding and difficult, and they were unwilling, therefore, to respond with deeply cognitive or visceral inquiries into British identities. Perhaps because national identity is difficult to define (Jacobson 1997; Scourfield et al. 2006; Maylor 2010; Anderson 2012; Burkett 2013); and even analyse (Anderson 2006), some young people chose to shy away from grappling with Britishness. Mr Martin also acknowledged a limitation with the project would be that students would not be able to express all that they found important about Britishness and identity in one portrait alone.

These findings are valuable and hopeful in a time when academic freedom is discouraged (Ross and Vinson 2013), and neoliberalism has given rise to individualism, privatisation, competition and profit, with schooling increasingly seen in terms of economics, and students as commodities and their teachers as mere machines (Kirylo 2013). Concerns continue to be raised regarding education and "the gritty sense of limits it faces within a capitalist society" (Giroux 2013: 5). Researching students' views about effective pedagogies can also enrich the education system (Gamman 2004), allowing students to embrace the education they want and need. The apprehension both teachers felt pre-teaching soon dissipated as most students energetically embraced critical pedagogical approaches. Instead of passively accepting a hegemonic narrative of Britishness, students utilised the space to debate the current discourses on British identities, and revealed personal definitions and experiences from diverse racial, ethnic and class positioning.

If a democratic goal of education is to inspire morally and socially responsible citizenry, critical pedagogy helps students to become "critical, self-reflective and knowledgeable" active members of society (Giroux 2013: 3). Moreover, the Art project manifested how "knowledge" created through art can move beyond "aesthetic and formalist concerns" towards "critical practice whereby contextual enquiry exposes the social, cultural and political terrain within which it is situated" (Grierson 2008: 25). The teachers worked with students on exploring concepts of Britishness and incorporated critical pedagogy strategies to encourage students to challenge prevailing societal stereotypes. Classroom dilemmas of identity exploration included unwillingness on the part of teachers to "impose" a "correct" version of Britishness on the students, as well as students' reluctance to withdraw from the "banking" method of teaching they were traditionally familiar with where students expect the teacher to be the oracle of knowledge, clinging to the idea that teacher knows best.

This book illustrates the usefulness of critical pedagogy "as theoretical and political practice" (Giroux 2013: 3) when learning about Britishness in inclusive and meaningful ways. Critical pedagogy emphasises "critical analysis, moral judgements, and social responsibility", thereby going "to the very heart of what it means to address real inequalities of power at the social level and to conceive of education as a project for freedom"

(Giroux 2013: 158). Critical pedagogy seeks counter-narratives from students and teachers to "critique the world in which they live and, when necessary, to intervene in socially responsible ways in order to change it" (Giroux 2013: 14). Inspired by Freire (1985, 2000), and Giroux (1988, 2001, 2013), I have argued for teachers and students to employ a language of critique, hope and possibility about the potential of resistance, challenge and change: "a vocabulary in which it becomes possible to imagine power working in the interest of justice, equality, and freedom" (Giroux 2013: 5).

For students to become critically reflective and active citizens is a core aim of critical pedagogy, as evident in the works of Paulo Freire, John Dewey and Ira Shor. In contrast to traditional banking methods of education (Freire 1985), like "rote learning and skills drills" that "bore and miseducate students" (Shor 1992: 18), I came to understand how teachers and students used approaches heavily grounded in critical pedagogy to yield remarkable results about contemporary South East London discourses on Britishness, as well as about pedagogies. I therefore have argued critical pedagogy has the capabilities and capacities to give rise to oft-silenced voices, stories and experiences, working towards implementing social change through collaborative and transformative advocacy and activism (Wink 2005). I have shown students need "a challenging curriculum that will assist them to make sense of their lives and identities" (Smyth and McInerney 2007: xi).

There is a danger that in solely championing British culture, history, values and identity from a middle-class White Eurocentric perspective, students' ethnic, class and cultural heritages are viewed as marginal and insignificant. Moreover, if history is taught according to the perspective of the British textbooks, then world history and universal human rights are eliminated from the picture (Osler 2009). Privilege and power operate in a way where "objectivity and neutrality" is presumed to be the domain of the "White, male, class-elitist, heterosexist, imperial, and colonial" elite who are presented as espousers of "reason, rationality and truth" (Kincheloe 2007: 19). This myth of "reason, rationality and truth" impacts upon educational policies, for example in the 1980s and 1990s, politicians opposed the sociology of education because of its focus on social classifications and structures, rather than on educational "standards" (Arnot and Barton 1992).

Prime Minister John Major (1992) called for the "reform of teacher training" and dismissed the study of social identities: "Let us return to basic subject teaching, not courses in the theory of education. Primary teachers should learn how to teach children to read, not waste their time on the politics of gender, race and class". In the 1990s, young people though were experiencing "the resurgence of racism on the streets and housing estates of urban Britain" (Dadzie 1997: 10), at a time when political rhetoric was discounting the significance of race and class. Yet when it comes to schooling, "race, gender, class, religion, and a host of other factors inform and influence what happens in schools and class-rooms" (Hess 2009). British identities are high on the educational policy agenda, but race and racism are ignored. Yet nation and race are insepa-rable (Carnegie 2002).

My research findings, over twenty-five years after Major's speech, show training teachers about race, class and intersectional identities is unavoidable. The Art students' discourses, in the next chapter, will show that Britishness discussion is inseparable from old and new notions of race and racism. Examining how "being White and the discourse of Whiteness are perpetuated" (Lander 2014: 94), that "race is not some-thing with which we are born; it is something learned and achieved in interactions and institutions" (Lewis 2004: 629), is significant to the learning of Britishness, if students like Kadisha and Joe see Britishness as sometimes synonymous with Whiteness. Students were able to hold a conversation on the meanings of Britishness, critically question the mul-tiple meanings of Britishness and learn what Britishness meant to others. Respectful and caring dialogue between students, and with the teacher, allowed for critical consciousness to flourish in a Freirean classroom as students mulled over multiple meanings of Britishness.

With the arrival of recent refugees to Europe, new ways of under-standing modern multicultural societies need investigating, making updated teacher training even more pressing, particularly training that enables students and teachers to build upon critical pedagogy strategies like *reflection, dialogue* and *action*. Schools are too often seen as places that perpetuate traditional asymmetrical models of power/powerlessness with processes and practices that "actively silence students...marginalize and ensure failure for working-class and minority students" (Giroux and McLaren 1989: xviii). Yet critical pedagogy can work towards combat-ing this silencing, marginalisation and oppression by validating student voice. Young people like Ellie, Kadisha, Joe and Chris might have come to the project thinking "*when we speak we are afraid/our words will not be heard/nor welcomed*" (Lorde 1995), but, the next chapter will show, the teachers' critical pedagogy strategies enabled students to grow in confidence: to not be afraid, to speak and to have their words heard and welcomed. To learn "to survive" (Lorde 1995). To better understand discourses of Britishness, the next chapter will further detail and discuss the "profound and rigorously syncretic cultural dialogues" (Back 1996: 241) of ethnically diverse young people.

NOTES

1. "Racial essentialism" perpetuating the idea that "humans are divided into biologically discrete races that have essential traits (i.e., intelligence, temperament, morality, and so on) that define and delimit their nature of being" (Cokley 2002: 35), whether it be about Black or White youth, needs disrupting.
2. In the past, for example, Italian, Irish and Swedish migrants to the USA were described as non-White (Ignatiev and Garvey 1996).
3. "What we think are our personal interpretations and dispositions are actually, in Marcuse's (1964) terms, ideologically sedimented...Louis Althusser (1969) and Pierre Bourdieu (1977) argue that what seem to us to be natural ways of understanding our experiences are actually internalized dimensions of ideology...Ideologies are manifest in language, social habits, and cultural forms" (Brookfield 2009: 38).
4. They had commenced the project with the new cohort of GCSE students and were tackling it slightly differently by looking at more documentaries beforehand to get to know multiple viewpoints on Britishness. To enable students to appreciate the sheer diversity of opinion, Mr Martin had shown his new GCSE class a documentary on Britishness showing pensioners in the North of England discussing Britishness, bingo and the cost of living which "surprised" the London students and gave them new insights into identity.

REFERENCES

Ajegbo, K., D. Kiwan, and S. Sharma. 2007. *Diversity and Citizenship: Curriculum Review*. London: Department for Education and Skills.

Allahar, A. 2006. The Social Construction of Primordial Identities. In *Identity and Belonging: Rethinking Race and Ethnicity in Canadian Society*, ed. B.S. Bolaria and S.P. Hier. Toronto: Canadian Scholars' Press.

Anderson, B. 2006. *Imagined Communities: Reflections on the Origin and Spread of Nationalism*. London: Verso.

Anderson, B. 2012. Introduction. In *Mapping the Nation*, ed. G. Balakrishnan. London: Verso Books.

Arnot, M., and L. Barton. 1992. Introduction. In *Voicing Concerns: Sociological Perspectives on Contemporary Education Reforms*, ed. M. Arnot and L. Barton. Wallingford: Triangle Books.

Back, L. 1996. *New Ethnicities and Urban Culture: Racisms and Multiculture in Young Lives*. London: Routledge.

Baron Cohen, D., and M. Souza. 2008. Cultural Literacy: An Arts-Based Interdisciplinary Pedagogy for the Creation of Democratic Multicultural Societies. In: *International Dialogues about Visual Culture, Education and Art*, ed. R. Mason, and T. Eça. Bristol: Intellect.

Barrett, M. 2002. Children's Views of Britain and Britishness in 2001: Some Initial Findings from the Developmental Psychology Section Centenary Project. Annual Conference of the Developmental Psychology. University of Sussex, British Psychological Society.

Baumann, G. 1999. *The Multicultural Riddle: Rethinking National, Ethnic and Religious Identities*. New York and London: Routledge.

Booth, E. 2015. Creativity in the Arts and Arts Education. In *The Routledge International Handbook of the Arts and Education*, ed. M. Fleming, L. Bresler, and J. O'toole. Abingdon: Routledge.

Bradley, H. 1996. *Fractured Identities: Changing Patterns of Inequality*. Cambridge: Polity Press.

Brookfield, S.D. 2009. The Concept of Critically Reflective Practice. In *Handbook of Adult and Continuing Education*, ed. A.L. Wilson and E.R. Hayes. San Francisco: Wiley.

Burkett, J. 2013. *Constructing Post-imperial Britain: Britishness, 'Race' and the Radical Left in the 1960s*. Basingstoke: Palgrave Macmillan.

Carnegie, C.V. 2002. *Postnationalism Prefigured: Caribbean Borderlands*. New Brunswick: Rutgers University Press.

Chilton, G., and P. Leavy. 2014. Arts-Based Research Practice: Merging Social Research and the Creative Arts. In *The Oxford Handbook of Qualitative Research*, ed. P. Leavy. Oxford: Oxford University Press.

Cokley, K. 2002. To Be or Not to Be Black: Problematics of Racial Identity. In *The Quest for Community and Identity: Critical Essays in Africana Social Philosophy*, ed. R.E. Birt. Lanham: Rowman & Littlefield.

Cooling, T. 2013. Teachers and Christian Religious Values. *In The Routledge International Handbook of Education, Religion and Values*, ed. J. Arthur and T. Lovat. Abingdon: Routledge.

Craig, G., and M. O'Nseill. 2013. The Official 'Invisibilisation' of Minority Ethnic Disadvantage. In *Social Policy Review 25: Analysis and Debate in Social Policy*, ed. G. Ramia, K. Farnsworth, and Z. Irving. Bristol: Policy Press.

Dadzie, S. 1997. *Blood, Sweat and Tears: A Report of the Bede Anti-racist Detached Youth Work Project*. Leicester: Youth Work Press.

Darder, A., M.P. Baltodano, and R.D. TORRES. (eds.). 2009. *The Critical Pedagogy Reader*. New York and London: Routledge.

Edensor, T. 2002. *National Identity, Popular Culture and Everyday Life.* Oxford: Berg.

Freedman, K. 2008. Leading Creativity: Responding to Policy in Art Education. In *International Dialogues About Visual Culture, Education and Art,* ed. R. Mason and T. Eça. Bristol: Intellect.

Freire, P. 1985. *The Politics of Education: Culture, Power and Liberation.* Westport, CT: Bergin & Garvey.

Freire, P. 2000. *Pedagogy of the Oppressed.* New York: Bloomsbury Publishing.

Freire, P., and A.M.A. Freire. 2004. *Pedagogy of Hope: Reliving Pedagogy of the Oppressed.* London and New York: Continuum.

Gamman, R. 2004. Children and the Curriculum. In *Children at the Margins: Supporting Children, Supporting Schools,* ed. T. Billington and M. Pomerantz. Stoke on Trent: Trentham Books.

Gillborn, D. 1995. *Racism and Antiracism In Real Schools: Theory, Policy, Practicex.* Buckingham: Open University Press.

Gilroy, P. 2002. *There Ain't No Black in the Union Jack.* Abingdon: Routledge.

Giroux, H.A. 1988. *Teachers as Intellectuals: Toward a Critical Pedagogy of Learning.* Westport: Bergin & Garvey.

Giroux, H.A. 2001. *Theory and Resistance in Education: Towards a Pedagogy for the Opposition.* Westport, CT: Bergin & Garvey.

Giroux, H.A. 2013. *On Critical Pedagogy.* New York and London: Bloomsbury Academic.

Giroux, H.A., and P. McLaren (eds.). 1989. *Critical Pedagogy, the State, and Cultural Struggle.* Albany: State University of New York Press.

Grierson, E. 2008. Creativity and Culture: Redefining Knowledge Through the Arts in Education for the Local in a Globalized World. In *International Dialogues About Visual Culture, Education and Art,* ed. R. Mason and T. Eça. Bristol: Intellect.

Heater, D. 2001. The History of Citizenship Education in England. *The Curriculum Journal* 12: 103–123.

Hess, D.E. 2009. *Controversy in the Classroom: The Democratic Power of Discussion.* New York and London: Routledge.

Hickman, R., and K.A. Eglinton. 2015. Visual Art in the Curriculum. In *The Routledge International Handbook of the Arts and Education,* ed. M. Fleming, L. Bresler, and J. O'Toole. Abingdon: Routledge.

hooks, b. 2010. *Teaching Critical Thinking: Practical Wisdom.* New York and London: Routledge.

hooks, b. 2015. *Talking Back: Thinking Feminist, Thinking Black.* New York: Routledge.

Howard, G. 2006. *We Can't Teach What We Don't Know: White Teachers, Multiracial Schools.* New York and London: Teachers College Press.

Hussain, Y., and P. Bagguley. 2005. Citizenship, Ethnicity and Identity: British Pakistanis After the 2001 'Riots'. *Sociology* 39: 407–425.

Ignatiev, N., and J. Garvey (eds.). 1996. *Race Traitor*. New York and London: Routledge.

Jacobson, J. 1997. Perceptions of Britishness. *Nations and Nationalism* 3: 181–199.

Kara, H. 2015. *Creative Research Methods in the Social Sciences: A Practical Guide*. Bristol: Policy Press.

Karlsen, S., and J.Y. Nazroo. 2015. Ethnic and Religious Differences in the Attitudes of People Towards Being 'British'. *The Sociological Review* 63: 759–781.

Kincheloe, J.L. 2007. Critical Pedagogy in the Twenty-First Century. In *Critical Pedagogy: Where are We Now?* ed. P. Mclaren and J.L. Kincheloe. New York: Peter Lang.

Kincheloe, J.L. 2008. *Critical Pedagogy Primer*. New York: Peter Lang.

Kirylo, J.D. (ed.). 2013. *A Critical Pedagogy of Resistance: 34 Pedagogues We Need to Know*. Rotterdam: Sense Publishers.

Lander, V. 2014. Initial Teacher Education: The Practice of Whiteness. In *Advancing Race and Ethnicity in Education*, ed. R. Race and V. Lander. Basingstoke: Palgrave Macmillan.

Lewis, A.E. 2004. What Group? Studying Whites and Whiteness in the Era of "Color-Blindness". *Sociological Theory* 22: 623–646.

Lorde, A. 1995. *The Black Unicorn: Poems*. New York: W.W. Norton.

Love, B.J. 2004. Brown Plus 50 Counter-Storytelling: A Critical Race Theory Analysis of the "Majoritarian Achievement Gap" Story. *Equity & Excellence in Education* 37: 227–246.

Major, J. 1992. *Mr Major's Speech to 1992 Conservative Party Conference* [Online]. Available: http://www.johnmajor.co.uk/page1208.html. Accessed 8 Mar 2016.

Manning, A., and A. Georgiadis. 2012. Cultural Integration in the United Kingdom. In *Cultural Integration of Immigrants in Europe, Cultural Integration of Immigrants in Europe*, ed. Y. Algan, A. Bisin, A. Manning, and T. Verdier. Oxford: Oxford University Press.

Mauro, M.K. 1998. The Use of Art Therapy in Identity Formation. In *Tapestry of Cultural Issues in Art Therapy*, ed. A.R. Hiscox, and A.C. CALISCH. London: Jessica Kingsley Publishers.

Maylor, U. 2010. Notions of Diversity, British Identities and Citizenship Belonging. *Race Ethnicity and Education* 13: 233–252.

Maylor, U., B. Read, H. Mendick, A. Ross, and N. Rollock. 2007. Diversity and Citizenship in the Curriculum: Research Review. Research Report 819. London: The Institute for Policy Studies in Education, London Metropolitan University.

McGann, E.P. 2006. Color Me Beautiful. *Journal of Emotional Abuse* 6: 197–217.

McNiff, S. 1998. *Art-Based Research*. London: Jessica Kingsley.

Modood, T. 1998. New Forms of Britishness: Post-immigration Ethnicity and Hybridity in Britain. In *The Expanding Nation: Towards a Multi-ethnic Ireland*, ed. R. Lentin. Dublin: Trinity College.

Nandi, A., and L. Platt. 2014. *Britishness and Identity Assimilation Among the UK's Minority and Majority Ethnic Groups* [Online]. ISER Working Paper Series, No. 2014-01. Available: https://www.econstor.eu/dspace/bitstream/10419/91705/1/776496069.pdf. Accessed 8 July 2014.

Osler, A. 2009. Patriotism, Multiculturalism and Belonging: Political Discourse and the Teaching of History. *Educational Review* 61: 85–100.

Parekh, B. 2000. *The Future of Multi-Ethnic Britain: Report of the Commission on the Future of Multi-Ethnic Britain*. London: The Runnymede Trust/Profile Books.

Patel, T. G., and D. Tyrer. 2011. *Race, Crime and Resistance*. London: Sage.

Pearce, S. 2012. Confronting Dominant Whiteness in the Primary Classroom: Progressive Student Teachers' Dilemmas and Constraints. *Oxford Review of Education* 38: 455–472.

Phillips, A., and G. Ganesh. 2007. *Young People and British Identity*. London: Ipsos MORI/Camelot Foundation.

Ratcliffe, P. 2011. From Community to Social Cohesion: Interrogating a Policy Paradigm. In *Promoting Social Cohesion: Implications for Policy and Evaluation*, ed. P. Ratcliffe and I. Newman. Bristol: Policy Press.

Rattansi, A. 2000. On Being And not Being Brown/Black-British: Racism, Class, Sexuality and Ethnicity in Post-imperial Britain. *Interventions: International Journal of Postcolonial Studies* 2: 118–134.

Ross, E.W., and K.D. Vinson. 2013. *Resisting Neoliberal Education Reform: Insurrectionist Pedagogies and the Pursuit of Dangerous Citizenship*. Cultural Logic: Marxist Theory & Practice.

Sanderson, P., and P. Thomas. 2014. Troubling Identities: Race, Place and Positionality Among Young People in Two Towns in Northern England. *Journal of Youth Studies* 9: 1–19.

Scourfield, J., B. Dicks, M. Drakeford, and A. Davies. 2006. *Children, Place and Identity: Nation and Locality in Middle Childhood*. Abingdon: Routledge.

Shor, I. 1992. *Empowering Education: Critical Teaching for Social Change*. Chicago: University of Chicago Press.

Smyth, J., and P. McInerney. 2007. *Teachers in the Middle: Reclaiming the Wasteland of the Adolescent Years of Schooling*. New York: Peter Lang.

Solomon, R.P., J.P. Portelli, B.-J. Daniel, and A. Campbell. 2005. The Discourse of Denial: How White Teacher Candidates Construct Race, Racism and 'White Privilege'. *Race Ethnicity and Education* 8: 147–169.

Solórzano, D.G., and T.J. Yosso. 2002. Critical Race Methodology: Counter-Storytelling as An Analytical Framework for Education Research. *Qualitative Inquiry* 8: 23–44.

Stahl, G., and S. Habib. 2017. Moving Beyond the Confines of the Local: Working-Class Students' Conceptualizations of Belonging and Respectability. *Young* 25 (3): 1–18.

Taylor, E. 2016. The Foundations of Critical Race Theory in Education. In *Foundations of Critical Race Theory in Education*, ed. E. Taylor, D. Gillborn, and G. Ladson-Billings. New York and London: Routledge.

Thomas, P. 2009. The Last Britons? Young Muslims and National Identity. 59th Political Studies Association Annual Conference: Challenges for Democracy in a Global Era, University of Manchester, Manchester, UK, April. 7–9.

Tisdell, E.J., M.S. Hanley, and E.W Taylor. 2009. Different Perspectives on Teaching for Critical Consciousness. In *Handbook of Adult and Continuing Education*, ed. A.L. Wilson and E.R. Hayes. San Francisco: Wiley.

Tourinho, I., and R. Martins. 2008. Controversies: Proposals for a Visual Arts Critical Pedagogy. In *International Dialogues about Visual Culture, Education and Art*, ed. R. Mason and T. Eça. Bristol: Intellect.

Ward, P. 2004. *Britishness Since 1870*. London: Routledge.

Wink, J. 2005. *Critical Pedagogy: Notes from the Real World*. Boston: Pearson/Allyn & Bacon.

Yokley, S.H. 1999. Embracing a Critical Pedagogy in Art Education. *Art Education* 52: 18.

CHAPTER 7

Local and Global Belongings

Abstract This chapter builds upon the previous two chapters by demonstrating some more outcomes of a critical pedagogy approach to the teaching and learning of Britishness. I show that when exploring British identities, young people's concerns about social divisions and inequalities arise in their discourses. Learning and teaching about Britishness gives young people a valuable opportunity to reflect critically upon how they situate themselves locally, nationally and globally. Positionality and intersectionality impact how the students explain their sense of Britishness. Students' sense of national identity is dwarfed by their sense of local identity, and transnational postcolonial identities influence ways of belonging to Britain. The conversations between the students suggest benefits to critical pedagogy, particularly if teachers want to give students space to confidently interrogate identity issues.

Keywords Belonging · Identity · Social inequalities · Social class Race

YOUNG PEOPLE AND BRITISHNESS: A LARGELY UNEXAMINED TOPIC

Investigating the classroom pedagogies of students and teachers exploring Britishness, I observed they were examining complex discourses of local, national and global identities in discussions and explorations of Britishness.

© The Author(s) 2018
S. Habib, *Learning and Teaching British Values,*
DOI 10.1007/978-3-319-60381-0_7

For teachers and students, to engage *critically* "in written, spoken, or visual form" (Yokley 1999: 24) about everyday Britishness was important to learn about contemporary belongings and identities. Their conversations shaped my perceptions of Britishness as I absorbed the stories of the students and started (re)defining my own ideas on Britishness (Brooke and Hogg 2012), for often "one does research in order to learn more about others, but in doing so also learns more about oneself" (Gregory 2005: 5). This chapter demonstrates young people's concerns about social divisions and inequalities impacting upon their sense of belonging to their locality, London, and to Britain.

As teachers avoided endorsing official political narratives of Britishness, students were more enthusiastic about telling their own stories. Student identity is found to be inextricably bound up with their intersectional experiences that are classed, gendered and racialised; often students from marginalised communities are accustomed to battling the stigmas and consequences of labels imposed upon them by the powerful and the privileged (Darder et al. 2009; Ferguson 2012; Stahl and Habib 2017). Critical pedagogues recognise schooling is not about employing routine teaching methods, but demands knowledge of the "social, economic, psychological and political dimensions of the schools, districts, and systems...about information systems in the larger culture that serve as pedagogical forces in the lives of students and other members of society", and of understanding marginalised communities and oppressive hegemonic orders (Kincheloe 2007: 17).

Following Back (1996: 6), I cannot reveal the "whole story" on Britishness, but this account should be "read as an open contemplation on the cultural dynamics of post-imperial London". Throughout this book, I have presented research participants discursively exploring complexities of race and social class. In this penultimate chapter, I continue to stress the importance of critically engaging in open discussions about identities and racisms, to negotiate ways of belonging to Britain. When discussing national identity, home and belonging, I find young people often affirm local place attachments and a local sense of citizenship (Osler and Starkey 2005). Positionality and intersectionality impact how the students explain their sense of Britishness. Students' sense of national identity is dwarfed by their sense of local identity, and transnational postcolonial identities influence ways of belonging to Britain. The conversations between the students suggest benefits to critical pedagogy, particularly if teachers want to give students space to confidently interrogate identity issues.

There needs to be more literature on school students' definitions and narratives of Britishness or attachments to nation (Scourfield et al. 2006; Lam and Smith 2009). If citizenship has increasingly impacted upon youth consciousness, since its introduction in 2002 as a school subject (Huq 2009), and if "childhood and nationalism are intertwined" (Scourfield et al. 2006: 4), empirical research on school students' discourses of Britishness and classroom experiences of learning about Britishness are important. Research on Britishness can challenge "ethnocentrism, cultural racism or xenophobia" (Carrington and Short 1995: 220). The empirical studies I draw on here refer to the category of *youth* in a broad sense, for youth are frequently the sociopolitical focus of debates on citizenship and belonging in modern multicultural societies (Fortier 2008; Butcher and Harris 2010). Young people are "everybody's business", with society placing "hopes for building a better world" upon them (Smyth and McInerney 2007: 37). Yet, young people are frequently maligned in media and political rhetoric (Smyth and McInerney 2007; Grattan 2009), with policies of social control proposed and implemented—justified in the interest of social harmony—to discipline them.

BOUNDARIES OF BRITISHNESS

Britishness as complex, contested and unfixed came to be evident in Jacobson's (1997) study of young British Pakistani Londoners. Embracing an "attitudinal approach" of "lay people's understandings", she found Britishness was articulated through rejection, ambivalence and affirmation in relation to civic, racial and cultural boundaries (Jacobson 1997: 181). Even if postmodern notions of identity are multiple, unfixed and "infinitely malleable", she argued, Britishness is not "subject to limitless reinterpretation" (Jacobson 1997: 187). More recently, Maylor (2010) highlighted multiple ways school students define Britishness: being born in Britain, holding a passport, citizenship, Whiteness, British parentage or family and historical heritage dating back to Anglo-Saxon times. Bradford's ethnic minority youth have been shown to assert their Britishness by referring to their rights to belong as citizens (Hussain and Bagguley 2005).

Faas (2008: 42) found some White students preferred the term Englishness as it connoted "concepts of blood and birth". Back (1996: 242) once predicted ethnic minority young people's "claiming" of

England as home could "produce a reworking in the definition of what Englishness means". Sanderson and Thomas's research reveals the complexities of racialised English and British identities, as sometimes "British" seems "to prompt a 'White' association almost twice as often as 'English'" (2014: 8). Muslim youth also racialised "British" and "English" by referring to Whiteness, but felt more comfortable with "British" than "English" for the former symbolised multicultural diversity (Sanderson and Thomas 2014).

Building on Jacobson (1997) and Vadher and Barrett (2009) interviewed young British Indians and Pakistanis. Arguing Jacobson's civic and cultural boundaries is more complex than she describes; they outlined new boundaries, affirming multiple identities/positionings, including racial, civic/state, instrumental, historical, lifestyle and multicultural (Vadher and Barrett 2009: 450). Racism and threats of racism figured in their participants' perceptions of British identity, with some young people expressing they felt they were not fully accepted as British (Vadher and Barrett 2009). The participants' identifications with Britishness differed according to contexts like socialising with friends, holidays abroad and national sport fandom (Vadher and Barrett 2009).

Finding schools neglect White British diversity when teaching the National Curriculum, the Ajegbo Report (2007), proposed schools teach British values alongside cultural diversity. Further reviews need to be conducted throughout Britain and beyond to learn about students' perceptions of nation and belonging. Belongings and identities are expressed differently by young people throughout the villages, towns and cities of Britain. Children in South Wales, for instance, construct identities in relation to "dominant discourses" of belonging to Wales, as well as "class-based notions of what it means to come from the valleys" (Scourfield et al. 2005: 222), while London youth have been shown as displaying "higher levels of national identification" than those in surrounding counties like Surrey and Kent (Barrett 2002: 6).

YOUNG LONDONERS ON IDENTITIES AND BELONGINGS

Like Jacobson (1997), I use an attitudinal approach by focusing on what ordinary people—particularly those absent in political conversations on Britishness—reveal about British identity. The young people I researched include White British, ethnic minority and dual heritage students, all exploring ways in which individual and collective identities matter to their everyday lives as young Britons. While government discourses on Britishness originate from an anti-extremism and securitisation agenda, the findings I discuss in this chapter reveal students have grave concerns about belonging to Britain, and want to discuss their conceptions of intersecting identities and social locations.

RACIAL BOUNDARIES OF BRITISHNESS: WHITENESS IN BERMONDSEY

Anti-racist and Multicultural Britishness

The young people often relayed Britishness in Bermondsey as belonging to White people, making connections between local place, race and nation. Even if there is "inherent definitional slipperiness and instability" about Whiteness (Rasmussen et al. 2001: 8), undeniably racial superiority and privilege have influenced notions of Britishness (Cohen 1994; McClintock 1995). Yet, like "any other racial label, whiteness does not exist as a credible biological property" (Rasmussen et al. 2001: 8), nor do racial groups have "coherent and consistent self-conscious group identities" (Lewis 2004: 626). Maylor (2010) reports discourses of racism evident in students' discussions on Britishness, while Hand and Pearce (2009: 461) cite examples of teachers witnessing students engaging in "a form of patriotism verging on racism or xenophobia". Terms like race and Whiteness are "inconsistently" defined in empirical and theoretical scholarship (Rasmussen et al. 2001: 8), perhaps because concepts like racism are "notoriously difficult" to define (Back 1996: 9). Ethnic belonging when tied to an "exclusive and regressive form" of national identity becomes symbolic of British racism (Hall 1996: 446).

Racialised belonging is not a new narrative. Imperialism and colonialism and its lasting legacies (Neely and Samura 2011) result in the continuation of political discourses "homogenising groups, de-historicising and not seeing their struggles, reducing their distinctiveness and viewing them as bearers of particular kinds of cultural norms" (Garner 2012: 451). Political narratives, through official documents, equate "enhanced immigration and asylum controls" with "improved sense of citizenship and community", but mixed messages emerge as advantages of migrants entering the UK are also outlined (Walters 2004: 239). New (and old) migrants encounter "hostility and welcome" (Sarup 2005: 95), learning nation is "always subject to contestation, especially about who belongs to it" (Day and Thompson 2004: 83). Ethnic minority communities negotiate new hostile contestations. Recent examples concern students impacted upon by the "War on Terror" rhetoric provoking "new excuses for anti-Islamic racism" (Scourfield et al. 2005: 222).

When exploring Britishness, the Art students Kadisha and Joe raised personal identifications and positionings about racial and multicultural belongings. Joe stated fierce pride for his White British heritage, explaining he loved "everything" about this project. His teacher observed Joe was more exceptionally engaged and excited about this class work than usual. The title he chose for his artwork about the army suggested grand sentiments about Britishness and belonging: *Pride of Britain: Man for Man we are the best.* For Joe, Britishness was heavily interconnected to ethnic and racial markers: "I consider every White person to be British straight away". Kadisha, born in Britain to Jamaican parents, understood Whiteness as complex and diverse. She challenged Joe's belief that every White person can straightforwardly be categorised as British. When Kadisha raised White diversity, Joe responded with racialised stereotypes of nationality:

Joe: I can tell a Polish person from a Welsh person from a Scottish person...Just by looking at them. The colour of their skin. Welsh people are pale. Scottish people are pale. Polish people are massive and hench. Most of them. White British... English people are... think they are hard and are crazy about football.

Joe homogenised the Welsh, Polish and Scottish according to physical appearance, passionately claiming "White British" identity for the English. His ideas evoke nineteenth-century discourses that attempted to "identify the different 'races' of which the British population were composed, using hair and eye colour and skull measurements (Beddoe 1885)" (Miles and Brown 2006: 27).

Joe displayed an affective national belonging, essentialising and racialising non-White identities: "I don't think any Black person in this school would consider themselves to be British". Multiple identifications confounded Joe: "They always talk about their countries and half of them have never been to their countries (nor) want to go their countries". He created a dichotomy between himself and his Black peers: "Their passion for their countries is passion I have for my country". Joe's discourses revealed "self-generated preoccupations" of patriotism: "us and them, loyalty and enmity, fidelity and betrayal" (Johnston 2007: 26). Socio-psychological approaches can be usefully combined in understanding national identity's affective dimension. Vogler (2001: 20) argues sociology should investigate "strong emotions such as love, hate, shame and anger", not just sociopolitical and sociocultural aspects of identity.

When I asked Joe about whether ethnic minority communities might feel British, he disagreed. Reductive and racist right-wing anti-migrant rhetoric about "coming over here" and "claiming our benefits" emerged in Joe's discourses of Britishness:

Joe: Not what I've seen...Nah. The majority say it's about where they come from. I feel like Britain's getting used in the sense that people are coming over here, claiming our benefits. And I don't think we should be letting people in unless they've got a good job...

Linking the rise of immigrants with the rise of (youth) unemployment, particularly by National Front propaganda (Hewitt 1986), has long been a problematic narrative. Media and political rhetoric powerfully propagate disturbing ideas about belonging and Britishness, omitting the consequences of Empire to maintain "cultural hegemony" (Wemyss 2009). Media content is known for transmitting "particular cultural, social, ethnic, and political values, knowledge, and advocacies" (Gay 2002: 109). Through tabloid news, British ethnic minorities are paradoxically accused of both claiming British benefits and taking British jobs. Cole (2016: 10) refers to Althusser's concept of *interpellation* as necessary to understand contemporary racisms: "Interpellation is the process via which the politicians and the media, for example, claim to be speaking on behalf of the people: 'what the British people have had enough of'". Joe had internalised racist ideologies about Black Britons. He was unperturbed about repeating racist discourses in a paired interview with a Black peer conducted by a British Asian researcher.

Joe polarised White British and Black British students, excluding Black students from Britishness by arguing that they have more "passion", and hence stronger identifications, for their African ancestral homelands. To belong to a nation necessitates not only *identification* with its culture, but also *recognition* (Gellner and Breuilly 2008). Students, like Kadisha (Black British) and Chris (Mixed Heritage), were negotiating belonging to Britain with the racism they experienced, expressing *identification* while simultaneously seeking *recognition*.

Another student, Bradley, born in Bermondsey with Nigerian heritage, pointed out though he was "proud" to be British and felt he belonged to Bermondsey; it was nonetheless a "racist" area. Ethnic minority youth in Bradford have been known to experience similar struggles, knowing they belong as citizens, but that the White British do not recognise them as British (Hussain and Bagguley 2005). Although Joe claimed fixed ideas about Britishness and Whiteness, later in the interview, he revealed a conflicted understanding of British identities.

When the young people were asking me about my sense of Britishness, Joe was unsurprised that I felt British, even if I was visibly not British in his earlier view: "You probably... you do (feel British)... you've grown up in Britain...born in Britain. You are British". He observed that I might *identify* with Britishness. Joe was reluctant to offer this "recognition", unable to comprehend multicultural Britishness, multiple identifications and postcolonial belongings that constitute contemporary British identities. Joe insisted Britishness and Whiteness were interconnected, but then conceded that Britishness identification can move beyond appearance, stating "accent" can evidence Britishness. Both Kadisha and Joe regarded appearance as significant in ascertaining whether someone belongs to Britain. Discourses of Britishness are therefore complex and contradictory, as students concentrate on accent and appearance, present Whiteness as Britishness and sometimes reluctantly concede ethnic minorities can identify with and be recognised as British.

EXPLORING BRITISHNESS THROUGH EXAMINING HISTORY

At the end of the interview, there was a reflective pause before Kadisha further asked about my identity:

Kadisha: Do you feel like you are British? (laughs)
SH: (laughs) I do, yeah, I think I do.
Joe: Why is that? Is it 'cos you've been brought up in Britain?
SH: Yeah... born in Britain...brought up in Britain...and you know how you Joe talk about the docks and Bermondsey.... I feel very much from... being part of Lancashire... because I guess you can tell. I'm from North Manchester....Lancashire...so I feel very strongly and passionately about being from that area...
Joe: I bet you know a lot of the history...

Joe expressed pleasure in discussing the history of Lancashire cotton and how people came from New Commonwealth countries like Pakistan to work in the mills after World War Two. Throughout the interview, he emphasised his Britishness, but at one point informed us, at length, of his grandfather's French identifications: "Now I think about it... like on my mum's side I think I'm a bit French". As he elaborated upon his grandfather's "connections" with France during the war, it emerged Joe was not "a bit French", but that his grandad had briefly lived with a French family in England. Joe was enthusiastic about providing a non-British link to his heritage; perhaps to show he too could be "diverse". My colleagues have frequently pointed out White British students often keenly highlight Irish ancestry to lay claim to cultural diversity.

Joe displayed passion for researching identity and history and revealed ambitions to join the army to discover new places and fulfil patriotic dreams: "I wanna train... go see new places...Yeah, fighting for our country". He believed "unless you felt you were hundred percent British", you would not fight for Britain. He claimed ethnic minorities would not join the army. Joe had internalised the "Invisible Empire" that dominates discourses of Britishness (Wemyss 2009). This rhetoric refuses to recognise that West Indian immigrants to Britain, as well as their relatives, had served Britain during World War Two (Ward 2004, Modood 2005), and Indians worked in the war factories and served in the navy (Ward 2004). The War had "encouraged migration at the same time as it created a new sense of a socially cohesive British identity", but excluded and Othered the Black and Asian migrants arriving in Britain (Ward 2004: 124). Joe doubted attachments his ethnic minority peers had for Britain could be strong. Questioning whether ethnic minorities belong to Britain is historical and crosses class boundaries.[1]

Kadisha's engagement with discourses of identities highlights the importance of also giving Black British females space to articulate themselves.[2] Joe showed interest in Kadisha's journey of discovering more about Jamaican culture and traditions, listening intently when she was critical of Britishness that excludes the contributions of minority ethnic people:

Kadisha: See the thing is Britain's history isn't just Britain's... like the country was made up on a lot of other cultures. So you can't just blank them out because other cultures helped make Britain.

SH: Like?

Kadisha:	Africans. During slavery time when they came and made... I don't know in particular the names of it... but I know they made loads of statues and buildings...
Joe:	They basically were the people who built it up... they done all the graft... because they couldn't get people to graft for them...

Kadisha was negotiating transnational attachments. She suggested ambivalence about Britishness: "I don't think it means anything to me really...Just the place I was born in... the place I live in". Yet, her artwork revealed Britishness was significant, proving Kadisha was caught up in the tensions of belongings. Belonging, after all, concerns both identification and acceptance (Gellner and Breuilly 2008). Joe acknowledged that Britain is the place where Kadisha comes from, yet he also perceived Kadisha as not being visibly British. Kadisha seemed to be working out her positionality by discussing counter-narratives of home and belonging and pushing the boundaries of this Britishness project to ensure it was inclusive and transnational. Like Joe, Kadisha frequently mentioned she enjoyed learning about issues of history and heritage. She explained she was keen to delve deeper into the histories of her "parents and ancestors", and learning about culture and identities allowed her to "look at things differently".

We can take lessons from students' conceptions of British identities. The discourses of Britishness expressed by Kadisha and Joe highlight the significance of historicised belongings. When preparing how to approach the teaching of Britishness, teachers could explore with their classes how reflecting upon British histories, we learn to understand the present and begin to shape the future: "while remaining firmly located in the present, we need to make a critical appraisal of our history and use its resources to develop a new sense of national identity that is faithful to the past and yet resonates with present experiences and aspirations" (Parekh 2000: 6). When exploring British histories, present complexities and future possibilities of nation, it is important to research how ethnic minorities "are regarded, and regard themselves, as part of the nation" (Carrington and Short 1998: 149). This becomes paramount if national identity is "continuously constructed and reshaped in its (often apathetic) interaction with outsiders, strangers, foreigners and aliens – the 'others'. You know who you are, only by knowing who you are not" (Cohen 1994: 1).

The next section demonstrates British identities require both deconstructions of race and class.

CULTURAL AND CLASS BOUNDARIES OF BRITISHNESS

The Chav in Bermondsey: Where Class and Race Meet

Alongside media, policy and political discourses, academia also has historically been guilty of neglecting detailed and empathetic study of the ways in which the White working classes are disparaged, racialised and marginalised (Haylett 2001). In recent years though, there has been an increase in academic research and media reportage about socially marginalised White working-class youth (Bottero 2009). Some scholars of globalisation studies argue class and place are less important to our social experiences, yet "class still plays a significant role in many attempts to theorize youth" (Shildrick et al. 2010: 3). Social class inequalities relay not just economic experiences but also cultural revelations and encounters (Atkinson et al. 2012; Stahl and Habib 2017). This section will expand on students' ambivalence when describing the chav caricature which they believed symbolised Britishness in Bermondsey, but which students Ellie and Chris also challenged as a populist mythical narrative that seeks to misrepresent and malign the working classes.

The term chav became a familiar media "buzz word", to describe the White working classes, yet regional synonyms such as "charver" have been around longer (Nayak 2009). The etymology is disputed with some interpreting chav as an acronym for "council housed and violent" (Tyler 2008; Plan B 2012b). Those popularising this term attempt to deny its pejorative connotations (Tyler 2013), yet it is commonplace vocabulary to abuse White working-class communities in England, synonymous with the "White trash" of the USA (Tyler 2008). Chav is the new *folk devil* (Hayward and Yar 2006; le Grand 2013), almost replacing the term "underclass" in media discourses, for chav has increased in use, while "underclass" has decreased considerably (Hayward and Yar 2006). The "underclass" label is known to connote "a discourse of familial disorder and dysfunction; of dangerous masculinities and dependent femininities; of antisocial behaviour; of moral and ecological decay" (Haylett 2001: 358), and now, these same demeaning discourses are used in reference to those described as chavs.

Media and political discourses amplify a contradictory identity of those they stigmatise as chavs: racialised as embodying dirty, poverty-stricken Whiteness (Tyler 2008), while simultaneously being epitomised as "a bunch of racist bigots" (Jones 2011: 9) or "filthy White" racists (Tyler 2008: 25). During the summer 2011 riots in English cities, social commentators used classed and racialised language about young people (Pearson 2012: 60):

> Bagehot picks up on the historian David Starkey's comments on the BBC that young white working class people had 'become black': 'The whites have become black. A particular sort of violent, destructive, nihilistic gang-ster culture has become the fashion… This language, which is wholly false, which is this Jamaican patois that has intruded England. This is why so many of us have this sense of literally a foreign country'.

Such media discourses judging Black and White youth and the communities that they inhabit inevitably impacts their everyday lives as they come to be classed and racialised by the state. Such negative rhetoric affects ways local areas are "governed and policed", as well as ways "agencies providing services to the residents in the area perceive the residents" (Rooke and Gidley 2010: 102).

The "demonization of the working class" was exacerbated by Margaret Thatcher's government in the 1980s when the working classes were vehemently attacked, along with their "communities, industries, values and institutions" (Jones 2011: 40). New Labour also promoted a negative representation of the working classes through rhetoric that incentivised them to free themselves from working-class roots and join middle-class Britain (Jones 2011). Discourses mocking the chav need deconstructing for the way they associate the young White working class as subject to "welfare dependency, moral degeneracy, academic failure, fecklessness, and excessive and tasteless consumption" (Shildrick et al. 2010: 4). The emergence and popularity of the chav caricature proves social class divisions remain significant in Britain (Lawler 2005; Hollingworth and Williams 2009; Jones 2011). The political landscape promoting denigration of the working classes—through humiliating images—will have arisen from political policies contributing to representing the working classes as dirty and shameful (Jones 2011).

Chav bashing must be politically contextualised and interrogated in the light of Britain's "deepening economic inequality" (Tyler 2008: 18).

In his TEDxObserver talk on disadvantaged youth, music and aspirations, East London hip hop artist Plan B argues for a change in classed antagonism and abuse: "...in this country we openly say the word chav. The papers openly ridicule the poor and less unfortunate" (Plan B 2012a, c). Children, as young as aged eight, refer to chavs when discussing social difference: "private school children often perceived children who lived in council estates to be 'chavs', who were seen as badly behaved, with parents that did not care about them" (Sutton et al. 2007). Chav bashing is justified through a "rationalised" critique of the racist attitudes and behaviours of those categorised as chavs: "The process of differentiating between respectable and non-respectable forms of Whiteness attempts to abject the White poor from spheres of White privilege" (Tyler 2008: 25).

London areas "coded as working class and minority ethnic" are often represented in ways to perpetuate moral panics about gangs in the "latest development in an ongoing history of the pathologisation of urban spaces" (Archer et al. 2010: 2). Ellie and Chris discussed Bermondsey as a place that was tarnished with the chav label. As well as being marginalised due to race and class, therefore, chavs are further outcast because of the place where they belong. Associating "street crime, disease, drugs, over-breeding" with chav spaces has become a common trope, a place where "South Asian communities, new migrants and asylum seekers are displaced" (Nayak 2009: 32). It was not just Bermondsey resident Jade Goody's[3] social class and appearance that were ridiculed by media discourses and wider society, but also her belonging to a "chav" place she came to represent: "That dark place was her childhood in Bermondsey, a grubby corner of south-east London" (The Economist 2009).

Inner city places are often represented as "dark places and described as urban jungles, shanty towns, a 'blot' on the ostensibly White landscape" (Nayak 2009: 32); the students recognised that Bermondsey was similarly a "blot" in the wider White middle-class landscape. Racialising the White working classes is a process that relies upon "the politics of space": "chav space" and "chav place" "are used discursively as a way of fixing people in racialized class positions" (Rooke and Gidley 2010: 95). The young people in the Art classes were growing in confidence to interrogate the stigmatisation and demonisation of the place where they felt they belonged. If Jade Goody and her family came to be seen by wider society as representing the White working classes (Raisborough et al. 2013), then similarly, her locale suffered from the same pathologisation.

The next section will show the Art student, Ellie, like Jade, encountered the burdens and stigmas of pathologisation of place and White working-class identity.

Class Boundaries: Imprisoned Identities

For the Art students, Britishness in Bermondsey frequently revolved around chav identity in public discourses. The Bermondsey chav is complexly perceived by the students through the intersectionality of race, place and social class. Focus on the chav caricature by some students relayed their working-class experience of Britishness and belonging. Sometimes, social class is referenced through coded language (Hollingworth and Williams 2009), similar to race. The chav caricature perpetuates "class boundaries", through "mockery... contempt, disgust or even hatred" (le Grand 2013: 219). Ellie, a White female student, articulated social struggles encountered by the stigmatised working classes because of the imposition of the undesirable and demeaning label chav. The concept of "double consciousness" that is used for "Black folk" (Du Bois 2007), could also apply to White working-class students like Ellie examined herself through society's contemptuous lens.

Chavs are "visible" to wider society, often through "stylistic markers" (le Grand 2013: 218). Designer brands, fashion and appearance might matter to young people performing identities (Archer et al. 2010; Shildrick et al. 2010), and those involved in chav subcultures can be regarded as expressing class identity through stylistic markers (McCulloch et al. 2006). The chav label becomes more than fashion, as chav embodiment or chav performativity come to be translated by society, often pejoratively. Young people branded chavs are judged by "moral-aesthetic" standards, as representing "lifestyles, behaviour, body techniques, speech, values and social background" (le Grand 2013: 218) that are socially undesirable and shameful.

Ellie struggled to escape the class imprisonment of what she powerfully denounced as "stereotypes and judgements". Feeling that society was reminding her of her place by humiliating discourses, imposing upon her the classed baggage that came with the term chav. Ellie's compelling and poignant artwork reflected deep displeasure and frustrated resentment at being labelled unfairly and prematurely. In the artwork on Britishness, she constructed a bar restraining her eyes, restricting her to a specific identity, enclosing her, confining her and repressing her self-identity, like prison bars:

Ellie: "… so it's like you're caged in and you can't express yourself how you want to be perceived because other people do it for you".

She saw society denigrating as "chavy", for example, because she wears a Tiffany chain. Ellie's vivid description of the positioning of the Tiffany chain in her artwork evoked a Freirean symbolism. The chain reflected her oppressed and marginalised experiences, and her lack of voice and inability to defend herself: "…it's like tight around my neck and my mouth… so I can't talk to myself … I can't breathe… I'm like tied up". Ellie's artwork, with its Tiffany chains and Burberry branded bullets, as well as the terrifyingly opened jaws of the Lacoste crocodile pointed towards confinement in an unfairly imposed sense of identity, as she battled social class prejudices. Ellie's sense of Britishness was tied up with judgements and stereotypes about social class, belonging and Bermondsey, just as her artwork and its title—"Stereotypes and Judgements"—presented.

Often, chav discourse attempts to present the chav caricature as representative of White working-class youth, blaming the individual for their class position (Shildrick et al. 2010). However, working with young people, we learn "identity is not a voluntary project of self-making", but "always set within a social, cultural and economic context, which sets limits on the kinds of identities that are available to particular selves: people position themselves within, and are positioned by, discourses" (Allen and Mendick 2012: 4). Ellie identified her working-class White identity as a stigmatised identity, but powerfully embraced it at the same time by painting what is caricatured by wider society. When inquiring into Britishness then, she was conceding Britishness in Bermondsey was an identity tainted by harsh social judgements and stereotypes, and significantly, she was engaging in a type of complex reclaiming and re-positioning of it on her own terms. Blue tones in Ellie's artwork, she explained, suggested coldness experienced when people label her a chav:

Ellie: I think that when someone's cold towards another person… it stops them from actually getting to know them because they have a presumption in their head.

She felt her British-Bermondsey identity was viewed negatively by wider society, imprisoning in her a false identity. Ellie positioned herself within a discourse of Britishness that reflected social oppression, recognising that she is stigmatised because of her White working-class female Bermondsey body.

Ellie felt strongly about stereotypes imposed on British youth as limiting and controlling identities. She believed wider society brands her as a representative of chav culture, a gross stereotype giving rise to her sense of injustice, rage and even violence. The gun and the chains in Ellie's artwork symbolised violent feelings of anger and frustration at being defined by others:

Ellie: "And then I've got a gun because... people... I don't think people think of guns related to chavs but I think they think like angry and like negative...and I think a gun represents that well. And that was painted in red to represent anger".

Ellie pointed out complexities of identity and belonging: though she did not reside in Bermondsey, because of the fashion she followed, she had been labelled "a Bermondsey girl", and perhaps because she felt attachments to Bermondsey as here she attended school. Ellie believed "a Bermondsey girl" was synonymous with "a chav". She detested the stereotyping of the White working-classes through the chav representation because it was unpleasant and undesirable: "something I didn't like about Britain". Yet, simultaneously Ellie embraced chav culture in her artwork, as she defended and protected it from wider societal disparagement throughout the interview.

Acquisition of wealth and celebrity status cannot displace the stereotypes and judgements that seem rigidly attached to those labelled as chav. Openly empathising with those labelled as chav, Ellie also referred to the "stereotypes and judgements" imposed upon "chav celebrity" Jade Goody. Even as a celebrity, Jade Goody was "constituted as illegitimate, undesirable and lacking" (Allen and Mendick 2012: 2), sneered by society as financially rich but culturally poor (le Grand 2013). Ellie was not alone in her frustration at the chav label. Another student Emma Jones entitled her artwork "Chav Britain" which consisted of an "angry expression" on her face, and "chav patterns in tattoo shapes", against a backdrop of a landscape of London. Emma explained chav "immediately" comes into her mind when thinking about British identity. She included positive images of London buildings in the background of her painting as a contrast to the negative image of a chav, thus demonstrating resistance and contestation. White British female student Sammie-Jo Earrey also referenced the Burberry logo in her artwork alongside a butterfly, stating Burberry represented stereotyping, while the butterfly symbolised her desire for "freedom" from the imprisonment of chav identity.

Ideas about Britishness and what it means to be British, therefore, can be difficult, troubling and stifling for students from all ethnic and cultural backgrounds. Students from ethnic minority communities, working-class communities and Gypsy, Roma or Traveller families encounter obstacles and barriers such as low expectations, school exclusion and social deprivation which can impact upon their educational achievement (Knowles and Lander 2011). Teachers sometimes dismiss the White working classes as low in aspiration and ambition (Archer et al. 2010), and the middle-classes perceive chavs as having no value for education (Hollingworth and Williams 2009). Ellie, who personally felt subjected to this malicious and vicious stereotype regarding education and class, believed it an unjust and incomplete understanding of Bermondsey. Being British in Bermondsey may have been seen by the world at large as lacking in aspirations, but Ellie thought this a demeaning misrepresentation, arguing the school's students take pride in opportunities for advancement. The growing intake of sixth-formers, and increasing number of university applicants year by year, reflected the life ambitions of these Bermondsey students, and also supported Ellie's arguments about aspirations.[4]

Through the labelling of areas as "chav spaces", and youth as chavs, we can see the "persistent classing gaze which fixes working class people in place" (Rooke and Gidley 2010: 95). Ellie observed this pathologisation of place too and countered it with her aspiration-speak. These were her counter-narratives about belonging to Bermondsey, London and Britain. Recognising popular media discourses have labelled Bermondsey as "grubby" and its inhabitants as chavs; students, like Ellie, were fighting stereotyping, wanting to succeed in their studies at school, despite low expectations of their aspirational selves. Seen to originate from an area synonymous with racism and chavs, the students felt Bermondsey had especially been painted as racist and chav-like due to the media representation of Big Brother's Jade Goody (2002, 2007) and subsequent sensationalising of Bermondsey by the popular press. For these students, Britishness in Bermondsey was about battling unfair representation and offensive classed and racialised caricatures perpetuated by media and wider society discourses.

CLASS, RACE AND PLACE

The kaleidoscopic images emerging from the Art students reflected the multi-layered, multifaceted and vibrant nature of contemporary Britishness. Critical pedagogues, like myself and the teachers I worked with, are keen to move away from notions of national identity revolving around ethnicity or monoculture. British identity needs to be reworked and rewritten in fluid and changing contexts "in which identities are constantly being negotiated and reinvented within complex and contradictory notions of belonging" (Giroux 1995: 55). This research with the Art students shows race, class and place[5] need to be consciously examined and deconstructed (Brahinsky 2011; Nayak 2003; Jackson 2005) if we are to work towards developing cohesive communities in multicultural societies. Teachers engage with students from multicultural backgrounds amidst political and media rhetoric declaring multiculturalism is dead, yet multiculturalism is the lived experience of many students in inner city schools.

Teachers and students witness "Britain's inability to reckon with a metropolitan paradox", where cities like London become "both the stage for some of the most profound, and I would say beautiful, realisations of dialogue and radical multiculture; and yet, at the same time, it also provides an arena where brutal and enduring forms of racism take hold" (Back 2009: 205). Ethnic minority teenagers perhaps sense they are only included when it suits national narratives (Back 1996: 148): they see their hyphenated identities are deemed by politicians as "at best as problematic and at worst as mutually exclusive". This might account for why African and Caribbean students in Britain, particularly females, sometimes regard ethnic heritage as a more valuable category of identification than nationality, revealing pride and emotional attachments for African or Caribbean heritage (Lam and Smith 2009). Critical theorists like Cohen (1988) and Wright (1985) have vigorously emphasised that racism is not a mere appendage to British history, but a central feature. If racism is perceived as inherent in British identity (Anthias and Yuval-Davis 1992), then learning and teaching about British identities cannot ever ignore racism.

Power and inequalities are inevitable factors of global cities as they contain disadvantaged places and people (Sassen 2005), with capitalist ideologies especially contributing to the inequalities in places

(Harvey 1996). Young people are hemmed in by policies of education, housing and welfare negatively affecting their experiences of multicultural Britain (Berkeley 2011). Kadisha and Joe's conversation on Britishness, place and race highlight the importance of exploring social inequalities, as well as learning about the power of media and political discourses in representing multicultural Britain negatively. Racist discourses of Britishness amplified by political and media rhetoric also reveal teaching about racism is necessary and urgent. The Art students revealed the ramifications of media and political discourses on the psyche of young working-class Londoners.

The complexity and multiplicity of the contested concept of Britishness can be explored in detail by valuing students' lived experiences and giving them safe spaces to voice their questions, confusions and contradictions about class, race and place. By emphasising identities as unfixed and fluid, sometimes contradictory and ambiguous, contextual and interdependent (Hall 1991; Kershen 1998; Parekh 2000; Lawler 2008), we can give young people the necessary permission to openly talk about nuanced and evolving identities and belongings. We are then in the muddle together, collectively working out what it means to be British, interrogating the taken for granted definitions propagated by the political elite.

Britishness is not a static or stable concept, and thus young people's representations of Britishness will be highly subjective, contextual and inevitably subject to change. If "narrating the nation" yields a narration of the self (Byrne 2007b), I expect young people throughout Britain would similarly relay stories on Britishness that yield narratives of personal identities intertwined with their social experiences. Conversations about Britishness are necessary to come to a shared understanding of the meaning of Britishness (Keddie 2013). However, definitions and discourses of Britishness will vary according to place and time. While a shared vision of Britishness may provide elements of temporary societal cohesion, this vision can only be time and context-bound, and not accepted by all in society. It is perhaps more useful to problematise and interrogate "narrow, fixed and racialised views of national identity and assumptions", especially when they perpetuate myths that "associate an affiliation with Britishness with generating social cohesion and conversely, a lack of affiliation with Britishness with generating social conflict" (Keddie 2013: 2).

It is important to present how definitions of Britishness are fleeting as time passes, evolving as experiences mould us, and multiple as we encounter new events, ideas and people. Researchers can take heart knowing although "those traces of life are opaque and that the person who made them is always to an extent unknowable", it "doesn't mean that all is lost" (Back 2004: 205). It is important to allow our students to learn about identity itself, about the multiple, fluid and shifting nature of identity, so they are able to bring plenty of examples from their own lives. Students need a space to interrogate how identities are influenced and affected by social structures too, and how this impacts upon their everyday lives. We can give students the chance to critique cultural mores, as they reflect upon social constraints and challenges for freedom.

NOTES

1. Ward (2004: 125) explains the attempts at "reasonableness" made by a retired judge relaying views on Britishness to the Welshpool Conservative Club in 1970: "The judge explained his desire to exclude in two ways. First, that there were too many immigrants to be 'absorbed' into Britishness, and second, that the immigrants did not want to be British anyway".
2. Black British females' identities and identifications were once an under-researched area (Rattansi 2000).
3. Bermondsey resident, Jade Goody, who achieved fame through her participation in the TV programme Big Brother (Channel 4, 2002) was caricatured as a chav by media and public rhetoric.
4. The GCSE pass rate of 5 A*–C achieved by students is now higher in Southwark than the England national average (Public Health England 2015), but around the time my research was conducted, according to Public Health England, the GCSE pass rate was lower than average (2007, 2008, 2009).
5. Critical Marxists in the 1970s identified the importance of power and domination in any discussions on space, arguing the social and spatial cannot be divorced; work has been done on race and space in distinct fields, but needs collaboration and interdisciplinarity (Neely and Samura 2011).

REFERENCES

Allen, K., and H. Mendick. 2012. Young People's Uses of Celebrity: Class, Gender and 'Improper' Celebrity. *Discourse: Studies in the Cultural Politics of Education* 34: 77–93.

Anthias, F., and N. Yuval-Davis. 1992. *Racialized Boundaries: Race, Nation, Gender, Colour and Class and the Anti-racist Struggle*. London and New York: Routledge.

Archer, L., S. Hollingworth, and H. Mendick. 2010. *Urban Youth and Schooling*. Maidenhead: McGraw-Hill Education.

Back, L. 1996. *New Ethnicities and Urban Culture: Racisms and Multiculture in Young Lives*. London: Routledge.

Back, L. 2009. Researching Community and Its Moral Projects. *Twenty-First Century Society* 4: 201–214.

Barrett, M. 2002. Children's Views of Britain and Britishness in 2001: Some Initial Findings From the Developmental Psychology Section Centenary Project. *Annual Conference of the Developmental Psychology*. University of Sussex: British Psychological Society.

Berkeley, R. 2011. True Multiculturalism Acts as a Bulwark Against Further Extremism [Online]. *Left Foot Forward*. Available: http://leftfootforward.org/2011/02/david-cameron-wrong-on-multiculturalism/. Accessed 24 Feb 2016.

Bottero, W. 2009. Class in the 21st Century. In *Who Cares About the White Working Class?* ed. K.P. Sveinsson. London: Runnymede Trust.

Brooke, R., and C. Hogg. 2012. Open to Change: Ethos, Identification and Critical Ethnography in Composition Studies. In *Ethnography Unbound: From Theory Shock to Critical Praxis*, ed. S.G. Brown and S.I. Dobrin. Albany: State University of New York Press.

Butcher, M., and A. Harris. 2010. Pedestrian Crossings: Young People and Everyday Multiculturalism. *Journal of Intercultural Studies* 31: 449–453.

Carrington, B., and G. Short. 1995. What Makes a Person British? Children's Conceptions of Their National Culture and Identity. *Educational Studies* 21: 217–238.

Carrington, B., and G. Short. 1998. Adolescent Discourse on National Identity: Voices of Care and Justice? *Educational Studies* 24: 133–152.

Cohen, R. 1994. *Frontiers of Identity: The British and the Others*. London and New York: Longman.

Darder, A., M.P. Baltodano, & R.D. Torres (eds.). 2009. *The Critical Pedagogy Reader*. New York and London: Routledge.

Day, G., and A. Thompson. 2004. *Theorizing Nationalism*. Houndmills: Palgrave Macmillan.

Faas, D. 2008. Constructing Identities: The Ethno-National and Nationalistic Identities of White and Turkish Students in Two English Secondary Schools. *British Journal of Sociology of Education* 29: 37–48.

Ferguson, S.J. (ed.). 2012. *Race, Gender, Sexuality & Social Class: Dimensions of Inequality*. Los Angeles: Sage.

Fortier, A.-M. 2008. *Multicultural Horizons: Diversity and the Limits of the Civil Nation*. London and New York: Routledge.

Garner, S. 2012. A Moral Economy of Whiteness: Behaviours, Belonging and Britishness. *Ethnicities* 12: 445–464.

Gay, G. 2002. Preparing for Culturally Responsive Teaching. *Journal of Teacher Education* 53: 106–116.

Gellner, E., and J. Breuilly. 2008. *Nations and Nationalism*. New York: Cornell University Press.

Grattan, A. 2009. Segregated Britain: A Society in Conflict with Its 'Radicalised' Youth? *Youth & Policy: Focus on Youth Work in Contested Spaces* 102: 35–52.

Gregory, E. 2005. Introduction: Tracing the Steps. In *On Writing Educational Ethnographies: The Art of Collusion*, ed. J. Conteh, E. Gregory, C. Kearney, and A. Mor-Sommerfeld. Stoke on Trent: Trentham Books.

Hall, S. 1991. Old and New Identities, Old and New ethnicities. In *Culture, Globalization and the World-System*, ed. A.D. King. Minneapolis: University of Minnesota Press.

Hall, S. 1996. New Ethnicities. In *Stuart Hall: Critical Dialogues in Cultural Studies*, ed. K.-H. Chen and D. Morley. London: Routledge.

Hand, M., and J. Pearce. 2009. Patriotism in British Schools: Principles, Practices and Press Hysteria. *Educational Philosophy and Theory* 41: 453–465.

Haylett, C. 2001. Illegitimate Subjects?: Abject Whites, Neoliberal Modernisation, and Middle-Class Multiculturalism. *Environment and Planning D* 19: 351–370.

Hayward, K., and M. Yar. 2006. The 'Chav' Phenomenon: Consumption, Media and the Construction of a New Underclass. *Crime, Media, Culture* 2: 9–28.

Hollingworth, S., and K. Williams. 2009. Constructions of the Working-Class 'Other' Among Urban, White, Middleclass Youth: 'Chavs', Subculture and the Valuing of Education. *Journal of Youth Studies* 12: 467–482.

Hussain, Y., and P. Bagguley. 2005. Citizenship, Ethnicity and Identity: British Pakistanis After the 2001 'Riots'. *Sociology* 39: 407–425.

Jacobson, J. 1997. Perceptions of Britishness. *Nations and Nationalism* 3: 181–199.

Johnston, S. 2007. *The Truth About Patriotism*. Durham and London: Duke University Press.

Jones, O. 2011. *Chavs: The Demonization of the Working Class*. London: Verso Books.

Keddie, A. 2013. The Politics of Britishness: Multiculturalism, Schooling and Social Cohesion. *British Educational Research Journal* 40: 539–554.

Kershen, A.J. (ed.). 1998. *A Question of Identity*. Aldershot: Ashgate.

Kincheloe, J.L. 2007. Critical Pedagogy in the Twenty-First Century. In *Critical Pedagogy: Where are We Now?* ed. P. Mclaren and J.L. Kincheloe. New York: Peter Lang.

Knowles, G., and V. Lander. 2011. *Diversity Equality and Achievement in Education*. London: Sage.

Lam, V., and G. Smith. 2009. African and Caribbean Adolescents in Britain: Ethnic Identity and Britishness. *Ethnic and Racial Studies* 32: 1248–1270.

Lawler, S. 2005. Introduction: Class, Culture and Identity. *Sociology* 39: 797–806.

Lawler, S. 2008. *Identity: Sociological Perspectives*. Cambridge: Polity.

le Grand, E. 2013. The 'Chav' as Folk Devil. In *Moral Panics in the Contemporary World*, ed. J. Petley, C. Critcher, J. Hughes, and A. Rohloff. New York: Bloomsbury Publishing.

Lewis, A.E. 2004. "What Group?" Studying Whites and Whiteness in the Era of "Color-Blindness". *Sociological theory* 22: 623–646.

Maylor, U. 2010. Notions of Diversity, British Identities and Citizenship Belonging. *Race Ethnicity and Education* 13: 233–252.

McClintock, A. 1995. *Imperial Leather: Race, Gender, and Sexuality in the Colonial Contest*. New York and London: Routledge.

McCulloch, K., A. Stewart, and N. Lovegreen. 2006. 'We Just Hang Out Together': Youth Cultures and Social Class. *Journal of Youth Studies* 9: 539–556.

Miles, R., and M. Brown. 2006. Representations of the Other. In *Identity and Belonging: Rethinking Race and Ethnicity in Canadian Society*, ed. B.S. Bolaria and S.P Hier. Toronto: Canadian Scholars' Press.

Modood, T. 2005. Ethnicity and Political Mobilization in Britain. In *Ethnicity, Social Mobility, and Public Policy: Comparing the USA and UK*, ed. G.C. Loury, T. Modood and S.M. Teles. Cambridge: Cambridge University Press.

Nayak, A. 2003. *Race, Place and Globalization: Youth Cultures in a Changing World*. Oxford: Berg.

Nayak, A. 2009. Beyond the Pale: Chavs, Youth and Social Class. In *Who Cares about the White Working Class?* ed. K.P. Sveinsson. London: Runnymede Trust.

Neely, B., and M. Samura. 2011. Social Geographies of Race: Connecting Race and Space. *Ethnic and Racial Studies* 34: 1933–1952.

Osler, A., and H. Starkey. 2005. *Changing Citizenship: Democracy and Inclusion in Education*. Maidenhead: Open University Press.

Parekh, B. 2000. Defining British National Identity. *The Political Quarterly* 71: 4–14.

Pearson, G. 2012. Everything Changes, Nothing Moves: The Longue Duree of Social Anxieties. In *The English Riots of 2011: A Summer of Discontent*. ed. D. Briggs. Hook: Waterside Press.

Plan B. 2012a. Plan B: 'Find Out What Kids are Good At. It Will Change Their Lives'. *The Guardian*, 17 Mar 2012.

Plan B. 2012b. Plan B: don't call me a chav [Online]. *Radio Times*. Available: http://www.radiotimes.com/news/2012-06-17/plan-b-dont-call-me-a-chav. Accessed 28 Mar 2016.

Plan B. 2012c. Youth, Music and London: Plan B at TEDxObserver. TEDx Talks.

Rattansi, A. 2000. On Being and not Being Brown/Black-British: Racism, Class, Sexuality and Ethnicity in Post-imperial Britain. *Interventions: International Journal of Postcolonial Studies* 2: 118–134.

Rasmussen, B.B., E. Klinenberg, I.J. Nexica, and M. Wray. 2001. Introduction. In *The Making and Unmaking of Whiteness*, ed. B.B. Rasmussen, E. Klinenberg, I.J. Nexica, and M. Wray. Durham and London: Duke University Press.

Rooke, A., and B. Gidley. 2010. Asdatown: The Intersections of Classed Places and Identities. In *Classed Intersections: Spaces, Selves, Knowledges*, ed. Y. Taylor. Farnham: Ashgate.

Sanderson, P., and P. Thomas. 2014. Troubling Identities: Race, Place and Positionality Among Young People in Two Towns in Northern England. *Journal of Youth Studies* 17: 1–19.

Sarup, M. 2005. Home and Identity. In *Travellers' Tales: Narratives of Home and Displacement*, ed. J. Bird, B. Curtis, M. Mash, T. Putnam, G. Robertson, and L. Tickner. London: Routledge.

Scourfield, J., J. Evans, W. Shah, and H. Beynon. 2005. The Negotiation of Minority Ethnic Identities in Virtually All-White Communities: Research with Children and Their Families in the South Wales Valleys. *Children and Society* 19: 211–224.

Scourfield, J., B. Dicks, M. Drakeford, and A. Davies. 2006. *Children, Place and Identity: Nation and Locality in Middle Childhood*. Abingdon: Routledge.

Shildrick, T., S. Blackman, and R. Macdonald. 2010. Young People, Class and Place. In *Young People, Class and Place*, ed. R. Macdonald, T. Shildrick, and S. Blackman. London and New York: Routledge.

Smyth, J., and P. McInerney. 2007. *Teachers in the Middle: Reclaiming the Wasteland of the Adolescent Years of Schooling*. New York: Peter Lang.

Stahl, G., and S. Habib. 2017. Moving Beyond the Confines of the Local: Working-Class Students' Conceptualizations of Belonging and Respectability. *Young* 25 (3): 1–18.

Sutton, L., N. Smith, C. Dearden, and S. Middleton. 2007. A Child's-Eye View of Social Difference [Online]. *Joseph Rowntree Foundation*. Available: https://www.jrf.org.uk/report/childs-eye-view-social-difference. Accessed 28 Mar 2016.

Tyler, I. 2008. Chav Mum Chav Scum. *Feminist Media Studies* 8: 17–34.

Tyler, I. 2013. *Revolting Subjects: Social Abjection & Resistance in Neoliberal Britain*. London: Zed Books.

Vadher, K., and M. Barrett. 2009. Boundaries of Britishness in British Indian and Pakistani Young Adults. *Journal of Community & Applied Social Psychology* 19: 442–458.

Vogler, C. 2001. Social Identity and Emotion: The Meeting of Psychoanalysis and Sociology. *The Sociological Review* 48: 19–42.

Ward, P. 2004. *Britishness Since 1870*. London: Routledge.

Wemyss, G. 2009. *The Invisible Empire: White Discourse Tolerance and Belonging*. Farnham: Ashgate.

Yokley, S.H. 1999. Embracing a Critical Pedagogy in Art Education. *Art Education* 52: 18.

CHAPTER 8

Conclusions and Recommendations

Abstract This chapter summarises the important reasons why society needs to recognise and elevate culturally diverse young people's contributions to the multiple debates on Britishness. I continue to argue this should be a priority in any Fundamental British Value policy or practice. When teachers are supported in their endeavours to provide students with opportunities to explore multicultural Britishness, students critically and collaboratively engage with identity issues, advance their own viewpoints, learn about alternative perspectives, and strengthen bonds with peers and teachers. Students feel empowered by having their critical counter-narratives validated and valued. The empirical research detailed in this book leads to the resounding conclusion that where students hear others' stories and tell their own, schools can become critical sites of opportunity for reflection, resistance and hopeful futures.

Keywords Multiculturalism · Youth voice · Identity · Critical pedagogy Counter-narratives

Young Britons' Needs and Aspirations

Scholars of identity should continue to ask important questions about racial and classed belongings and identities, while educators must consider how these questions translate into classroom pedagogies. Questions like "whose heritage we should now be counting as British?"

© The Author(s) 2018
S. Habib, *Learning and Teaching British Values,*
DOI 10.1007/978-3-319-60381-0_8

(Morley and Robins 2001: 2) persist in contemporary Britain. Or in what ways can teaching about British citizenship negotiate sensitive coverage of colonial histories and contemporary cultural diversity (Heater 2001)? Or are we addressing concerns about the National Curriculum viewed as inherently Eurocentric and diversity featuring low on most schools' priority list (Maylor et al. 2007)? Whose Britishness or FBV we should teach in schools? How might we successfully define Britishness and at the same time condemn "nasty" racist discourse? This book has demonstrated the significance of creating spaces to critically interrogate Britishness and FBV from ideological and pedagogical perspectives.

The perspectives and experiences of trainee teachers, Art teachers and young people, discussed throughout this book, maintain the gravity of asking questions, of providing safe spaces for trainee teachers, teacher educators, teachers and students to interrogate, clarify and re-define pedagogies of Britishness and the meanings of contemporary multicultural Britishness. Critical pedagogy, I emphasise in this book, is a "theoretical and political practice", not just a teaching technique (Giroux 2013: 3). The teacher's role in giving students a protected space to question prevailing modes of racialised and classed power and privilege is vital and welcomed by young people. The previous chapters have shown the ways discourses on Britishness and FBV might be addressed sensitively and discursively, and always critically. This book has highlighted how empowering critical pedagogy can be participatory and interactive, as well as helping to combat traditionally low rates of student involvement in the classroom (Shor 1992). I have argued classrooms have the potential to be sites of struggle with opportunities for resistance and critique, moments of hope and possibility and beginnings of social change (Giroux 1995; Giroux 2013).

Young people often perceive their views on belonging to Britain as neither heard nor respected (Harris et al. 2003). Yet this book shows identity exploration is important for young people, especially if they feel "marginalised" and "devalued" by wider society (Batsleer 2008: 17). This book has demonstrated notions of nationalism and national identity require examination, not only as peripheral phenomena on the sidelines of national consciousness, but also through thinking over their impact on everyday existences (Billig 1995; Cameron 1999). Recognising and encouraging culturally diverse young people's contributions to the debates on Britishness should be a priority in any FBV policy or practice. Young people's perceptions of identities and belongings are necessary for bringing about social justice (Leistyna 2009; Smyth and McInerney 2007). Young people are frequently honest about lived realities, and political engagement will mean they become society's future change-makers (Smyth and McInerney 2007).

Official reviews or inquiries, and subsequent reports, also often neglect youth voice (Ratcliffe 2011; Osler 2015), even when documenting young people's identities, belongings and attachments. Teaching Britishness, for example, was proposed by politicians as a way to develop young people's sense of citizenship and national identity in the multicultural society (Golmohamad 2009). This book advocates young people being given spaces to working critically through conceptions of Britishness, belonging and social inequalities with their peers and teachers. Just as anti-racist work should "address black people, their needs, aspirations, world views, and how they wish to live" (Gurnah 1992: 97), learning and teaching Britishness should focus on young British people's needs, aspirations and world views. In the past, schools have not taken to exploring a shared British identity (Maylor et al. 2007) which explains the gap in the literature regarding students' definitions and discourses of Britishness. The work with London young people, trainee teachers and Art teachers—that I have described in this book—emphasises the urgency of working towards an inclusive society without essentialising, stereotyping or creating a maligned Other (Mavroudi 2010).

COMPLEX IDENTITIES: FLUID, MULTIPLE AND EVOLVING

When Commonwealth citizens from India, Pakistan and the Caribbean came to establish homes in post-war Britain, the notion that British identity was an exclusively White identity came to be problematic (Cohen 1994). Nevertheless, the supposed "common sense" view prevailed that "Britishness was a finite collective identity and could not accommodate all of these immigrants" (Ward 2004: 125). Current melancholic nostalgia (Gidley 2014)—for a mythical Britishness—potentially excludes the lived experiences of ethnic minority and White working-class communities. The UK Conservative-Liberal Democrat Coalition government (2010–2015) keen to promote "our island story" through British history teaching in schools, for example, was critiqued for its narrow and exclusive vision of belonging which failed to acknowledge the legacy of our imperial past (Sales 2012; Bhambra 2014).

Ideas about teaching Britishness arose from social concerns like young people's political disenfranchisement, fragmented multicultural society (Golmohamad 2009), "radicalisation" of young Muslim males and the educational failure of White working-class males (Jerome and Clemitshaw 2012). Such discourses about troubled, failing and lost generations of potentially criminal youth are not new, for "there is a long history of social anxiety that finds its crystallising focus in a preoccupation with the rising youth generation, and the crime and violence for which it is responsible" (Pearson 2012: 45). Promotion of Britishness in political and policy rhetoric takes attention away from the urgent need for anti-racist education, particularly as the post-Brexit sociopolitical climate has made racism more visible.

Unsurprisingly, "xenophobia and nationalism are thriving" (Gilroy 2005: 2) and continue to thrive. Race—a "category of social visibility…made and affirmed through processes of seeing and being seen"— needs deeper interrogation and contestation (Brahinsky 2011: 146) in educational institutions with teachers and with students. An underlying uneasiness about possible hegemonic attempts to impose an unwelcome patriotic—and even "racist"—agenda on schools is troubling for teachers in training and for existing teachers who are suddenly being asked to teach FBV. The trainee Art teachers I met mentioned Brexit as problematic. There was consensus among the trainees that multicultural Britishness was the norm, pointing towards the need for teacher educators to explore themes of identity, belonging and multiculturalism with trainee teachers.

Multicultural Education: Moving from FBV Towards Critical Pedagogy

Contemporary debates on national identity reveal political condemnation of "unintegrated" ethnic minority communities, blamed for social disharmony and criticised for not sharing a sense of collective belonging with indigenous peoples (Vasta 2013). Observing schools, teachers and students struggle with the challenges of diversity (Sleeter 2014), as well as with themes of national and global identities and attachments, I write knowing now is a crucial time to research increasing sociopolitical tensions juxtaposing with lived complexities of multicultural belongings and national identities. I follow Brubaker (2004: 11) in that race, nation and ethnicity "should be conceptualized not as substances or things or entities or organisms or collective individuals... but rather in relational, processual, dynamic, eventful, and disaggregated terms". This book, therefore, takes the strong view that even if "identities may be socially, culturally and institutionally assigned" (Weedon 2004: 6), identities are, nevertheless, unfixed and fluid, sometimes contradictory and ambiguous, contextual and interdependent (Kershen 1998; Parekh 2000; Lawler 2008).

This book has understood government is often "compromised by its attempts to placate racism and xenophobia within its increasingly disenchanted electorate" (Back et al. 2002: 452). Subsequent policies and practices might manifest that government "flirtations with multicultural democracy are combined, where opportune, with appeals to the remnants of racially exclusive nationalism and the phantoms of imperial greatness" (Back et al. 2002: 452). Thus, contemporary Britishness is critiqued for sometimes evoking "a particular narrative of British history" (Croft 2012: 167) that intentionally seeks to "distort the character and history" (Parekh 1999: 323) of the nation. Examining misrepresented characters and histories of the nation can counteract "the power of the rhetoric of 'Britishness'" (Andrews and Mycock 2008: 143), for—as this book has substantiated—there is no singular way to experience Britishness. To continue to "move beyond theorizing how diasporic identities are constructed and consolidated" to investigating how diasporic identities are "practised, lived and experienced" (Braziel and Mannur 2003: 9) is therefore a productive approach for teachers and researchers.

Exploration of Britishness and identity issues through a framework of critical pedagogy requires, I have illustrated in the previous chapters, what Giroux (2013: 4) refers to as "the construction of critical agents". Students and teachers perform as critical agents; they collaboratively interrogate common sense assumptions about the nature of legitimate knowledge, social relations and ideologies (Giroux 2013). Teachers, like students, are in danger of falling victim to what Gramsci (1971) outlines are hegemonic forces of *spontaneous consent*. Through affiliating with the social institutions and social norms that maintain the status quo and promoting the prevailing social order, teachers are consenting (sometimes without consciousness) to maintain power and privilege for the elite. There are implications for how teacher training institutions address concepts of multiculture, race and diversity, alongside Britishness. Many new teachers have little or no training to grasp complex concepts like race and ethnicity (Lander 2014), making schools problematic places for students needing space to explore the nuances and multiplicities of identities. Others argue ethnicity, as a term, is no longer applicable "now that hybridity and cultural mixing have become the norm" (Mason 2008: 106), which also needs exploring in teacher education and with young people.

The "message" ethnic minority young people once received through schooling "that 'Britain' and 'the British' are categories that can never truly include them" (Gillborn 1995: 2) prevails in contemporary discourses of education policy and practice, particularly with regards to FBV. Britishness discourses are in danger of being "depressingly insular and nationalist... premised on the qualifications of being white and indigenous" (Ware 2009: 8). Young people might undergo a sense of emotional disconnection from Britishness if they are trapped by ideas of Britishness they view to be fixed, and not offering fluidity: "Britain represents an old, hierarchical, traditional, political discourse that does not fit with the fresh, inventive, messy and often chaotic world of a teenager" (Phillips and Ganesh 2007: 13). Britishness or Englishness might become "almost meaningless" to British youth who are busy "embracing diversity in seemingly inexhaustible combinations" in their local spaces and cities (Back 1996: 250).

Both pre-service and in-service teachers are struggling to make sense of FBV policies and practices without having received appropriate training to challenge the majoritarian narrative of FBV (Elton-Chalcraft et al. 2017). Educational institutions are sites where the government's *majoritarian* stories and myths of a post-racial society can be critically examined through analysing everyday and institutional racisms (Gillborn 1995; Solórzano and Yosso 2002). We also cannot assume because a school contains culturally and ethnically diverse demographics that teaching staff understand diversity (Maylor 2010). Sometimes new teachers may not know about critical pedagogy. Or some teachers may not understand the benefits of incorporating critical pedagogies in their teaching-learning practices. Unfortunately, many educationalists are unaware of the "suppression of historical consciousness and critical thinking" in schooling (Giroux 2013: 42). Teacher training programmes can introduce student teachers to the importance of "the historical nature of their own fields" (Giroux 2013: 42), and to critical pedagogy, to work towards creating a democratic and fair classroom, where students are valued for the diverse knowledge they bring to collaborative learning opportunities.

There is a danger the government is espousing versions of Britishness, of culture and of citizenship alien to how these notions are experienced by our students. Counter-hegemonic strategies can help in the battle for social change and social justice (Anyon 2011). Critical reflection, particularly about prevailing ideologies, can also encourage students and their teachers to critique the status quo together, to "learn to recognise how uncritically accepted and unjust dominant ideologies are embedded in everyday situations and practices" (Brookfield 2009: 36). Reflection leads to action. In this case, exploration of Britishness is a starting point, and students can move onto critical action in order to tackle the social injustices and social inequalities they see as damaging to their school and local community. Bearing in mind Karl Marx's eleventh thesis: "*the philosophers have only interpreted the world in various ways; the point, however, is to change it*" (Brett 2007: 6), change is required.

Often though, in the current climate of "fear-driven security policies", teachers might be hesitant to teach controversial topics (Freedman 2008: 41), resulting in silenced students. As has been seen in the USA's school system, for instance, Sikh students are marginalised in the curriculum, and even though they have been long settled in the USA, post-9/11 Islamophobia has impacted upon their everyday existences alongside their Muslim peers (Verma 2010). In the UK, the "controversial" (Mason 2016: 2) Prevent strategy focusing on "non-violent extremism" (HM Government 2011) calls for teachers and lecturers to report students displaying signs of "radicalisation", subsequently creating fear and mistrust in schools (Mumisa 2014; Richardson 2015; Bolloten and Richardson 2015; Reclaiming Schools 2015; Garner 2015; Birt 2015; Neustatter 2016). Yet terms like "radicalisation" and "de-radicalisation" are contested and problematised in definition, discourse, and in the accompanying "assumptions" (Sedgwick 2010; Kundnani 2012; Baker-Beall et al. 2015).

Muslim students are reported, for example, for proclaiming pro-Palestinian support (Broomfield 2016) or for reading course books on terrorism in the university library (Ramesh and Halliday 2015). A Muslim teacher was reported for telling a colleague she was planning to attend a charity fundraising dinner for Syria (Bowcott 2016). Critics of Prevent question representation and social control of Muslim bodies seen as transgressing "normal" Britishness:

> The problem of radicalisation comes to be tied to a notion that the radicalised subject is vulnerable to extremist messages due to their dislocation, their dis-identification from the normalcy of British society. Thus positioned, it becomes those who (are seen to) exist outside of a framework of British norms and behaviours who may potentially threaten the unity of the British state. (Martin 2015: 194)

FBV and Prevent are collocations that have become impossible to separate, especially as government has used Prevent to establish FBV policy. The Prevent duty (HM Government 2011, 2015) has been extensively criticised for casting all Muslims as a "suspect community"; unions, including the TUC, UCU, NUT and NUS, have passed motions opposing Prevent for stifling freedom of speech and activism, encouraging racism and Islamophobia and hindering safe learning spaces (UCU Left 2015). At the NUT annual conference, teachers "voted overwhelmingly to reject the government's Prevent strategy" (Adams 2016).

If there is a danger, as Richard Johnson believed, a national culture is "defined in exclusive, nostalgic, and frequently racist terms" (Apple 1993: 233), the exploration of Britishness can be done innovatively and creatively to develop critical citizens who aspire to improve society and actively engage in social change, and who also move beyond exclusivity, nostalgia and racist discourses. Visual arts critical pedagogues advocate a "nomadic consciousness", whereby students frequently create "situated connections", but will not "accept the limitations of a national, fixed identity" (Tourinho and Martins 2008: 65). There will be critical pedagogues in the classroom who embrace their students' "situated connections" and allow students to reject a "national, fixed identity" in favour of multiple belongings and attachments. The danger is teachers will be "Prevent-ed" from encouraging students to express honestly how they feel about nation state and national identity. To move away from Prevent ideology, I advocate the argument of Baron Cohen and Souza (2008: 79) that "arts-based pedagogical training is essential" for teachers if society is to develop "a new, self-reflexive, expressive, dialogic and empathetic humanity". More "autonomy" and "participation" are necessary both for teachers and students in order for knowledge to be co-constructed and for individual and collective learning to take place about local, national and global issues (Gamman 2004). Teachers and students of Art exploring Britishness would benefit from knowing critical race approaches also embrace the visual, thereby allowing students to (re)present their *experiential knowledge*, privileging their "racialized, gendered, and classed experiences as sources of strength" (Solórzano and Yosso 2002: 26).

COUNTER-NARRATIVES OF BRITISHNESS

To incorporate features of critical pedagogy into lessons when embarking on a journey of learning with school students is in itself an act to challenge prevailing *master narratives*. To provide counter-stories is to dismantle hegemonic master narratives which "legitimise and privilege the fears of the bourgeoisie, their fear of those Others who might invade or disrupt their homely spaces, their habitus" and to challenge powerful "discourses of fear" surrounding youth and ethnic minorities (Sandercock 2005: 232). If "state-induced forms of subordination have created the conditions for movements of resistance" (Rosaldo 1996: 239), then encouraging counter-narratives through critical pedagogy when teaching and learning sensitive, controversial and complex issues permits teachers and students to contest imposition of the FBV agenda. In the spirit of culturally relevant pedagogy, the collective and collaborative become core to teaching and learning, to reflection and discussion, to social justice and social change (Ladson-Billings 1995). This focus on the collective, not the individual, can aid teachers and students in their resistance to neoliberal educational policies and practices.

The pedagogical-political act of Britishness teaching must not submit to hegemonic policies that become symbolic representational tools to perpetuate "symbolic violence" on powerless citizens (Bourdieu and Passeron 1990) already struggling with identity formation in a classed and racialised social world. If there exists a "politics of forgetting that erases how disparate social identities have been produced, legitimated and marginalized with different relations of power" (Giroux 1995: 47), then these disparate social identities cannot be abandoned in the name of pursing national common identity and culture. Britishness cannot become a "marker of certainty" that "affirms monoculturalism and restores the racially coded image" (Giroux 1995: 50) of what it means to be British. Moving forwards, we must continue to give young people—our future generation—greater space to discuss national identity, as well as the critical tools to deconstruct classed and racialised belongings to Britain.

How do young people experience belonging to Britain? What happens when some young people do not fully subscribe to the supposed core characteristics of a nation (Young 2000)? Young people must be encouraged to explore these narratives. Silencing students' stories hinders the encouragement, engagement and enfranchisement of future generations. Student (dis)engagement is a real concern in schools: students from disadvantaged and marginalised communities often lack the cultural capital to succeed, and thus "new social spaces" are urgently needed to enable the disengaged students to develop love for learning (Smyth et al. 2013; Lingard and Keddie 2013). Facilitating open discussion in order to promote respect and diversity is a common theme supported by critical pedagogy approaches. In schools, there is a danger that on a wide range of issues affecting students there is "...silencing of students' own stories, needs, contexts, thoughts, and concerns, in favour of the stereotypes and assumptions which were features of the hegemonic discourse" (Carlile 2012: 395). This silencing of students' stories should be actively challenged and changed for students to become critical citizens of the future. Rather than education creating "cheerful robots", society must demand critical young people who learn about the world which they inhabit and come to understand the workings of "justice, values, ethics and power" (Giroux 2013: 3).

When learning about British identities, we need to keep asking questions. Kincheloe (2007: 16) argues critical pedagogues will forever be asking questions about social justice, privilege/power and praxis "operating in different historical times and diverse pedagogical locales". Teachers and students' identities evolve, as demonstrated by the teachers and students who undertook a pedagogical journey of learning about the self and the other. Moreover, "educational spaces are unique and politically contested" (Kincheloe 2007: 16). Freire's concept of *situationality* where *social* beings are encouraged to reflect upon their *social* contexts and act critically upon these "temporal-spatial conditions which mark them and which they also mark" (Freire 2000: 90) applies to Britishness exploration. Calls to rework and rewrite the national collective imagination must be received cautiously when there is a chance that appropriating national identity becomes "a vehicle to foster racism, nativism, and political censorship" (Giroux 1995: 47). Teaching Britishness cannot solely be an exercise in determining a national collective "imagination" because, as this book shows and as critical pedagogues advocate, the unique character of local context plays a major role in identity formation.

Where schools are situated in heavily disadvantaged areas, innovative and alternative pedagogies can be used by teachers to increase educational engagement and achievement (Smyth et al. 2013). Teachers, after all, are a "potentially powerful force for social change" (Giroux 2013: 42). Currently there is an over-focus on levelling and testing students, as well as on topping the school examination league tables; instead schools could create give teachers the training and support needed to develop pedagogies that are impactful, positive and engaging. A curriculum "attentive to the lives and needs of young people rather than the performative imperatives of the system" (Smyth et al. 2013: 309) works towards enabling students to be more engaged and enthusiastic about learning. This book has revealed teachers and students practising critical pedagogies can enhance learning and critical reflection and shed light upon young people's classed and racialised British belongings.

Critical pedagogical philosophies and practices are necessary for maintaining trainee teachers' and young people's enthusiasm for exploring identities, and as embedded in Art teachers' lesson planning and delivery when teaching Britishness. When teachers are supported in their endeavours to provide students with opportunities to explore multicultural Britishness, this book shows students critically and collaboratively engage with identity issues, advance their own viewpoints, learn about alternative perspectives and strengthen bonds with peers and teachers. Students feel empowered by having their critical counter-narratives validated and valued. The empirical research detailed in this book leads to the resounding conclusion that where students hear others' stories and tell their own, schools can become critical sites of opportunity for reflection, resistance and hopeful futures.

References

Andrews, R., and A. Mycock. 2008. Dilemmas of Devolution: The 'Politics of Britishness' and Citizenship Education. *British Politics* 3: 139–155.

Anyon, J. 2011. *Marx and Education*. New York: Routledge.

Apple, M.W. 1993. The Politics of Official Knowledge: Does a National Curriculum Make Sense? *Teachers College Record* 95 (2): 222–241.

Back, L. 1996. *New Ethnicities and Urban Culture: Racisms and Multiculture in Young Lives*. London: Routledge.

Back, L., M. Keith, A. Khan, K. Shukra, and J. Solomos. 2002. New Labour's White Heart: Politics, Multiculturalism and The Return of Assimilation. *The Political Quarterly* 73: 445–454.

Baker-Beall, C., C. Heath-Kelly, & L. Jarvis. (eds.). 2015. *Counter-Radicalisation: Critical Perspectives.* London and New York: Routledge.

Batsleer, J.R. 2008. *Informal Learning in Youth Work.* London: Sage.

Bhambra, G.K. 2014. *Connected Sociologies.* London: Bloomsbury Academic.

Billig, M. 1995. *Banal Nationalism.* London: Sage.

Birt, Y. 2015. Safeguarding Little Abdul: Prevent, Muslim Schoolchildren and the Lack of Parental Consent. Available from: https://www.yahyabirt1.wordpress.com/2015/06/04/safeguarding-little-abdul-prevent-muslimschoolchildren-and-the-lack-of-parental-consent/2016, 04 June 2015.

Bolloten, B., and R. Richardson. 2015. The Great British Values Disaster - Education, Security & Vitriolic Hate [Online]. Institute of Race Relations. Accessed 03 July 2015.

Bourdieu, P., and J.C. Passeron. 1990. *Reproduction in Education, Society and Culture.* London: Sage Publications.

Brahinsky, R. 2011. Race and the City: The (Re)development of Urban Identity. *Geography Compass* 5: 144–153.

Braziel, J.E., and Mannur, A. 2003. Nation, Migration, Globalization: Points of Contention in Diaspora Studies. In *Theorizing Diaspora*, ed. J.E. Braziel and A. Mannur. Oxford: Blackwell Publishing.

Brett, P. 2007. *"Endowing Participation With Meaning": Citizenship Education, Paolo Freire and Educating Young People as Change-Makers.* http://www.citized.info/pdf/commarticles/Endowing%20Participation%20Peter%20Brett.pdf.

Brookfield, S.D. 2009. The Concept of Critically Reflective Practice. In *Handbook of Adult and Continuing Education*, ed. A.L. Wilson and E.R. Hayes. San Francisco: Wiley.

Broomfield, M. 2016. Anti-terror police question schoolboy for wearing pro-Palestine badge. The Independent, 14 Feb 2016.

Brubaker, R. 2004. *Ethnicity Without Groups.* Cambridge and London: Harvard University Press.

Cameron, K. (ed.). 1999. *National Identity.* Exeter: Intellect.

Carlile, A. 2012. 'Critical bureaucracy' in action: embedding student voice into school governance. *Pedagogy, Culture and Society* 20: 393–412.

Cohen, R. 1994. *Frontiers of Identity: The British and the Others.* London and New York: Longman.

Croft, S. 2012. *Securitizing Islam: Identity and the Search for Security.* Cambridge: Cambridge University Press.

Elton-Chalcraft, S., V. Lander, L. Revell, D. Warner, and L. Whitworth. 2017. To Promote, or not to Promote Fundamental British Values?—Teachers' Standards, Diversity and Teacher Education. *British Educational Research Journal* 43: 29–48.

Freedman, K. 2008. Leading Creativity: Responding to Policy in Art Education. In *International Dialogues about Visual Culture, Education and Art*, ed. R. Mason and T. Eca. Bristol: Intellect.

Freire, P. 2000. *Pedagogy of the Oppressed*. New York: Bloomsbury Publishing.

Gamman, R. 2004. Children and the Curriculum. In *Children at the Margins: Supporting Children, Supporting Schools*, ed. T. Billington and M. Pomerantz. Stoke on Trent: Trentham Books.

Garner, R. 2015. Teachers forced to act as 'front-line storm troopers' to spy on pupils under guidelines aimed at combating terrorism. Independent, 06 April 2015.

Gidley, B. 2014. Integration. In *Migration: The COMPAS Anthology*, ed. B. Anderson and M. Keith. Oxford: COMPAS.

Gillborn, D. 1995. *Racism and Antiracism in Real Schools: Theory, Policy, Practice*. Buckingham: Open University Press.

Gilroy, P. 2005. *Postcolonial Melancholia*. New York: Columbia University Press.

Giroux, H.A. 1995. National identity and the politics of multiculturalism. *College Literature* 22: 42–57.

Giroux, H.A. 2013. *On Critical Pedagogy*. New York and London: Bloomsbury Academic.

Golmohamad, M. 2009. Education for World Citizenship: Beyond National Allegiance. *Educational Philosophy and Theory* 41: 466–486.

Gramsci, A. 1971. *Selections from the Prison Notebooks of Antonio Gramsci*, ed. and trans. Quintin Hoare and Geoffrey Nowell Smith. New York: International Publishers.

Gurnah, A. 1992. On the Specificity of Racism. In *Voicing Concerns: Sociological Perspectives on Contemporary Education Reforms*, ed. M. Arnot and L. Barton. Wallingford: Triangle Books.

Harris, C., P. Roach, R. Thiara, D. Amory, and R. Yusuf. 2003. *Emergent Citizens? African-Caribbean and Pakistani Young People in Birmingham and Bradford*. Leicester: The National Youth Agency.

Heater, D. 2001. The History of Citizenship Education in England. *The Curriculum Journal* 12: 103–123.

HM Government June 2011. Prevent Strategy.

HM Government March 2015. Revised Prevent Duty Guidance: For England and Wales.

Jerome, L., and G. Clemitshaw. 2012. Teaching (About) Britishness? An Investigation into Trainee Teachers' Understanding of Britishness in Relation to Citizenship and the Discourse of Civic Nationalism. *Curriculum Journal* 23: 19–41.

Kershen, A.J. (ed.). 1998. *A Question of Identity*. Aldershot: Ashgate.

Kincheloe, J. L. 2007. Critical Pedagogy in the Twenty-First Century. In *Critical Pedagogy: Where are We Now?*, ed. P. Mclaren and J.L. Kincheloe. New York: Peter Lang.

Kundnani, A. 2012. Radicalisation: The Journey of a Concept. *Race and Class* 54 (2): 3–25.

Ladson-Billings, G. 1995. But That's Just Good Teaching! The Case for Culturally Relevant Pedagogy. *Theory into Practice* 34: 159–165.

Lander, V. 2014. Initial Teacher Education: The Practice of Whiteness. In *Advancing Race and Ethnicity in Education*, ed. R. Race and V. Lander. Basingstoke: Palgrave Macmillan.

Lawler, S. 2008. *Identity: Sociological Perspectives*. Cambridge: The Polity Press.

Leistyna, P. 2009. Preparing for Public Life: Education, Critical Theory, and Social Justice. In *Handbook of Social Justice in Education*, ed. W. Ayers, T. M. Quinn, and D. Stovall. New York: Routledge.

Lingard, B., and A. Keddie. 2013. Redistribution, Recognition and Representation: Working Against Pedagogies of Indifference. *Pedagogy, Culture & Society* 21: 427–447.

Mason, R. 2008. Contemporary Artworks as Sites for Identity Research. In *International Dialogues About Visual Culture, Education and Art*, ed. R. Mason and T. Eca. Bristol: Intellect.

Mason, R. (ed.). 2016. *Muslim Minority-State Relations: Violence, Integration, and Policy*. Basingstoke: Palgrave Macmillan.

Mavroudi, E. 2010. Nationalism, the Nation and Migration: Searching for Purity and Diversity. *Space and Polity* 14: 219–233.

Maylor, U. 2010. Notions of Diversity, British Identities and Citizenship Belonging. *Race Ethnicity and Education* 13: 233–252.

Maylor, U., B. Read, H. Mendick, A. Ross, and N. Rollock. 2007. Diversity and Citizenship in the Curriculum: Research Review. Research Report 819. London: The Institute for Policy Studies in Education, London Metropolitan University.

Morley, D., and K. Robins. 2001. Introduction: The National Culture in Its New Global Context. In *British Cultural Studies: Geography, Nationality and Identity*, ed. D. Morley and K. Robins. Oxford: Oxford University Press.

Mumisa, M. 2014. It Is the Government's Prevent Programmes and Religious Quietism, Not Radicalism, Which Have Been Driving Young British Muslims into the Hands of Extremists [Online]. The Huffington Post. Available: http://www.huffingtonpost.co.uk/michael-mumisa/muslim-extremism-b-5862188.html. Accessed 02 March 2016 .

Neustatter, A. 2016. Rules to fight extremism 'creating fear among teachers and pupils'. The Guardian. https://www.theguardian.com/education/2016/jan/12/rules-extremism-teachers-pupils-spy-radicalisation-muslimsprevent. Accessed 25 Jan 2016.

Osler, A. 2015. The Stories We Tell: Exploring Narrative in Education for Justice and Equality in Multicultural Contexts. *Multicultural Education Review* 7: 12–25.

Parekh, B. 1999. The Incoherence of Nationalism. In *Theorizing Nationalism*, ed. R. Beiner. New York: State University of New York Press.

Parekh, B. 2000. Defining British National Identity. *The Political Quarterly* 71: 4–14.

Pearson, G. 2012. Everything Changes, Nothing Moves: The Longue Duree of Social Anxieties. In *The English Riots of 2011: A Summer of Discontent*, ed. D. Briggs. Hook: Waterside Press.

Phillips, A., and G. Ganesh. 2007. Young People and British Identity. London: Ipsos MORI/Camelot Foundation.

Ramesh, R,. and J. Halliday. 2015. Student accused of being a terrorist for reading book on terrorism. The Guardian, 24 Sep 2015.

Ratcliffe, P. 2011. From Community to Social Cohesion: Interrogating a Policy Paradigm. In *Promoting Social Cohesion: Implications for Policy and Evaluation*, ed. P. Ratcliffe and I. Newman. Bristol: Policy Press.

Richardson, R. 2015. British Values and British Identity: Muddles, Mixtures, and Ways Ahead. *London Review of Education* 13: 37–48.

Sales, R. 2012. Britain and Britishness: Place, Belonging and Exclusion. In *Muslims in Britain: Making Social and Political Space*, ed. W. Ahmad and Z. Sardar. Abingdon: Routledge.

Sandercock, L. 2005. Difference, Fear and Habitus: A Political Economy of Urban Fears. In *Habitus: A Sense of Place*, ed. J. Hillier and E. Rooksby, 2nd ed. Aldershot: Ashgate.

Sedgwick, M. 2010. The Concept of Radicalization as a Source of Confusion. *Terrorism and Political Violence* 22 (4): 479–494.

Shor, I. 1992. *Empowering Education: Critical Teaching for Social Change*. Chicago: University of Chicago Press.

Sleeter, C.E. 2014. Multiculturalism and Education for Citizenship in a Context of Neoliberalism. *Intercultural Education* 25 (2): 1–10.

Smyth, J., and P. McInerney. 2007. *Teachers in the Middle: Reclaiming the Wasteland of the Adolescent Years of Schooling*. New York: Peter Lang.

Smyth, J., P. McInerney, and T. Fish. 2013. Blurring the Boundaries: From Relational Learning Towards a Critical Pedagogy of Engagement for Disengaged Disadvantaged Young People. *Pedagogy, Culture & Society* 21: 299–320.

Smyth, J., and P. McInerney. 2013. Whose Side Are You On? Advocacy Ethnography: Some Methodological Aspects of Narrative Portraits of Disadvantaged Young People, in Socially Critical Research. *International Journal of Qualitative Studies in Education* 26: 1–20.

Solórzano, D.G., and T.J. Yosso. 2002. Critical Race Methodology: Counter-Storytelling as an Analytical Framework for Education Research. *Qualitative Inquiry* 8: 23–44.

Tourinho, I., and R. Martins. 2008. Controversies: Proposals for a Visual Arts Critical Pedagogy. In *International Dialogues About Visual Culture, Education and Art*, ed. R. Mason and T. Eca. Bristol: Intellect.

Vasta, E. 2013. Do We Need Social Cohesion in the 21st Century? Multiple Languages of Belonging in the Metropolis. *Journal of Intercultural Studies* 34 (2): 196–213.

Verma, R. 2010. Unlearning the Silence in the Curriculum: Sikh Histories and Post 9/11 Experiences. In: *Critical Global Perspectives: Rethinking Knowledge about Global Societies.* ed. B. Subedi. Charlotte: Information Age Publishing.

Ward, P. 2004. *Britishness Since 1870.* London: Routledge.

Ware, V. 2009. Chasing Britishness: A Post-colonial Project. *British Politics Review: Journal of the British Politics Society* 4: 8.

Weedon, C. 2004. *Identity and Culture: Narratives of Difference and Belonging: Narratives of Difference and Belonging.* Maidenhead: Open University Press.

Young, I.M. 2000. *Inclusion and Democracy.* Oxford: Oxford University Press.

BIBLIOGRAPHY

Big Brother. 2002. Directed by Channel 4.
Celebrity Big Brother. 2007. Directed by Channel 4.
King, J. 2004. Dysconscious Racism: Ideology, Identity and the Miseducation
  of Teachers. In *The RoutledgeFalmer Reader in Multicultural Education*, ed.
  G. Ladson-Billings and D. Gillborn. Abingdon: RoutledgeFalmer.

© The Editor(s) (if applicable) and The Author(s) 2018   165
S. Habib, *Learning and Teaching British Values,*
DOI 10.1007/978-3-319-60381-0

INDEX

9 783319 603803